Short Circuits

THE JOHN D. AND CATHERINE T. MACARTHUR FOUNDATION SERIES ON DIGITAL MEDIA AND LEARNING

Inaugural Series Volumes

Six edited volumes were created through an interactive community review process and published online and in print in December 2007. They are the precursors to the peer-reviewed monographs in the series. For more information on these volumes, visit http://mitpress.mit.edu/books/series/john-d-and-catherine-t-macarthur-foundation -series-digital-media-and-learning.

Short Circuits
Crafting e-Puppets with DIY Electronics

by Kylie Peppler, Katie Salen Tekinbaş,
Melissa Gresalfi, and Rafi Santo

The MIT Press
Cambridge, Massachusetts
London, England

MIT Press books may be purchased at special quantity discounts for business or sales promotional use. For information, please email special_sales@mitpress.mit.edu.

This book was set in Melior LT Std 9.5/13 by Toppan Best-set Premedia Limited, Hong Kong. Printed and bound in the United States of America.

Library of Congress Cataloging-in-Publication Data is available.
ISBN: 978-0-262-02783-0

10 9 8 7 6 5 4 3 2 1

CONTENTS

SERIES FOREWORD

In recent years, digital media and networks have become embedded in our everyday lives and are part of broad-based changes to how we engage in knowledge production, communication, and creative expression. Unlike the early years in the development of computers and computer-based media, digital media are now *commonplace* and *pervasive*, having been taken up by a wide range of individuals and institutions in all walks of life. Digital media have escaped the boundaries of professional and formal practice, and of the academic, governmental, and industry homes that initially fostered their development. Now they have been taken up by diverse populations and noninstitutionalized practices, including the peer activities of youth. Although specific forms of technology uptake are highly diverse, a generation is growing up in an era when digital media are part of the taken-for-granted social and cultural fabric of learning, play, and social communication.

This book series is founded upon the working hypothesis that those immersed in new digital tools and networks are engaged in an unprecedented exploration of language, games, social interaction, problem solving, and self-directed activity that leads to diverse forms of learning. These diverse forms of learning are reflected in expressions of identity, in how individuals express independence and creativity, and in their ability to learn, exercise judgment, and think systematically.

The defining frame for this series is not a particular theoretical or disciplinary approach, nor is it a fixed set of topics. Rather, the series revolves around a constellation of topics investigated from multiple disciplinary and practical frames. The series as a whole looks at the relation between youth, learning, and digital media, but each contribution to the series might deal with only a subset of this constellation. Erecting strict topical boundaries would exclude some of the most important work in the field. For example, restricting the content of the series only to people of a certain age would mean artificially reifying an age boundary when the phenomenon demands otherwise. This would become particularly problematic with new forms of online participation where one important outcome is the mixing of participants of different ages. The same goes for digital media, which are increasingly inseparable from analog and earlier media forms.

The series responds to certain changes in our media ecology that have important implications for learning. Specifically, these changes involve new forms of media *literacy* and developments in the modes of media *participation*. Digital media are part of a convergence between interactive media (most notably gaming), online networks, and existing media forms. Navigating this media ecology involves a palette of literacies that are being defined through practice but require more scholarly scrutiny before they can be fully incorporated pervasively into educational initiatives. Media literacy involves not only ways of understanding, interpreting, and critiquing media, but also the means for creative and social expression, online search and navigation, and a host of new technical skills. The potential gap in literacies and participation skills creates new challenges for educators who struggle to bridge media engagement inside and outside the classroom.

The John D. and Catherine T. MacArthur Foundation Series on Digital Media and Learning, published by the MIT Press, aims to close these gaps and provide innovative ways of thinking about and using new forms of knowledge production, communication, and creative expression.

FOREWORD

When we try to pick out anything by itself, we find it hitched to everything else in the universe.

—John Muir

At a recent national meeting, a group of National Writing Project (NWP) educators participated in a workshop based on a Design Challenge from this *Short Circuits: Crafting e-Puppets with DIY Electronics* curriculum. The workshop, led by *Short Circuits* authors Kylie Peppler and Melissa Gresalfi, was organized so that we started with a few provocations about systems and "systems thinking," got an overview of circuits and switches, and then had some time (as well as scaffolded support and materials) to dive into our first puppet-making task. After that, we would debrief about what we had just done and reflect on the implications for systems thinking and for learning.

The actual making task had us use a precut shape to create a hand puppet integrating an interactive switch that would turn a light on and off when activated. Seemingly a straightforward task, the group of us in the room got to work, and we were clearly excited to be making and playing in this way. As we dived in, however, the complexity of the design task in front of us became clear, and what I remember was how this otherwise very talkative group of educators got kind of quiet (well, at least for a moment). After all, it wasn't just conductive thread, LEDs, and switches we were putting together with batteries on felt. Rather, the task required that all of these components be embedded within overlapping systems of circuits, switches, and an emerging puppet character with related movements, each of which had unique systemic requirements all of its own!

As educators, engaging with the content that we'd like to explore with students is a key piece of the work we do together at the NWP. The design of this workshop, then, was meant to support us in having a chance to engage as learners while also imagining what's possible as teachers. So, while we were clearly impressed by the challenge in front of us, the room of educators certainly did not stay quiet for long, as everyone started sharing what they knew as well as what they were trying, showing each other what they were figuring out and were exploring, and in the best active learning and making kind of way, pushing each other's thinking while creating a range of unique and wonderful creations.

One of these teachers, Kim Douillard—a second- and third-grade teacher and director of the San Diego Area Writing Project—documented her own learning by taking photos of what she was doing as she was doing it and then posted them, along with a reflection about them, on her blog (see http://digitalis.nwp.org/site-blog/systems-thinking/5813). In her post-workshop reflection, she wrote:

> Our educational system (and our government) seems to spend a lot of time in the simple cause and effect model, rather than helping our students think more deeply about systems and the ways there are multiple factors, interconnections, and possibilities at work in the outcomes we see. So the making of puppets in this workshop was about more than learning how circuits work or developing language and writing related to the puppet, it was also a way to think about systems and the problem solving and iteration that it takes to understand and make changes to the overall system.

Engaging in these kinds of design tasks that integrate new technologies and design processes while looking at the work through a systems-thinking lens is the goal of this *Short Circuits* curriculum. And as the authors of this volume tell us, systems are based on the interactions of a set of components within that system, and there is agency involved in recognizing systems and these components as potential levers of change. To me, then, Kim's reflection is an example of the agency that can be engaged in this work; she started with making a puppet but ended up also considering issues of governance and systems of education. This also underscores what I believe is the ultimate ambition of this volume and the larger set of the Interconnections series overall; i.e., to support us—adults and youths alike—in making these kinds of connections and being agents of change in our own systems and interconnected worlds.

This same kind of interconnected approach, underscored by agency, was taken up by the team that came together to work on the initial design and research project of which this *Short Circuits* volume is a result. As will be described further in the introduction, it was a project that brought together a variety of experts, including researchers, scholars, youths, and teachers (including those from the NWP network) into a shared space where they had opportunities to co-construct and create together while integrating and/or exploring the range of experiences and approaches they brought with them. In this way, everyone involved in this curriculum's development ended up being teachers as well as "constructionist" learners, in Seymour Papert's sense of the word, and an approach to which the *Interconnections* collection is dedicated:

> Constructionism—the N word as opposed to the V word—shares constructivism's connotation of learning as "building knowledge structures" irrespective of the circumstances of the learning. It then adds the idea that this happens especially felicitously in a context where the learner is consciously engaged in constructing a public entity, whether it's a sand castle on the beach or a theory of the universe. (Papert and Harel, 1991)

Short Circuits, therefore, seems to me to be both a curriculum that falls somewhere along this continuum between sandcastles and universal theories and an offering made from a moment captured in time and within a context meant to be used and be iterated upon within new moments and contexts. Offering soundly tested suggestions, recommendations, and scaffolded steps alongside quotes from the field and active encouragement to play, tinker, test, and "mod" (modify) its many activities and challenges, this curriculum, like its partner curricula in the *Interconnections* collection, actively explores the outcome that it seeks. It is a living document into which you are invited to breathe, and build, your own life and meaning-making.

> Christina Cantrill, Senior Program Associate for National Programs, National Writing Project

ACKNOWLEDGMENTS AND PROJECT HISTORY

ACKNOWLEDGMENTS

This book collection would not have been possible without the involvement of so many people, who were as inspired as we were by the idea of having youths develop powerful new ways for seeing and acting in the world. It's the result of years of collaboration with research and design partners across the United States, cycles of testing and feedback from teachers, and helpful insights from advisors and friends. In particular, we'd like to thank the following:

- Connie Yowell (Director of Education for U.S. Programs at the John D. and Catherine T. MacArthur Foundation), for the ongoing support provided to this project through the MacArthur Foundation's Digital Media and Learning (DML) initiative. The project would have been impossible without not only the funding provided, but also the incredible networks of colleagues within the DML field that she has done so much to foster.

- This material also is based in part upon work supported by the National Science Foundation under Grant No. 0855886, awarded to Kylie A. Peppler.

- Nichole Pinkard (Associate Professor of Interactive Media, Human Computer Interaction, and Education, DePaul University), for seeing the need for the project from the beginning and catalyzing this incredible group of partners to come together to work on it.

- The hard-working team of graduate research assistants at Indiana University who have contributed to this project over the years, including Sinem Siyyahan, Diane Glosson, Charlene Volk, Mike Downton, Leon Gordon, Jackie Barnes, Sophia Bender, and Kate Shively, not to mention the broader Learning Sciences student body, who have all engaged in conversations with us around this work one way or another.

- Our colleagues and teacher leaders at the National Writing Project (NWP), who worked with us to pilot the activities in this book and helped us integrate their valuable insights into the final manuscript: Christina Cantrill, Paul Oh, Steve Moore, Lori Sue Garner, Janie Brown, Deidra Floyd, Laura Beth Fay, Carol Jehlen, Travis Powell, Laura Lee Stroud, Eric Tuck, Kevin Hodgson, Janelle Bence, Laura Fay Beth, Cliff Lee, Chad Sansing, and Trina Williams.

- The many institutions in Bloomington, Indiana, that have worked with us to pilot the activities in these books, including the Boys and Girls Club, under the leadership of Matthew Searle; and the Bloomington Project School, under the leadership of Daniel Baron.

- Our advisory board, which has provided valuable feedback both on the treatment of the ideas in these books and how they fit into the broader field: Linda Booth Sweeney, Natalie Rusk, Amon Millner, and Cindy Hmelo-Silver.

HISTORY OF THE GRINDING NEW LENSES PROJECT

One of the important lessons to be learned from working on systems thinking is that nothing is created in a vacuum; the same is true of all the work shared in this book. In this section, we briefly share the background on the Grinding New Lenses (GNL) project, which has led to this book collection and shaped its focus.

Taking a systems perspective, it's somewhat challenging to tell a linear story about what led to this work. But a good place to start might be a school called Quest to Learn (Q2L; q2l.org), which was opened by Katie Salen and Institute of Play in New York City in 2009 (www.instituteofplay.org) with support from the MacArthur Foundation's Digital Media and Learning initiative (Salen et al., 2010). The school was designed as a proof of concept to answer a unique question: How can school-based learning be designed based on powerful learning principles found in the best games—ones that inspire engagement, collaboration, critical thinking, and, of course, systems thinking?

In answering this question, Q2L did a number of things differently from traditional schools. To begin with, it reorganized the curriculum so that disciplines with natural intersections that were usually kept separate were joined together. Mathematics and English language arts became "Codeworlds," a class that focused on symbolic and representational systems. Another class called "The Way Things Work," taught science and math combined, and still another class called "Being, Space, and Place" was put together to teach history and English literature. Assessment and testing also was done differently—instead of finals at the end of each semester, each class broke up into teams that needed to work collaboratively on a week-long "boss level," which challenged the youths to integrate insights from the rest of the course. More broadly, the school made the idea of youths as designers and makers of systems central to the overall setup of Q2L's learning environment an idea that was reflected in the after-school activities, the course design, the boss levels, and the school's integration of design thinking throughout the curriculum. All the different parts of the school aimed to have kids use what they were learning to make or design something concrete.

While the Q2L school represented great innovations in learning and was lucky to have the freedom to do a lot of things differently, it was just one school. How could what was being learned there be shared, tested, and added to by the wealth of innovative educators and schools in the world already doing great work? In many ways, the GNL project, titled from the idea that systems thinking offers a powerful new "lens" to see the world, came from a desire to do just this. In the initiative, Kylie Peppler and Melissa Gresalfi, researchers and educational designers from Indiana University's Learning Sciences program (**education.indiana.edu/learnsci**), began to work with Katie Salen from Institute of Play (**instituteofplay.org**), Nichole Pinkard from DePaul University, and the Digital Youth Network (DYN; **digitalyouthnetwork.org**) to develop a series of modular toolkits that used the design of digital media as a means to develop systems thinking skills, all based on the existing approaches taken in the Q2L school. With the financial support of the MacArthur Foundation and the help of additional partners like the NWP (**www.nwp.org**) (a network of educators and local writing project sites that serve up to 100,000 teachers annually), the initiative worked for three years to make this idea a reality.

The main goal of the initiative was twofold: to create a series of scalable modular toolkits that used the power of designing with new media to promote engagement in design and systems thinking dispositions in young people; and to conduct research on what kind of curricular supports lead to the development of systems thinking dispositions through design activities.

Ultimately, four sets of modular curricula were developed in close coordination with teachers in the NWP network at every step of the process. Each of these uses a different technology and provides unique ways to engage in design with various approaches to understanding systems. The *Gaming the System* curricula involves game design with the Gamestar Mechanic (G*M) platform (Salen, 2007) and focuses on understanding games as systems and young people as designers of those systems. A second set of curricula, *Script Changers* focuses on the idea of using narrative and stories to understand systems, and uses the Scratch programming environment (Resnick et al., 2009) as a way to tell digital stories about systems by way of a computational system. The final two sets of curricula, *Short Circuits* and *Soft Circuits,* use physical computing technology like light-emitting diodes (LEDs), sensors, and the wearable technology controlled by the LilyPad Arduino (Buechley, 2006) to show how youths can create electronics embedded in paper, clothing, and other everyday objects and understand how these creations operate as systems.

Using an approach called Design-Based Research (DBR) (Brown, 1992), which employs approaches found in the world of engineering to engage in an iterative and cyclical design process around learning activities in which each implementation yields lessons that are incorporated into final designs, we piloted and tested the modules in many contexts. A particularly positive benefit of DBR is that it acknowledges that you're not necessarily going to get things right the first time (we certainly didn't!) but trusts a process of embracing failures and missteps as learning opportunities that are really gifts in disguise. For us, the process of being active learners about what worked and why was a central part of the work that we did in developing the activities being shared here.

Many of the activities were, as mentioned, initially developed and tested in New York City at Q2L; others were developed and piloted at local schools like the Bloomington Project School in Indiana, as well as at a local Boys and Girls Club that serves a wide range of youths from varied ethnic and socioeconomic backgrounds. A significant amount of testing was done in close coordination with our NWP partners in sites across the United States and through extended, project-specific summer workshops hosted at DePaul University in Chicago and elsewhere. Testing and refinement also was done in Chicago in schools affiliated with partners at the DYN. Additionally, DYN's parent institution, DePaul University, hosted a summer camp that served as a major testing ground for the curricula. Over the course of four weeks in the summer of 2011, expert teachers from across the United States affiliated with the NWP worked with researchers from Indiana University and designers from Institute of Play to refine the modules based on lessons born of implementing them with almost 100 youths native to Chicago, again with a mix of kids from different backgrounds. These educators are too numerous to list here, but their voices and contributions to this volume are recognized both in our list of contributors and in the "Voices from the Field" sections that you will see throughout all three of these volumes. The exercises, ideas, and guiding pedagogical ideas throughout these books are infused with their perspectives.

In developing the volumes, we wanted to ensure that the work was grounded both in insights from the academic literature on systems thinking and the learning sciences, and also in the lived experiences of educators. The research team contained a number of members who had worked as educators for many years in both formal learning contexts like public schools and informal ones like after-school programs, libraries, and museums. Most importantly, though, the initiative's partnership with the NWP meant that the kind of educators interested in the sort of innovative approaches that we were developing were kept at the center of our designs. They played important roles in testing and refining the modules as previously described, as well as serving on an editorial advisory board (including, most prominently, the assistance of Christina Cantrill, Paul Oh, and Steve Moore) that offered insights, made substantial edits, gave productive feedback, and helped to create many of the activities and materials found in these volumes. They were indispensable to the core design team throughout the project. Through this partnership, we hope that the current volumes are useful to educators in a wide variety of settings to engage youths in design activities that will help them to become systems thinkers, with the ultimate goal of transforming the world that we live in today.

As you might have already noticed, this project brought together many different participants with divergent backgrounds, including game designers from Institute of Play; researchers with backgrounds in the arts, mathematics, and civic education at Indiana University; out-of-school educators at DYN; and professional teachers from the NWP. So, what common threads brought all of these partners together? While there was certainly a common interest in systems thinking as a critical skill for an increasingly complex world, the group also shared a common belief that kids in the twenty-first century had new opportunities for learning as a result of the changing technological landscape. Like many forward-thinking educators, we all saw that the ways that we've been educating young people as a society, through focusing on skill and drill rather than innovation and exploration, and through teaching to the test rather than teaching to youths' interests, were doing a major disservice to young people.

Each of these partners was involved in a broader movement started by the MacArthur Foundation in 2006 to investigate the ways that digital media was changing how kids learn and how these technologies might be leveraged to create new opportunities for learning that might have been previously unimaginable. The Digital Media and Learning (DML) initiative has supported over $80 million in grants to research and develop innovations in digital learning at the time of this writing. It has focused on youth-interest-driven activity in digital spaces as a source of inspiration for creating new learning environments that incorporated the kinds of engagement and higher-order skill development found in places like massively multiplayer online games or do-it-yourself online creative communities like those centered around fan fiction, video blogging, and many other forms of making, tinkering, and designing. The Q2L school and the G*M platform used in the game design module were two examples of learning environments that came out of the DML initiative. Both aimed to build off of interests that youths already brought to school with them, as well as focus on the kinds of twenty-first-century skills they'll need to thrive in the world.

We share this background to enable the reader to think about the activities and resources in this collection not as an isolated approach to teaching, but rather as part of a larger movement to rethink learning in a digital age. There is an incredible amount of innovation happening at the edges of education, and in places that people tend not to think of as learning spaces. We see youths learning in new ways connected to pursuing their interests, engaging deeply, and solving problems through engagement with technology. We want to bring that kind of learning into more formal learning spaces, and we know that we're not alone in this desire. If you're reading this, it's probably because you agree with us that education can be done differently, that youths can engage in problems that are meaningful for them, are connected to their lives, and prepare them for lifelong learning in a changing and complex world.

A TEACHER'S REFLECTION

In concluding this section on the history of the project, we wanted to share the voice and experience of one of the many talented educators that worked on this project. Laura Lee Stroud—a secondary teacher and English language arts instructional coach in the Round Rock Independent School District, as well as a member of the Central Texas Writing Project—reflected on her experience as a maker and learner while engaging with the GNL curriculum during the GNL summer camp in 2011. As part of a playtesting moment, Stroud joined a number of other teachers to construct her own understanding of tools like G*M, Scratch, and e-textiles, as well as facilitate understanding for youths at the camp:

> The Grinding New Lenses camp experience was unlike any experience I'd ever had the opportunity to engage in. NWP teachers from all over the nation gathered for one month in Chicago, away from our homes and families, hoping to learn about systems thinking concepts and internalize them into our existing teaching repertoires. The only thing that we all knew about each other and the work was that we believed in the lifelong learning process and that we had the NWP in common.

The group of educators, in partnership with researchers from Indiana University, Institute of Play, and the DYN, participated in conversations and activities that would evolve into the challenges described in these volumes. As the teachers explored platforms and tools in the service of systems thinking by doing what they soon would be asking youths to do, they also provided feedback, suggestions, and their own mods, contributing to the overall development of the modules as they exist today. As Stroud says, "As a professional, I was viewed as a professional and asked to help edit and revise the curriculum." This feedback and response process with the educators continued throughout the camp experience:

> After we were comfortable with the first layers of the curriculum we were to learn, we split into the modules we were to teach. We were partnered with another teacher and reviewed the materials, learned new vocabulary, and tried to familiarize ourselves with this newfound systems thinking perspective. Every day, in preparation for the summer camp youths, we processed the modules as learners and created the products—be it games, digital narratives with sprites as characters, or e-textile clothing and accessories.

Stroud was a facilitator of the *Soft Circuits* curriculum with youths, but also saw herself as a learner. By entering this brand new world of e-textiles (though it easily could have been a "brand new world of game development" or "brand new world of the programming of a digital story"), she discovered the gaps that existed in her own knowledge—about circuits and circuitry, for instance. This made her that much more sympathetic to the needs of her youths, which in turn allowed her to support them in relating the e-textiles work to their life experiences:

> As the youth entered the camps, for the most part not one teacher assumed the comfortable position of "expert" with our novice youths learning under us. Instead, we were positioned as learners alongside our campers. In some cases, our campers knew more about the content than did we the teachers. We had to remember our new value of supporter, encourager, observer, and researcher. We provided scaffolds for the new concepts, such as an immersion into the new vocabulary, and created a space in the modules for explicit vocabulary instruction. For example, the youths needed to know how to sew a "running stitch" before they could complete a circuit with conductive thread. In fact, in creating the e-cuff, we realized that many of the youths had never made a hem, which is created with a running stitch. As we tried to explain to them how we teachers learned to sew a running stitch, a

previously disinterested camper had a light bulb moment as she realized she in fact knew how to sew. She'd worked with her mother in a beauty shop in which they sewed in extra hair for clients. She not only knew how to create a running stitch, she was able to teach the other children how to do it, too! This experience reinforced for me the iterative process of discovering the strengths available within our classrooms that in turn make our instructional systems most productive.

Stroud concluded by saying:

When we teachers had group time to reflect on our experience, we found that we all struggled in one way or another and as a result we had a newfound level of respect for our youths' learning processes and struggles, as well as a wonderful glimpse into our own learning process.

LIST OF CONTRIBUTORS

Jackie Barnes, Indiana University
David Burton, Bloomington Project School
Christina Cantrill, National Writing Project
Avri Coleman, Digital Youth Network
Michael Downton, Indiana University
Deidra Floyd, Central Texas Writing Project
Leon Gordon, Indiana University
Katya Hott, E-Line Media
Steve Moore, Greater Kansas City Writing Project
Paul Oh, National Writing Project
Nichole Pinkard, DePaul University
Travis Powell, Oregon Writing Project
Scott Price, E-Line Media
Sinem Siyyahan, Arizona State University, Play2Connect Research Group
Charlene Volk, Indiana University
Scott Wallace, Bloomington Project School
Janis Watson, Indiana University
Malcolm Williams, Digital Youth Network

SYSTEMS THINKING CONCEPTS IN THIS BOOK COLLECTION

The goal of the *Interconnections: Understanding Systems through Digital Design* book collection is to make available an accessible set of activities that can help youths develop a "systems lens" for seeing the world—a lens they can use to make sense of problems around them. Our hope is that youths will be able to see, anticipate, and understand patterns in the systems that make up that world, and use those understandings to eventually design better systems.

In these modules, we share a range of practices and concepts related to systems thinking. These concepts by no means represent a comprehensive list of every major idea in systems thinking—instead, we have chosen to focus on a subset of key ideas that focus centrally on *understanding systems,* and, in some of the volumes, on more complex ideas related to *system dynamics.* Understanding systems involves recognizing the elements that structure a system, and, more important, the ways that those elements interconnect to impact each other and the overall function of a system. These understandings are mostly oriented toward analyzing a system at a particular point in time, which is a common focus in these modules. In contrast, the study of system dynamics is fundamentally concerned with understanding the behavior of systems *over time.* Examining how a system changes and the kinds of patterns that emerge over time is crucial to understanding how to intervene effectively in systems. As is detailed next, not all the modules deal with these ideas in the same way—the *Gaming the System* module focuses almost exclusively on supporting youths' understanding of systems, while the *Script Changers* module is more fundamentally concerned with understanding (and orchestrating) system changes over time.

The choices made about which concepts and practices to include were driven by the kinds of design activities that we envisioned for youths, and those ideas that are particularly easy to see via the tinkering and iteration processes associated with design. For example, all modules spend a significant amount of time helping youths to see the kinds of *interconnections* that take place among components of a system and the kinds of system dynamics that emerge through these interconnections. This focus is easily revealed through design work because youths can define interconnections, observe the functioning of the system, and then, through iterations on their designs, change the nature of these interconnections and immediately observe the resulting changes in system function. For example, when youths are designing a videogame (in *Gaming the System),* they can see immediately how changing the behavior of a single component (such as the health of an avatar, or the damage that an enemy can do) can immediately change how challenging the game is (the overall *function* of the game—the way it works). Likewise, in *Short Circuits* and *Soft Circuits,* youths can observe how changing the structure of light-emitting diode (LED) connections (i.e., the ways that they're linked to each other) can immediately affect the number of LEDs that can light up.

Although there is a lot of overlap among the concepts covered in the four books, each one tackles these ideas uniquely, and there are some particular systems thinking concepts that are covered only in some modules. In the following sections, we describe and define the "big ideas" that are addressed in the modules. In the table that follows, the specifics of those big ideas and where they are addressed in each book and module are portrayed.

1. IDENTIFY SYSTEMS.

A *system* is a collection of two or more components and processes that interconnect to function as a whole. For example, speed and comfort in a car are created by the interactions of the car's parts, so they are "greater than the sum" of all the separate parts of the car. The way that a system works is not the result of a single part; rather, it is produced by the *interactions* among the components and/or individual agents within it. A key way to differentiate whether something is a system or not is to consider whether the overall way that it works in the world will change if you remove one part of it.

2. USE LANGUAGE THAT REVEALS A SYSTEM'S CHARACTERISTICS AND FUNCTION.

A key indicator of youths' understanding of systems involves listening for the ways that they describe and make sense of a system. When using a systems thinking approach effectively, youths will be able to identify a system's *components*, the *behaviors* of those components, how those behaviors are shaped by the *system's structure*, and how these behaviors *interconnect* to form broader *system dynamics* that move the system toward a particular *function*. At times, a system is designed to meet a particular *goal,* which can be (but is not always) aligned with the actual function of the system.

3. MAKE SYSTEMS VISIBLE.

When we learn to "make the system visible"—whether through a system model drawn on the back of a napkin, a computer simulation, a game, a picture, a diagram, a set of mathematical computations, or a story—we can use these representations to communicate about how things work. At their best, good pictures of systems help both the creator and the "reader" or "audience" to understand not only the parts of the system (the components), but also, how those components work together to produce the whole.

4. SEEK OUT COMMON SYSTEM PATTERNS.

Beyond the core aspects of a system (i.e., components, behaviors, interconnections, dynamics, and function), there are a number of common patterns that are important for young people to look for when engaging with systems. Specifically, systems often have *reinforcing feedback loops* that cause growth or decline, as well as *balancing feedback loops* that create stability in a system. These loops are directly related to the *stocks and flows* of a system—what is coming into a system and what is going out. In particular, when more is flowing out of a system than is coming in, there begins to be a concern about *limited resources* within a system. Sometimes patterns in systems can be seen best by examining the ways that systems are *nested* within each other.

5. DESIGN AND INTERVENE IN SYSTEMS.

A key practice of a systems thinker involves both designing new systems and fixing systems that are out of balance. These interventions allow youths to go beyond simply interrogating existing systems in the world to use their understanding of how systems work to actually change the world around them, while doing so in a conscious way that respects the complexity of systems. The process of *designing* a system involves thinking deeply about the state of the system that you have envisioned, and how the particular components you have to work with might interconnect with other components for that state to be realized. This process of design involves more than understanding inter-connections, however; it is also about considering what to do when things go wrong—the most productive *leverage point* to intervene or change a system, why a proposed solution might *fail*, and what *unintended consequences* might occur based on your design.

6. SHIFT PERSPECTIVES TO UNDERSTAND SYSTEMS.

Systems thinkers regularly shift perspectives as they look at systems to get the full picture of what's happening. They think about the actors in a system and what *mental models* they bring to the system that affect the way that they participate. They shift among different *levels of perspective*—from events, to patterns, to structures, and finally to the mental models that give rise to a system—to better understand that system. And finally, they change the *time horizon* associated with looking at a system in order to find *time delays* from prior actions in a system.

		Gaming the System: Designing with Gamestar Mechanic						Script Changers: Digital Storytelling with Scratch						Short Circuits: Crafting e-Puppets with DIY Electronics				Soft Circuits: Crafting e-Fashion with DIY Electronics			
		CH 1	CH 2	CH 3	CH 4	CH 5	CH 6	CH 1	CH 2	CH 3	CH 4	CH 5	CH 6	CH 1	CH 2	CH 3	CH 4	CH 1	CH 2	CH 3	CH 4
1. Identify systems	Identifying the way that a system is functioning	x	x	x	x	x	x	x	x	x	x	x	x	x	x	x	x	x	x	x	x
2. Use language that reveals a system's characteristics and function	Distinguishing the goal of a system	x	x	x	x	x	x	x						x				x	x	x	
	Identifying components	x	x	x	x	x	x	x	x	x	x	x	x	x	x	x	x	x	x	x	x
	Identifying behaviors	x	x	x	x	x	x	x	x	x	x	x	x	x	x	x	x	x	x	x	x
	Identifying interconnections	x	x	x	x	x	x	x	x	x	x	x	x	x	x	x	x	x	x	x	x
	Perceiving dynamics									x		x									
	Considering the role of system structure			x												x		x			
3. Make systems visible			x	x				x	x	x	x	x	x	x	x	x	x	x	x	x	x
4. Seek out common system patterns	Reinforcing feedback loops										x										
	Vicious cycles										x										
	Virtuous cycles										x										
	Balancing feedback loops						x					x		x				x			
	Stocks and flows														x						x
	Limited resources in systems													x				x			
	Nested systems								x						x					x	
	Dynamic equilibrium																				x
5. Design and intervene in systems	Designing a system			x	x	x	x	x	x	x	x	x	x	x	x	x	x	x	x	x	x
	Fixes that fail											x									
	Leverage points											x			x				x		
	Unintended consequences												x								
6. Shift perspectives to understand systems	Mental models									x											
	Levels of perspective									x						x		x			
	Time horizons and delays								x												

ALIGNMENT TO COMMON CORE STATE STANDARDS

The following tables represent an at-a-glance view of the alignment of Design Challenges from all four books in the *Interconnections: Understanding Systems through Digital Design* collection to relevant Common Core State Standards (CCSS) for English Language Arts and Literacy in History/Social Studies, Science and Technical Subjects. Only relevant standards are included in these tables. (For the complete list of standards, go to **www.corestandards.org/ELA-Literacy**.)

The Common Core State Standards for English Language Arts and Literacy in History/Social Studies, Science, and Technical Subjects are the result of an initiative to provide a shared national framework for literacy development to prepare youths for college and the workforce. The CCSS span kindergarten through twelfth grade, divided into three bands: K–5, 6–8, and 9–12. The CCSS may be thought of as a "staircase" of increasing complexity that details what youths should be expected to read and write, both in English and in targeted content areas. The CCSS are built upon a set of guiding "anchor standards" that evolve through grade-level progression and emphasize informational text and argumentative writing, particularly at the middle and high school levels. In addition, the CCSS include a strand that emphasizes literacy skills associated with production and distribution via technology.

For newcomers, a useful way to enter into the English Language Arts standards is to read the online About the Standards page at the CCSS website (**www.corestandards .org/about-the-standards**), and then read the anchor standards for each grade band, as well as for the content areas.

Through the Design Challenges, youths are introduced to a range of core skills and information that stretch their learning potential and build on prior knowledge. Expect them to encounter material described in the English Language Arts standards for reading informational text for key ideas and detail, as well as the integration of knowledge and ideas; for producing and distributing writing with technology; and for speaking and listening tasks that prepare youths for college and careers through comprehension and collaboration, as well as the presentation of knowledge and ideas.

Because the *Interconnections* collection presents curricula that engage youths in literacy practices that fall in the English Language Arts domain, as well as the domains of History/Social Studies and Science and Technical Subjects, the letter-number designation that accompanies each standard in the table aligns with the CCSS letter-number designation as follows:

- R—Reading Literature
- RI—Reading Informational Text
- W—Writing
- SL—Speaking & Listening
- RST—Reading in Science and Technical Subjects
- WHST—Writing in History/Social Studies, Science and Technical Subjects

The standards included in these tables serve as a guide through which the Design Challenges can be understood in conjunction with the CCSS. They do not represent an exhaustive list of all possible alignments, but rather those most prevalent and immediate to the central tasks.

Common Core English Language Arts Standards	Gaming the System: Designing with Gamestar Mechanic					
	CH 1	CH 2	CH 3	CH 4	CH 5	CH 6
R.6-12.7 (anchor standard) Integrate and evaluate content presented in diverse formats and media, including visually and quantitatively, as well as in words.	x					x
RI.7.3 Analyze the interactions between individuals, events, and ideas in a text (e.g., how ideas influence individuals or events, or how individuals influence ideas or events).						x
RI.7.7 Compare and contrast a text to an audio, video, or multimedia version of the text, analyzing each medium's portrayal of the subject (e.g. how the delivery of a speech affects the impact of the words).						x
RI.7.9 Analyze how two or more authors writing about the same topic shape their presentations of key information by emphasizing different evidence or advancing different interpretations of facts.	x	x	x	x	x	
W.6-8.3 Write narratives to develop real or imagined experiences or events using effective technique, relevant descriptive details, and well-structured event sequences.	x	x	x	x	x	
W.7.6 Use technology, including the Internet, to produce and publish writing and link to and cite sources as well as to interact and collaborate with others, including linking to and citing sources.						x
RST.6-8.3 Follow precisely a multistep procedure when carrying out experiments, taking measurements, or performing technical tasks.	x	x	x	x	x	
RST.6-8.4 Determine the meaning of symbols, key terms, and other domain-specific words and phrases as they are used in a specific scientific or technical context relevant to grades 6–8 texts and topics.						
RST.6-8.7 Integrate quantitative or technical information expressed in words in a text with a version of that information expressed visually (e.g., in a flowchart, diagram, model, graph or table).	x	x	x	x		x
RST.6-8.9 Compare and contrast the information gained from experiments, simulations, video, or multimedia sources with that gained from reading a text on the same topic.	x	x	x	x	x	x
RST.11-12.9 Synthesize information from a range of sources (e.g., texts, experiments, simulations) into a coherent understanding of a process, phenomenon, or concept, resolving conflicting information when possible.						x
SL.6-12.4 (anchor standard) Present information, findings, and supporting evidence such that listeners can follow the line of reasoning and the organization, development, and style are appropriate to task, purpose, and audience.	x	x	x	x	x	x
SL.7.5 Include multimedia components and visual displays in presentations to clarify claims and findings and emphasize salient points.	x	x	x	x	x	

Common Core English Language Arts Standards	Script Changers: Digital Storytelling with Scratch					
	CH 1	CH 2	CH 3	CH 4	CH 5	CH 6
R.6-12.3 (anchor standard) Analyze how and why individuals, events and ideas develop and interact over the course of a text.			x	x	x	x
R.6-12.7 (anchor standard) Integrate and evaluate content presented in diverse formats and media, including visually and quantitatively, as well as in words.	x	x	x	x	x	x
RI.7.3 Analyze the interactions between individuals, events, and ideas in a text (e.g., how ideas influence individuals or events, or how individuals influence ideas or events).		x	x	x	x	x
W.6-12.2 (anchor standard) Write informative/explanatory texts to examine and convey complex ideas and information clearly and accurately through the effective selection, organization, and analysis of content.		x	x	x	x	x
W.6-8.3 Write narratives to develop real or imagined experiences or events using effective technique, relevant descriptive details, and well-structured event sequences.	x					
W.8.6 Use technology, including the Internet, to produce and publish writing and present the relationships between information and ideas efficiently as well as to interact and collaborate with others.	x	x	x	x		x
W.8.7 Conduct short research projects to answer a question (including a self-generated question), drawing on several sources and generating additional related, focused questions that allow for multiple avenues of exploration.						x
W.6-12.7 (anchor standard) Conduct short as well as more sustained research projects based on focused questions, demonstrating understanding of the subject under investigation.		x	x	x	x	x
W.6-12.9 (anchor standard) Draw evidence from literary or informational texts to support analysis, reflection and research.			x	x	x	x
RST.6-8.3 Follow precisely a multistep procedure when carrying out experiments, taking measurements, or performing technical tasks.	x	x	x	x	x	x
RST.6-8.4 Determine the meaning of symbols, key terms, and other domain-specific words and phrases as they are used in a specific scientific or technical context relevant to grades 6–8 texts and topics.						
RST.6-8.7 Integrate quantitative or technical information expressed in words in a text with a version of that information expressed visually (e.g., in a flowchart, diagram, model, graph or table).		x	x	x		x

Common Core English Language Arts Standards	Script Changers: Digital Storytelling with Scratch					
	CH 1	CH 2	CH 3	CH 4	CH 5	CH 6
RST.11-12.9 Synthesize information from a range of sources (e.g., texts, experiments, simulations) into a coherent understanding of a process, phenomenon, or concept, resolving conflicting information when possible.						x
SL.7.2 Analyze the main ideas and supporting details presented in diverse media and formats (e.g., visually, quantitatively, orally) and explain how the ideas clarify a topic, text or issue under study.		x	x	x	x	x
SL.7.4 Present claims and findings, emphasizing salient points in a focused, coherent manner with pertinent descriptions, facts, details, and examples; use appropriate eye contact, adequate volume, and clear pronunciation.						
SL.6-12.4 (anchor standard) Present information, findings, and supporting evidence such that listeners can follow the line of reasoning and the organization, development, and style are appropriate to task, purpose, and audience.		x	x	x	x	x
SL.7.5 Include multimedia components and visual displays in presentations to clarify claims and findings and emphasize salient points.			x	x		x
WHST.6-8.4 Produce clear and coherent writing in which the development, organization, and style are appropriate to task, purpose, and audience.						x
WHST.6-8.5 With some guidance and support from peers and adults, develop and strengthen writing as needed by planning, revising, editing, rewriting, or trying a new approach, focusing on how well purpose and audience have been addressed.						x
WHST.6-8.6 Use technology, including the Internet, to produce and publish writing and present the relationships between information and ideas clearly and efficiently.						x
WHST.6-8.7 Conduct short research projects to answer a question (including a self-generated question), drawing on several sources and generating additional related, focused questions that allow for multiple avenues of exploration.			x			x

Common Core English Language Arts Standards	Short Circuits: Crafting e-Puppets with DIY Electronics				Soft Circuits: Crafting e-Fashion with DIY Electronics			
	CH 1	CH 2	CH 3	CH 4	CH 1	CH 2	CH 3	CH 4
R.6-12.7 (anchor standard) Integrate and evaluate content presented in diverse formats and media, including visually and quantitatively, as well as in words.								x
RI.7.3 Analyze the interactions between individuals, events, and ideas in a text (e.g., how ideas influence individuals or events, or how individuals influence ideas or events).			x	x		x		
RI.7.4 Determine the meaning of words and phrases as they are used in a text, including figurative, connotative, and technical meanings; analyze the impact of a specific word choice on meaning and tone.						x		x
RI.7.5 Include multimedia components and visual displays in presentations to clarify claims and findings and emphasize salient points.			x	x			x	
RI.8.5 Analyze in detail the structure of a specific paragraph in a text, including the role of particular sentences in developing and refining a key concept							x	
RI.8.7 Evaluate the advantages and disadvantages of using different mediums (e.g., print or digital text, video, multimedia) to present a particular topic or idea.							x	
W.6-12.2 (anchor standard) Write informative/explanatory texts to examine and convey complex ideas and information clearly and accurately through the effective selection, organization, and analysis of content.	x				x			x
W.6-8.3 Write narratives to develop real or imagined experiences or events using effective technique, relevant descriptive details, and well-structured event sequences.	x	x			x			
W.7.6 Use technology, including the Internet, to produce and publish writing and link to and cite sources as well as to interact and collaborate with others, including linking to and citing sources.								x
W.8.6 Use technology, including the Internet, to produce and publish writing and present the relationships between information and ideas efficiently as well as to interact and collaborate with others.			x					x
W.8.7 Conduct short research projects to answer a question (including a self-generated question), drawing on several sources and generating additional related, focused questions that allow for multiple avenues of exploration.							x	
RST.6-8.3 Follow precisely a multistep procedure when carrying out experiments, taking measurements, or performing technical tasks.		x		x		x	x	x
RST.6-8.4 Determine the meaning of symbols, key terms, and other domain-specific words and phrases as they are used in a specific scientific or technical context relevant to grades 6–8 texts and topics.	x	x			x		x	x
RST.6-8.7 Integrate quantitative or technical information expressed in words in a text with a version of that information expressed visually (e.g., in a flowchart, diagram, model, graph or table).	x				x			x

Common Core English Language Arts Standards	Short Circuits: Crafting e-Puppets with DIY Electronics				Soft Circuits: Crafting e-Fashion with DIY Electronics			
	CH 1	CH 2	CH 3	CH 4	CH 1	CH 2	CH 3	CH 4
RST.6-8.9 Compare and contrast the information gained from experiments, simulations, video, or multimedia sources with that gained from reading a text on the same topic.								x
RST.11-12.9 Synthesize information from a range of sources (e.g., texts, experiments, simulations) into a coherent understanding of a process, phenomenon, or concept, resolving conflicting information when possible.	x				x	x		
SL.6-12.4 (anchor standard) Present information, findings, and supporting evidence such that listeners can follow the line of reasoning and the organization, development, and style are appropriate to task, purpose, and audience.	x		x		x		x	
SL.7.2 Analyze the main ideas and supporting details presented in diverse media and formats (e.g., visually, quantitatively, orally) and explain how the ideas clarify a topic, text, or issue under study.						x		
SL.7.4 Present claims and findings, emphasizing salient points in a focused, coherent manner with pertinent descriptions, facts, details, and examples; use appropriate eye contact, adequate volume, and clear pronunciation.				x				
SL.7.5 Include multimedia components and visual displays in presentations to clarify claims and findings and emphasize salient points.			x			x		
WHST.6-8.4 Produce clear and coherent writing in which the development, organization, and style are appropriate to task, purpose, and audience.			x					x
WHST.6-8.6 Use technology, including the Internet, to produce and publish writing and present the relationships between information and ideas clearly and efficiently.							x	

NEXT GENERATION SCIENCE STANDARDS

Because the *Interconnections* book collection presents curricula that engage youths in design activities that embrace the sciences, the standards included in this table serve as a guide through which the challenges can be understood in conjunction with the Next Generation Science Standards (NGSS; found at **www.nextgenscience.org/next -generation-science-standards**). They do not represent an exhaustive list of all possible alignments, but rather those most prevalent and immediate to the central tasks.

As the NGSS are explicit in assigning specific scientific topics and learning to specific grade levels, the correlations in these tables range from third grade to high school. The following tables were created to help identify which national science standards align to our Design Challenges, to what grade, and in which challenge each is addressed. Please note, however, that all the Design Challenges have been tested in a wide range of ability, grade, and age groups.

NGSS CODE DESIGNATIONS

- 3–5: Upper elementary grades
- MS: Middle school grades 6–8
- HS: High school grades 9–12
- ESS = Earth and Space Science
- ETS = Engineering, Technology, and Applications of Science
- PS = Physical Sciences

Next Generation Science Standards	Gaming the System: Designing with Gamestar Mechanic					
	CH 1	CH 2	CH 3	CH 4	CH 5	CH 6
ETS1 Engineering Design						
3-5-ETS1-1. Define a simple design problem reflecting a need or a want that includes specified criteria for success and constraints on materials, time, or cost.	x	x	x	x	x	x
3-5-ETS1-2. Generate and compare multiple possible solutions to a problem based on how well each is likely to meet the criteria and constraints of the problem.	x	x	x	x	x	x
3-5-ETS1-3. Plan and carry out fair tests in which variables are controlled and failure points are considered to identify aspects of a model or prototype that can be improved.	x	x	x	x	x	x
MS-ETS1-1. Define the criteria and constraints of a design problem with sufficient precision to ensure a successful solution, taking into account relevant scientific principles and potential impacts on people and the natural environment that may limit possible solutions.			x	x	x	x
MS-ETS1-2. Evaluate competing design solutions using a systematic process to determine how well they meet the criteria and constraints of the problem.	x	x	x	x	x	x
MS-ETS1-3. Analyze data from tests to determine similarities and differences among several design solutions to identify the best characteristics of each that can be combined into a new solution to better meet the criteria for success.				x	x	x
MS-ETS1-4. Develop a model to generate data for iterative testing and modification of a proposed object, tool, or process such that an optimal design can be achieved.	x	x	x	x	x	x

Next Generation Science Standards	Script Changers: Digital Storytelling with Scratch					
	CH 1	CH 2	CH 3	CH 4	CH 5	CH 6
ETS1 Engineering Design						
3-5-ETS1-1. Define a simple design problem reflecting a need or a want that includes specified criteria for success and constraints on materials, time, or cost.	x	x	x	x	x	x
3-5-ETS1-2. Generate and compare multiple possible solutions to a problem based on how well each is likely to meet the criteria and constraints of the problem.			x	x	x	x
3-5-ETS1-3. Plan and carry out fair tests in which variables are controlled and failure points are considered to identify aspects of a model or prototype that can be improved.				x	x	x
MS-ETS1-1. Define the criteria and constraints of a design problem with sufficient precision to ensure a successful solution, taking into account relevant scientific principles and potential impacts on people and the natural environment that may limit possible solutions.	x	x	x	x	x	x
MS-ETS1-2. Evaluate competing design solutions using a systematic process to determine how well they meet the criteria and constraints of the problem.			x	x	x	x
MS-ETS1-3. Analyze data from tests to determine similarities and differences among several design solutions to identify the best characteristics of each that can be combined into a new solution to better meet the criteria for success.					x	x
MS-ETS1-4. Develop a model to generate data for iterative testing and modification of a proposed object, tool, or process such that an optimal design can be achieved.		x	x	x	x	x
ESS3 Human Impacts						
MS-ESS3-3. Apply scientific principles to design a method for monitoring and minimizing a human impact on the environment.		x	x	x	x	x

Next Generation Science Standards	Short Circuits: Crafting e-Puppets with DIY Electronics				Soft Circuits: Crafting e-Fashion with DIY Electronics			
	CH 1	CH 2	CH 3	CH 4	CH 1	CH 2	CH 3	CH 4
PS2 Motion and Stability: Forces and Interactions								
3-PS2-3. Ask questions to determine cause and effect relationships of electric or magnetic interactions between two objects not in contact with each other.	x	x	x	x	x	x	x	x
MS-PS2-3. Ask questions about data to determine the factors that affect the strength of electric and magnetic forces.	x	x		x	x	x	x	x
PS3 Energy								
4-PS3-2. Make observations to provide evidence that energy can be transferred from place to place by sound, light, heat, and electric currents.	x	x	x	x	x	x	x	x
4-PS3-4. Apply scientific ideas to design, test, and refine a device that converts energy from one form to another.		x		x		x	x	x
MS-PS3-2. Develop a model to describe that when the arrangement of objects interacting at a distance changes, different amounts of potential energy are stored in the system.		x				x	x	x
HS-PS3-3. Design, build, and refine a device that works within given constraints to convert one form of energy into another form of energy.				x				x
ETS1 Engineering Design								
3-5-ETS1-1. Define a simple design problem reflecting a need or a want that includes specified criteria for success and constraints on materials, time, or cost.	x	x	x	x	x	x	x	x
3-5-ETS1-2. Generate and compare multiple possible solutions to a problem based on how well each is likely to meet the criteria and constraints of the problem.	x	x	x	x	x	x	x	x
3-5-ETS1-3. Plan and carry out fair tests in which variables are controlled and failure points are considered to identify aspects of a model or prototype that can be improved.		x	x	x	x	x	x	x
MS-ETS1-1. Define the criteria and constraints of a design problem with sufficient precision to ensure a successful solution, taking into account relevant scientific principles and potential impacts on people and the natural environment that may limit possible solutions.							x	
MS-ETS1-2. Evaluate competing design solutions using a systematic process to determine how well they meet the criteria and constraints of the problem.	x	x		x	x		x	
MS-ETS1-4. Develop a model to generate data for iterative testing and modification of a proposed object, tool, or process such that an optimal design can be achieved.		x		x		x	x	x

INTRODUCTION

You think that because you understand "one" that you must therefore understand "two" because one and one make two. But you forget that you must also understand "and."

—*Sufi teaching*

Few would argue with the idea that the world is growing more complex as the twenty-first century unfolds. We live in a time that not only requires us to work across disciplines to solve problems, but also one in which these problems are of unprecedented scale, coming from a world that is more interconnected than ever. In such a context, power rests in the hands of those who understand the nature of the interdependent systems that organize the world, and, more important, can identify where to act or how to intervene in order to change those systems. Effective intervention requires considering not just simple causal relations, but also the complex interconnections that work together in often-unexpected ways to produce an outcome. Taking action in our complex world requires a set of twenty-first century skills and competencies called "systems thinking."

Systems thinking is best characterized by the old dictum that the whole is always greater than the sum of its parts. It's an approach that involves considering not just the behavior of individual components of a system, but also the complex interconnections between multiple parts that work together to form a whole. Systems are ubiquitous in our world—which includes natural systems that deal with climate and biodiversity, economic systems that drive production and labor trends, and political systems that enact governance of communities and nations. And, of course, these systems are themselves connected to one another in important ways, so understanding the nature of these interconnections, not just within but also across systems, is becoming ever more vital. The promise of learning to reason about how systems work is that of creating a new and effective lens for seeing, engaging with, and changing the world.

Systems thinking allows one not just to understand better how systems function, but also to decide the best way to intervene to *change* systems. Systems thinkers have the potential to have a significant impact on the world around them—an impact that is often denied to those who think in simple cause-and-effect terms. As a consequence, we believe that to effectively and ethically educate children to thrive in the twenty-first century, we must create contexts in which young people are supported in learning to be creative and courageous about making changes to systems in the world and to understand that those changes will always have an impact on other parts of the system—everything is interconnected. It's not enough to instill this competency in current leaders—we must prepare the next generation to be effective and thoughtful stewards of the world that they will inherit soon. Helping young people to understand how systems work, how they are represented, and how they change—via direct or indirect means—is critically important to this larger project. Furthermore, it's important that young people learn about systems not in a distant and unfamiliar context, but in contexts that have meaning to today's youth—those rooted in popular culture, design, and new technologies. This approach is the basis of this collection.

Digital media are central in almost every aspect of daily life, most notably in how we communicate, understand political issues, reflect, produce, consume, and share knowledge. We are living in an era in which digital media is rapidly becoming a driving force in globalization, scientific advances, and the intersection of cultures. The growing accessibility of digital tools and networks, the prevalence of many-to-many distribution models, and the large-scale online aggregation of information and culture are leading to profound changes in how we create and access knowledge. Perhaps nowhere is this digital influence contested more than in education, where questions arise about the ability of traditional systems to prepare young people for the social, economic, and political demands of a complex and connected new century.

This collection, *Interconnections: Understanding Systems through Digital Design,* builds on the existing work of educators, management theorists, designers, and learning scientists who are aiming to promote systems thinking in young people. The project uses a design-based approach to learning and offers up a toolkit for supporting systems thinking in ways that are aligned to current Common Core State Standards (CCCS) and relevant to youth interests in digital culture. Through a collaborative effort across a leading group of designers and educators from Institute of Play, Indiana University's Creativity Labs, the Digital Youth Network (DYN), and the National Writing Project (NWP), we've developed an innovative approach to supporting the development of systems thinking in young people; one that allows them to see how systems are at play in the digital contexts that they regularly engage with and one that puts them in the position of designers of those systems. Most prior work on teaching systems thinking has focused on the biological, physical, and social sciences. By contrast, this collection aligns itself with a growing body of work emerging from the fields of game design, digital storytelling, and do-it-yourself (DIY) electronics as contexts for engaging in systems thinking. Creating animated digital stories about aspects of their community they would like to see changed, for example, provides young people with rich opportunities for observation, analysis, and problem solving.

Each of the four books in the collection is rooted in *constructionist* learning theory, which positions young people as active creators of their own understanding by engaging in the design, iteration, and sharing of media artifacts within communities of interest (Papert, 1980; Kafai, 2006). Each book teaches systems thinking concepts and skills in the context of a specific digital media platform and includes an average of six design "challenges" totaling between 25 and 40+ hours of project time.

The first book in the collection, *Gaming the System: Designing with Gamestar Mechanic*, orients readers to the nature of games as systems, how game designers need to think in terms of complex interactions between game elements and rules, and how to involve systems concepts in the design process. The core curriculum uses Gamestar Mechanic (G*M), an online game design environment with a strong systems thinking focus. *Script Changers: Digital Storytelling with Scratch*, focuses on how stories offer an important lens for seeing the world as a series of systems and provides opportunities for young people to create interactive and animated stories about the systems around them. The projects in this book use the Scratch visual programming environment as a means to tell stories about how to affect change in youths' local communities. The two final books, *Short Circuits: Crafting e-Puppets with DIY Electronics* and *Soft Circuits: Crafting e-Fashion with DIY Electronics,* both explore the fields of electronics and "e-textiles," which involves physical computing projects making fabrics and other everyday materials, including incorporating microprocessors into these materials and programming them with an accessible tool called Modkit.

WHAT IS SYSTEMS THINKING?

It has become increasingly clear that youths' experiences in school do not match the kinds of experiences that they are likely to have once they have completed school. The push to support "twenty-first-century" skills stems from this mismatch, and many have advocated for ensuring that young people learn to think about the world not as a simple set of cause-and-effect experiences, but rather as a set of complex systems. *Systems thinking* generally refers to a way of understanding the world as a set of systems that are made up of many components, each of which has distinct behaviors that change and interact, giving rise to emergent behavior. There are many advantages to understanding the world as a set of systems, but a chief one is that systems thinking allows youths to understand and interpret the world across content areas (Goldstone & Wilensky, 2008). Unfortunately, supporting youths to develop systems thinking has proven to be a significant challenge. First, systems thinking ideas are difficult (Hmelo-Silver & Pfeffer, 2004) and also can be counterintuitive (Wilensky & Resnick, 1999). Systems thinking requires youths to look for myriad contributions to system behaviors as opposed to simple cause-and-effect. Indeed, a key concept of systems thinking involves understanding that a small change can lead to a significant outcome—an idea that flies in the face of many core assumptions that we have about the world. Linda Booth Sweeney (2001) points out that most of our experiences in the world, particularly those we have as children, are explained in terms of linear causality. As a consequence, we have limited opportunities to practice talking about or interpreting our experience of the world as a set of systems.

While linking systems thinking to digital media and learning may seem novel, an integration of systems thinking in K–12 education began in the late 1980s and continues today through the efforts of many organizations and individuals, including the Waters Foundation, the Creative Learning Exchange, the Society for Organizational Learning Education Partnership, and various research groups at institutions like the Massachusetts Institute of Technology (MIT), Northwestern University, Rutgers, and Indiana University. There are also many passionate educators across the United States who have been informed by these initiatives, as well as by leaders in the field of systems dynamics, including Jay Forrester, Linda Booth Sweeney, Peter Senge, and George Richardson. According to Debra Lyneis of the Creative Learning Exchange, the field first began to take root in classrooms when Gordon Brown, a retired MIT dean of engineering, introduced a piece of modeling software called STELLA to a middle school teacher at Orange Grove Junior High School in Tucson, Arizona. That teacher, Frank Draper, and his principal, Mary Scheetz, worked for years to integrate systems thinking across grades in their school. The work was transformative, as Draper writes of his classroom experience:

> Since October 1988 our classrooms have undergone an amazing transformation. Not only are we covering more material than just the required curriculum, but we are covering it faster (we will be through with the year's curriculum this week and will have to add more material to our curriculum for the remaining five weeks) and the students are learning more useful material than ever before. "Facts" are now anchored to meaning through the dynamic relationships they have with each other. In our classroom, students shift from being passive receptacles to active learners. They are not taught about science per se, but learn how to acquire and use knowledge (scientific and otherwise). Our jobs have shifted from dispensers of information

to producers of environments that allow students to learn as much as possible.

We now see students come early to class (even early to school), stay after the bell rings, work through lunch, and work at home voluntarily (with no assignment given). When we work on a systems project—even when the students are working on the book research leading up to system work—there are essentially no motivation/discipline problems in our classrooms. (Draper, 1989)

At the same time, other initiatives rooted in digital media have used computer-based modeling and simulations as a powerful approach to teaching about systems. Leading designers have produced other kid-friendly modeling software packages such as StarLogo, NetLogo, and other tools to study the ways that these sorts of technologies can be used in the context of small and large groups in classrooms (Colella, Klopfer, & Resnick, 2001; Wilensky, 1999; Goldstone & Wilensky, 2008). The field also has extended its use of simulations to include participatory simulations (Colella, 2000) that use technology to allow youths to act as agents in simulations of complex systems. In addition, it has found ways to use simulation software to teach even children in early elementary classrooms the properties of complex systems (Danish et al., 2011).

Systems education now can be found in such diverse places as an elementary school in the Netherlands, public middle and high schools in New York City and Chicago, a private elementary day school in Toledo, a charter school in Chelmsford, Massachusetts, rural schools in northern Vermont and Georgia, suburban schools in Carlisle and Harvard, Massachusetts, and an entire school district in Tucson, Arizona. Some people believe that the middle school level is a good place to begin because of the developmental level of the youths and the flexibility of the middle school structure, but many (including Sweeney, 2001) advocate that both stories and simulations can be used to bring systems thinking to elementary schools, and others (including Lyneis, 2000) have developed robust systems thinking programs in high schools as well.

Throughout the process of coming to know something about their own capacity as systems thinkers, this book collection encourages educators and youths alike to manage and reflect on their evolving identities as learners, producers, peers, researchers, and citizens. The resulting focus is on learning how to *produce meaning*—both for themselves and for external audiences—within complex, multimodal, and systems-rich contexts. Creativity, expression, and innovation underlie this learning as learners practice and apply systems thinking concepts through the coding and decoding of linguistic, computational, social, and cultural systems. This approach challenges traditional barriers between consumer and producer/viewer and designer, allowing youths to gain the skills to act as full citizens within a connected, participatory landscape (Salen et al., 2010).

WHAT IDEAS ABOUT SYSTEMS WILL YOUTHS LEARN IN *SHORT CIRCUITS*?

Although typically systems thinking curricula are concerned with encouraging youths to describe the behavior of systems, the goal of the *Short Circuits* module is for youth to experience the internal structure and interconnections within systems. This is accomplished by creating design experiences that allow youths to tweak components of systems and examine the impact of those tweaks on other components of the system and on the overall function of the system as a whole. Specifically, our goal is that, by the end of the module, youths will have had opportunities to deeply engage with the following practices:

- **Identifying a system:** Understanding that systems are a collection of parts, or components, which interconnect to function as a whole

- **Identify the way a system is functioning:** Understanding what a system is actually doing—the "state" it is moving toward.

- **Distinguishing the goal of a system:** Identifying the ideal state or function of a system from the particular perspective of the designer.

- **Identifying components:** Considering what a system is made of—what are the parts that work together to make a system function as it does?

- **Identifying behaviors**: Identifying the different ways that each component can act.

- **Identifying interconnections:** Identifying the different ways that a system's parts, or components, interact with each other through their behaviors and, through those interactions, change the behaviors of other elements.

- **Considering the role of system structure:** Understanding that the way the system works (i.e., what it actually does) is the product of a set of complex interconnections between components that cannot simply be reduced to an account of the components themselves—these sorts of system dynamics emerge from the way the components interconnect, and these interconnections largely are determined by the way that the system's structure sets them up in relation to one another.

- **Designing systems:** Students are participating in an iterative design process that involves designing systems, tweaking elements of those designs, creating new iterations, and then reflecting on how changes they made fundamentally shape the ways that those systems function and whether they satisfy their own goals for the system.

- **Modeling systems:** Students create versions of existing systems as designed games; that creation involves the act of translating what they understand about the target system to a new domain with new representations.

These are just a subset of the ideas relevant to systems thinking that are covered in the *Short Circuits* module. Each challenge details the ideas about systems thinking that are specifically covered. In addition, these ideas are explored in more depth in the "Delving Deeper into Systems Thinking" chapter that appears at the end of the Design Challenges.

WHAT IS DESIGN THINKING?

To know the world one must construct it.
—Cesare Pavese

When a young person creates a video, a poster, an animation, a customized T-shirt, or a digital app, she is operating within the space of design. Design is a particularly important activity for learning because it positions the learner as an active agent in the creation process. As learners construct a public artifact, they externalize their mental models and iterate on them throughout the design process (Papert, 1980; Kafai, 2006). In contrast to prescriptive approaches to design, where youths all construct the same artifact in parallel or arrive at an idealized solution through design, the challenges in this book strike a balance between structure and free exploration (Colella, Klopfer, & Resnick, 2001). The activities presented here engage youths in design activities to encourage them to learn key systems thinking concepts. We also acknowledge that learning happens best when it's done in a collaborative setting and there are purposeful moments for reflection. As such, the challenges in each volume share a common structure of activities, based on the creative design spiral proposed by Rusk, Resnick, and Cooke (2009).

Resnick (2007) describes the creative process of design as an idea that is realized by iteratively imagining, creating, playing, sharing, and reflecting on the work. *Imagining* begins with youths' open exploration of the materials to ignite their creativity and imagination to take the work in unexpected and personally meaningful directions. *Creating* places an emphasis on building, designing, and making artifacts that can be shared with a broader community. The act of construction not only provides opportunities to develop and enrich creative thinking, but also presents youths with the chance to experience disciplinary content through hands-on reconstruction of their prior knowledge. *Play*, the next step in the design cycle, is where playful experimentation with ideas is done in a low-risk environment to explore and test the boundaries of the materials. The public presentation or *sharing* of work in progress or completed work is also critical to the learning and motivation in the design process, where youths become more engaged and find new inspiration and an audience for their ideas. Resnick also argues for systematic *reflection* on both the design and learning process, where youths discuss and reflect on their thinking. Making the thinking process visible through easy access to the design artifacts from various parts of the creative process is crucial to learning. Finally, Resnick describes this pathway through the design process as a spiral that is then iteratively repeated.

To this work, we add two more steps to the design cycle: Research and Publish. *Research* encapsulates the information gathering that is critical to high-quality teaching and learning. This includes the introduction and definition of key terms and vocabulary, the introduction of key concepts that are important to systems thinking and disciplinary content, and the activities used to gather this information (including the use of videos, diagrams, and other information sources). We also disentangle the sharing of the final product, which we call *Publish*, from more informal moments where sharing is done within the local community to assist in iteration. Current research has demonstrated that this is an important moment for learning and community building, and that there are some crucial differences in who is likely to post in the informal, interest-driven hours (Lenhart and Madden, 2007).

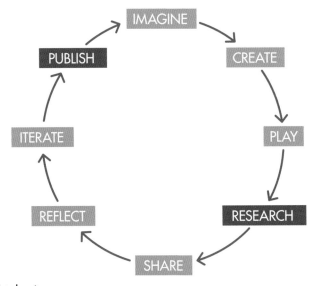

Design-based approach to learning.

As a methodology for learning about systems, design is all about providing constructive contexts in which to explore ideas, interactions, and expressions. Linking design to digital media tools expands this context further: digital tools often make it easier, faster, and less risky to test ideas. There is no need to worry about wasting expensive materials, and erasing a mistake is as easy as clicking a mouse. The act of designing incorporates complex technical, linguistic, and symbolic elements from a variety of domains, at a variety of different levels, and for a variety of different purposes. Designers explicate and defend design ideas, describe design issues and user interactions at a meta-level, imagine new possibilities, create and test hypotheses, and reflect on the impact of each of their creations as a distinctive medium in relation to other media. And each of these involves a melding of technological, social, communicational, and artistic concerns in the framework of a form of scientific thinking in the broad sense of the term. Designers make and think about complex interactive systems, a characteristic activity today, both in the media and in science.

The challenges included within this book emphasize a process of prototyping and iteration based on a design methodology: youths envision new solutions to open-ended problems, work through multiple versions of any idea, integrate ongoing feedback into the learning process, and identify the strengths and weaknesses of both their processes and solutions. In some cases, youths may choose to build on previous solutions or approaches of their peers, seeing themselves as contributors to a larger body of collaboratively generated knowledge.

DESIGNING A SUPPORTIVE LEARNING ENVIRONMENT

Before sharing the Design Challenges that we've developed, it's important to provide a set of guiding design principles for creating a supportive learning environment that are never stated explicitly, but form the base assumptions about what kind of pedagogy they're aiming to promote. As you adapt (and appropriate, of course), the activities in this book, we hope that the principles here might help guide you.

A design-oriented experience, particularly one created to support systems understandings has to be … well, designed. The curriculum modules shared in this book focus on activity structures and learning outcomes—what learners might be doing, with what tools, and in what kinds of configurations. Young people must experience the activities robustly when they take into account a set of larger principles defining the qualities of the learning context itself. The principles outlined next help to structure a learning setting that is itself understood as a dynamic system—one where the interactions among learners and mentors, peers, resources, and social contexts has been considered and where specific attention has been paid to the ways in which these different relationships reinforce or amplify each other.

The principles are intended to offer suggestions for how the experience of learning might be designed to support the learning resources offered later in the book. Please note that the principles should be understood as working together within a system—that is, no single principle does much on its own. It is in the relationships between principles that the robustness of the system resides. For example, creating learning experiences where a challenge is ongoing likely will fail miserably if it doesn't also include feedback that is immediate and ongoing. Organizing a classroom environment where authority is shared, expertise is distributed, and a broad range of ways to participate is allowed matters only if there are also visible ways for learners to share and exchange expertise and discover resources. The whole is far greater than the sum of its parts. The fact that the principles are listed separately should be understood as a limitation of the page, not as a feature of the principles.

1. Everyone is a participant.

Create a shared culture and practice where everyone contributes. Design learning experiences that invite participation and provide many different ways for individuals and groups to contribute. Build in roles and supports for teachers, mentors, and instructors to act as translators and bridge-builders for learners across domains and contexts. Make sure that there are opportunities for participants (especially new participants) to lurk and leech (i.e., observe and borrow), and that peer-based exchange, like communication and sharing, is easy and reciprocal. Provide a diverse set of resources to support teaching and peer-to-peer mentorship activities, allowing youths with various forms of expertise to take on leadership roles.

2. Feedback is everywhere; iteration is assumed.

Encourage youths to assume that their first draft is never the final version—they should make something and then gather feedback, rather than waiting to share their creation until they "get it right." Feedback should include structures for guidance and mentorship, which may take place via the online communities associated with the modules, or in classroom, after-school, or home settings. Make sure that there are plenty of ways for participants to share their work in progress with their peers, solicit feedback, teach others how to do things, and reflect on their own learning. Provide opportunities for participants to incorporate feedback in iterative design cycles. One key aspect of this latter element is allowing every participant's contribution to be visible to everyone else in the group through frequent posting, sharing, group discussion, or a combination of the three. Utilize the tools associated with the module platform to enable communication and exchange between peers who may or may not be part of the same program or setting to broaden the kind of feedback that youths receive.

3.   Create a need to know.

One of the more powerful features of challenge-based experiences is that they create a *need to know* by challenging youths to solve a problem whose resources are accessible but require work to find. They must develop expertise in order to access the resources, and they are motivated to do so either because they find the problem context itself engaging or because it connects to an existing interest or passion. Make sure that challenges are implemented within learning environments that support situated inquiry and discovery so that youths have rich contexts within which they can practice using concepts and content. As participants advance through a challenge, provide a diverse array of opportunities for them to build social and cultural capital around their progress. Allow youths to collaborate in many different ways as they explore different roles or identities related to the design project at hand.

4.   Learning happens by doing.

Modules emphasize performance-based activities that give rise to authentic learning tasks. These experiences provide opportunities for participants to develop knowledge and understanding through direct discovery and engagement with a complex but well-ordered problem space. These spaces often require participants to figure out the nature of the problem space itself, rather than proposing a specific problem to be solved.

Make sure that learners have access to robust mechanisms for discoverability; a number of resources to support this type of inquiry are included in this volume (on Systems Thinking Concept cards and Gaming the System Challenge cards), while additional resources—peer-produced tutorials and other materials—should be easy to find, use, and share. Think of ways to situate challenges within a context that has meaning or relevance for participants, whether in peer, interest-driven, or academic contexts. Provide participants with multiple, overlapping opportunities to interact with experts and mentors who model expert identities associated with the problem space. Explore teaming and competing structures like competitions and collaborations that mix collaborative and competitive elements in the service of problem discovery and solving.

5.   Create meaningful public contexts for sharing.

In addition to sharing and receiving feedback during the design and iteration cycles, encourage the sharing of final products and projects with both local and global audiences. Knowing that there will be an audience, especially one that youths care about, is motivating, but also promotes a sense of creating something with a particular audience in mind. This contrasts with creating things in a vacuum, which is too often the case in educational contexts.

Create infrastructures for youths to share their work, skills, and knowledge with others across networks. These channels might take the form of online public portfolios, streamed video or podcasts, student-led parent conferences, or public events where work is critiqued and displayed, to name only a few options. Allow participants to develop identities in contexts of their own choosing; create opportunities for acquiring status via achievements that are visible in a range of home, school, workplace, and peer group settings. Provide diverse forms of recognition and assessment, which might take varied forms, including prizes, badges, ranking, ratings, and reviews.

6.   Encourage play and tinkering.

Youths often learn best by experimentation, tinkering, and doing things that might look like they're "wasting time." As much as possible, build in open-ended spaces for playing and tinkering with the tools, materials, and platforms in addition to more structured challenges. Invite interaction and inquiry into the limits and possibilities of the platform, media, or form in which youths are working. Support learners in defining goals that structure the nature of their interaction and inquiry from moment to moment, as well as over a longer term.

7.   Position youths as change agents.

The whole process of design implies agency—that people are able to create innovative solutions in the face of problems, be they large or small. And a big idea behind a pedagogy of systems thinking is that young people who bring this lens to complex problems can envision better solutions than those who don't. Help youths reflect on the choices that they are making in the design or transformation of a system—empower them to see themselves as agents of change.

WHO IS THIS COLLECTION FOR?

These materials were designed for both in- and out-of-school spaces. Educators and mentors using the materials and tools in this book, such as conductive thread and sewable battery holders, do not need to be experts in sewing or needlework. The activities in this book are designed to spur a range of interactions between young people and the digital platform or tool, as well as between peers. Educators should serve as facilitators for youth discussion, reflection, and ideation. The principles of systems thinking encourage young people to figure things out, put puzzle pieces together, look for similar patterns, and work together to ask questions and find answers across disciplines. The activities have been designed to invite young people to teach one another, because the act of playing and making products for each other, be they games, stories, or physical objects, moves learning into a collaborative context. Youth can show others what they've discovered as they work on their projects, which provides an opportunity for them to act as experts. We recommend that educators try and support youth taking on these roles in the classroom, serving as teachers and mentors to their peers.

APPROACH TO CONVERSATION AND CRITIQUE IN THIS VOLUME

With the aim of creating a participatory environment where feedback is welcomed and iteration is assumed, several processes and protocols have been included that support productive conversation and critique within groups. For example, there are many points where youths share their work with each other, with the goal of getting feedback to refine and improve their designs. This can be a tricky endeavor, as they might be reluctant to let others see their work, and not all youths are practiced at offering feedback that goes beyond being simply laudatory or critical, to hit a point of being *constructively critical*. Although there are many ways to help them learn to find this "sweet spot" of feedback, in these Design Challenges, we encourage them to give a balance of "warm" and "cool" feedback to each other, taking turns as presenter and responder. In any community that does not have much experience providing constructive feedback and critique, the warm and cool feedback protocol can be a really effective tool. Next, we give details about this process, as well as a few related suggestions. All of these could be modeled and discussed beforehand with youths to support familiarity and ease of use.

Warm/cool feedback: This type of feedback begins with a few minutes of warm feedback from the responder, which should include comments about how the work presented seems to meet the desired goals. Next, the responder provides a few minutes of cool feedback, sometimes phrased in the form of reflective questions. Cool feedback may include perceived disconnects, gaps or problems in attaining the goal. This is an opportunity to include suggestions for making changes as well. You might note that people feel encouraged to improve something that they have worked on when they feel *good* about it. A young designer especially can become discouraged without some positive feelings and compliments about the design.

Consider role-playing this, with you—the teacher or mentor—taking on the part of the partner receiving feedback. Ask for a volunteer to give you examples of feedback, starting with warm feedback and then moving to cool. When processing the results afterward, focus first on what felt like helpful feedback. Then explore with the group what types of feedback seemed unhelpful. Provide examples of several feedback sentence starters that might lead to more constructive conversation. (e.g., "Have you thought about ...?" "What were you thinking when you ...?" "I was confused when ... Can you help me understand?")

WARM FEEDBACK

elements that work well
goals that were met
things to build on

COOL FEEDBACK

areas of wondering
gaps or disconnects
suggestions for improvement

"Yes, and ..." feedback: Another way to support youths in developing ideas together is to have them generate "Yes, and ..." feedback as opposed to "Yes, but ..." or negative feedback. This type of feedback reserves judgment, challenge, or dismissal, and instead focuses on refining the original idea that the youths generated. It is a technique often used in supporting iteration in a design process.

One way to demonstrate the difference between these two types of feedback is to create a silly or neutral situation in which one person presents an idea (such as "I think we should get rid of all money. We don't need it."), and then a larger group answers only with "Yes, but ..." feedback (e.g., "Yes, but how can we buy things online without money?"). Then ask the presenter to present the same idea again and have the larger group answer only with "Yes, and ..." feedback (e.g., "Yes, and then maybe we could then use [suggestion] when we want to buy something online."). Ask the presenter, and then the group, to describe the differences between the two experiences.

Response starters: At any given moment, not everyone in any community will agree completely about what's working or not working in a creative project. Sometimes this means that debate is necessary to clarify ideas, and healthy debate can support the development of critical thinking skills around systems at play in their communities. To help youths respond to each other civilly while still disagreeing—during both formal response times and informal collaborative work periods—you may want to post in the room a range of possible response starters that introduce disagreement respectfully, such as the following:

- "I see your point, and ..."

- "I am wondering about ..."

- "I understand that you see this as a way to ..., and from my perspective ..."

- "What if ...?"

- "Yes, and ..."

APPROACH TO ASSESSMENT IN THIS VOLUME

Assessment is designed to happen in three ways in these modules: informally, through *embedded discussions* within challenges; and formally, as *structured reflections* and design feedback in the challenges; and as *written assessments,* which can be administered as pre- and post-tests. Of course, all assessments can and should be used at the discretion of the educator. All of the assessment opportunities that we included here were designed to be formative, serving not just as an important opportunity for the educator to get information on how youths are learning, but for the youths themselves to gain insight into their own understanding of the key ideas being explored and the areas that they might want to work to improve.

With the goal of helping to prepare you to listen for and evaluate youths' understanding, we also include rubrics that offer an overview of what "novice" versus "expert" understanding of the concepts in each section would look like. These rubrics are intended to be used for instructional decision making, so that the educator can determine whether students are ready to move on, must talk more about a particular idea, or need more chances to show what they know.

Informal assessments are marked with this "Let's talk" icon. These assessments are designed to be formative and informal, in that they take place within the context of the Design Challenge as small-group or whole-group conversations. These conversations should serve both to help youths formalize some of the ideas that they've been working on and to create an opportunity for the educator to gauge what they understand about a particular idea.

Structured assessments indicated by the "hands on" icon, are times when youth write down and document what they understand about a particular idea. Structured assessments come in a variety of forms. For example, this might a piece of peer feedback about another person's design, a sketch or diagram about their own design, or perhaps a paragraph in which they reflect on a particular idea. These assessments are intended to help youth formalize their understanding of a particular idea, but are also designed to provide educators with a formal representation (i.e., a hard copy!) of what youth understand about a particular idea at a particular time. If desired, these assessments can be graded and returned to youth as a means of tracking performance toward a grade in the context of classroom use.

Written assessments are given only at the end of the module (and perhaps at the beginning, if the educator is interested in pre- and post-change information). The written assessment is designed to measure what youths have learned across the entire module, and it targets both youths' understanding of key systems-thinking content and what they've learned about a particular technology platform.

Information about ways that students might reason about the content can be found in the *What to Expect* sections of each Design Challenge. We share the end points of student reasoning (novice and expert) but, of course, rarely are youth novices or experts at everything at the same time. The goal of these rubrics is for the educator to be able to determine how students are thinking about the content to inform decisions about how to proceed, review, or intervene.

COMMON CORE STATE STANDARDS (CCSS) AND TIPS FOR INTEGRATION

You might be asking yourself: Why focus on the Common Core State Standards for English Language Arts in a book designed to support understanding of systems thinking concepts through the use of circuitry? What do electronic artifacts and literacy have in common?

On a basic level, the challenges in this book involve literacy practices related to narrative development. Youths will create a shadow puppet and then write a script for that puppet. They will need to understand nuances of character development and dialogue, skills that are featured in the CCSS.

Dig a little deeper and you'll see that youths will also need to read and create technical subject texts: the ability to create an e-puppet, for instance, is predicated on youths' ability to understand complex, step-by-step directions. Dig deeper still—not only are youths consuming these technical subject texts, but they're doing so within the context of thinking systemically. In addition, youths in these challenges are asked to learn while they design, with the goal and gaining and understanding science content knowledge. Knowing, for instance, the way in which electrical circuits function is crucial. The CCSS, in fact, build upon the layer of English Language Arts standards to create guidelines for literacy skills and knowledge specific to Science and Technical Subjects.

Literacy in the content areas like Science is critical, in the eyes of the CCSS, to support youths as they progress down a path toward college and career readiness. Creating with e-textiles, therefore, clearly involves a number of key literacy arenas—narrative writing, speaking and listening, analyzing technical subject texts—as outlined in the CCSS through standards such as:

- Writing 6–8.3: Write narratives to develop real or imagined experiences or events using effective technique, relevant descriptive details, and well-structured event sequences.

- Speaking and Listening 6–12.4: Present information, findings, and supporting evidence such that listeners can follow the line of reasoning and the organization, development, and style are appropriate to task, purpose, and audience.

- Reading and Science in the Technical Subjects 6–8.3: Follow precisely a multistep procedure when carrying out experiments, taking measurements, or performing technical tasks.

In addition, technology is woven throughout the standards—as a way to gain knowledge, as something to be understood through critical media analysis, and as a means to produce and disseminate work. The challenges in this book touch upon many of these areas. But perhaps most important, in these challenges youths use technology tools to *produce*, to create electronic artifacts. And during an age when composing means everything from writing text to producing a YouTube video, they may in fact be helping to shape a broader definition of "writing" today.

TOOLKIT

In this chapter, we transition from talking about the ideas and principles behind this book to share more about how they can be realized in practice. Here, we offer a toolkit and various tips on how to foster a productive climate of making with Do-It-Yourself (DIY) electronics.

Throughout this volume, we encourage instructors to follow the spirit, rather than the letter, of the upcoming Design Challenges. Every learning environment is different—a classroom is dramatically different from a library space, which is also different from an after-school program. Every group of youths is different—tweens are not teens, youths who grew up in a city are different from ones who grew up in rural areas, immigrant youths are different from youths born in their country of residence. And every educator is different in terms of style, history, and relationships to youths. So we don't assume that the activities we share will (or should) ever be implemented in the exact same way in every context. We assume that these materials will be adapted, reinvented, and even improved in your own classroom. This is part of why we spent a good deal of space talking about the "big ideas"—the concepts and principles that drove this work—in the first section of this book. We didn't simply see this sort of background as something interesting and informative (though we hope it is); rather, we offered it up as tools that you could use to bring this work to life. We hope that when you inevitably adapt our activities to fit your context and interests, you have a sense of what the spirit behind them is, and you have the opportunity to adapt the lessons (and even create new activities) with these key principles in mind.

This book contains a sequence of four crafting Design Challenges with DIY electronics that both build an early understanding of electronics and introduce core systems thinking concepts. Each of the Design Challenges builds off of the last, deepening and extending youths' understanding of systems thinking and electronics. The bulk of the Design Challenges follow a similar curricular trajectory (see the table on p. 22). Typically, youths will experience a short systems thinking activity followed by a mini-Maker Design Challenge, which is designed to introduce both the big ideas of systems thinking and the tools and materials needed for the Design Challenge. Youths then are invited to take part in a thematic activity to construct gadgets such as electronic puppets or DIY flashlights. The final part of most of the Design Challenges involves youths' reflecting on and sharing their work with a larger community by posting it online.

PLANNING YOUR TRAJECTORY IN SHORT CIRCUITS

Instructors can augment the learning experiences in this volume by offering complementary Design Challenges from another book in this collection, *Soft Circuits: Crafting e-Fashion with DIY Electronics*. Both volumes share a common introductory challenge ("Design Challenge 1: Introduction to the Electronic Circuit") and then branch into three unique Design Challenges in line with that volume's theme.

- **Crafting e-puppets:** In the current volume, youths begin by exploring thematic projects around electronic hand puppets (e-puppets) in "Design Challenge 2: It's Alive! Making e-Puppets"; then they create storyboards with an embedded recordable sound module in "Design Challenge 3: Speaking Stories"; and finally, they create an LED flashlight to facilitate putting on a unique shadow puppet show in "Design Challenge 4: DIY Flashlights and Shadow Puppets." Each of these challenges involves circuitry concepts that range in difficulty from understanding a simple circuit with a switch to creating circuits with multiple light-emitting diodes (LEDs) both in series and parallel.

- **Crafting e-fashion:** The projects in *Soft Circuits* explore wearable electronic textiles (e-textiles), including creating an electronic cuff/bracelet with a simple circuit and multiple LEDs in "Design Challenge 2," fashioning a T-shirt embedded with a small wearable computer called the LilyPad Arduino that controls the LEDs in "Design Challenge 3," and making a solar-powered backpack in "Design Challenge 4."

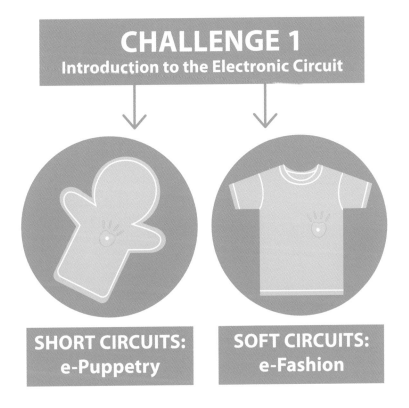

This volume focuses on a series of e-puppetry Design Challenges. Each of them is designed with unique systems thinking and circuitry content. We suggest beginning with Design Challenge 1 and then deciding which of the remaining Design Challenges best suits your setting. All Design Challenges can be used independently, but be warned: They were created with the assumption that you have read or introduced prior Design Challenges, so you will need to make some limited modifications if you use the Design Challenges out of order or in isolation.

Note For more information on the connections within each Design Challenge to the Common Core State Standards (CCSS) and Next Generation Science Standards (NGSS), please see the Preface. For more information on the circuitry concepts, targeted systems thinking concepts, estimated costs of consumable materials per child, and the relative technical difficulty captured in each Design Challenge, see the table on p. 22. This information is meant to help guide your larger decisions about which Design Challenges are right for your setting, influence your decision-making process, and inform the trajectory that you're planning.

Short Circuits Design Challenges at a Glance

	Strand	Estimated Cost per Child*	Technical Difficulty Rating	Targeted Systems Thinking Concepts Introduced	Other Targeted Concepts
Design Challenge 1: Introduction to the Electronic Circuit (Time: 105 minutes)	General introduction	$5	1	Circuits as systems Components Behaviors Functioning Goals Interconnections Limited resources Balancing feedback loops	Simple circuits Resistance Conductivity Electric current Short circuits
Design Challenge 2: It's Alive! Making e-Puppets (Time: 320–350 minutes)	e-puppetry	$7	2	Limited resources Leverage points Interconnections Balancing feedback loops	Switch e-textiles Debugging Character traits
Design Challenge 3: Speaking Stories (Time: 160 minutes)	e-puppetry	$16	1	Stories as systems Interconnections Systems structure Goal	Narrative Conflict Narrator Plot Resolution Context
Design Challenge 4: DIY Flashlights and Shadow Puppets (Time: 265 minutes)	e-puppetry	$12	2	Systems structure Interconnections Goal	Series circuit Parallel circuit Voltage Script Shadow play

*Note that estimated costs per child include only those costs for the basic project materials. Materials that are general start-up supplies are not included in these estimates. This is also calculated without factoring in price reductions for larger quantities. There are many ways to cut costs significantly; see suggestions throughout these materials.

WHAT ARE DIY ELECTRONICS?

The DIY movement has been popularized by *Make* magazine, and today there is a growing number of Makerspaces across the United States to promote personalized fabrication outside traditional manufacturing. These spaces promote a DIY approach to electronics that most often include physical materials and electronics in a project of one form or another. Our focus on e-textiles and other forms of merging papercrafts and electronics in this volume places an equal emphasis on both high- and low-tech materials, as well as merging the materials and activities from both traditionally female and male maker cultures (i.e., sewing/crafting and shop/electronics). The e-textiles introduced in Design Challenge 2 (and used widely in the *Soft Circuits* volume) are electronically enhanced garments, accessories, and other fabric-based items that are designed to combine traditional aspects of textile crafts with elements of embedded computing, conductive sewing/craft materials such as conductive thread or fabrics, sensors for light and sound, and actuators such as LEDs and speakers.

We see an additional benefit to exploring e-textiles and DIY electronics: namely, that they reveal insights about the production or design of technology itself and cultural assumptions that nowadays are often hidden or invisible to youths. Creative production with e-textiles encourages both youths and instructors to question their current understanding of functionality and aesthetics, make explicit their gender assumptions about crafts, and master the fundamentals of a new field by learning the visual, aural, and technological literacies necessary to inscribe themselves into the larger DIY and fashion culture. All in all, what takes place during such creative production becomes a critical reflection on how technology design decisions are made, how they are interrelated with craft production and engineering functionality, and how they intersect with personal decisions and cultural assumptions.

WHY USE DIY ELECTRONICS IN A SYSTEMS THINKING CURRICULUM?

These curricular Design Challenges involve a range of activities including role playing, small games, and group discussions to engage youths in ideas and practices of systems thinking. However, the core activities in which systems thinking is used are ones where youths create tangible design projects that incorporate DIY electronics, as we believe that the process of designing systems provides an important context for understanding how systems work.

To begin with, each DIY electronics project can be understood, in and of itself, as a *system*. Every project comprises interdependent elements—batteries, LEDs, conductive thread or wire, and sometimes even microcomputers—that take on specific roles as they work together to accomplish a goal. If any of these parts are removed, that has an impact on the whole system. These projects allow an educator to provide opportunities for youths to ground the ideas and practices of systems thinking in a real-world, tangible context where they can see things like interconnections and stocks and flows come to life.

Another important aspect of DIY electronics and e-textiles projects is that they allow youths to engage in personally meaningful creative activity. These projects let them bring in many of their own ideas, styles, and interests, whether by allowing them to tell stories they care about or by giving them avenues for exploring their own sense of aesthetics. Being able to make things that have personal relevance deepens engagement and learning outcomes.

DIY electronics also promote collaboration and peer-to-peer learning through online global communities such as those suggested at the Interconnections website (**digitalis .nwp.org/gnl**) where youths share, learn from one another, and give feedback on projects. Creating personally meaningful objects is certainly an important way to learn, but when youths can share them in a community context, it increases the likelihood that they'll persist and iterate on a project, gives them an audience to keep in mind when they're authoring, and lets their voice be heard on a global scale. Importantly, such a community is also a place where youths can be inspired by each other and even teach one another techniques and practices to improve their ability to be creators of technologies and crafts.

Finally, we like using these materials because DIY electronics and e-textiles have been linked to a host of other twenty-first-century skills beyond systems thinking, including computational thinking and design thinking. Specifically, when projects like those featured in the *Soft Circuits* volume incorporate the LilyPad Arduino, they support youths in exploring a range of computational thinking *concepts* (sequence, loops, conditionals), *practices* (working iteratively and incrementally, testing and debugging, reusing and remixing), and *perspectives* (expressing, connecting, questioning). In a world where interactions between digital and physical spaces are growing ever more fluid, these competencies become increasingly important. More broadly, these sorts of maker projects provide opportunities for youths to engage in design thinking, wherein they go through cycles of research, tinkering, iteration, feedback, revision, and publication. These design-thinking competencies are applicable to a range of creative, production-oriented activities that are becoming ever more ubiquitous in our information society.

For all these reasons, we believe that DIY electronics and e-textiles provide a strong avenue for developing systems thinking and twenty-first-century skills in youths.

The next sections are intended to help orient you to the tools and materials that you'll put to use in the Design Challenges in this book and give you suggestions for organizing your space, as well as how to pack general toolboxes to hold materials common across most Design Challenges so as to minimize setup/cleanup time.

TOOLS AND MATERIALS

The following sections are organized into general families of tools and materials used in all the Design Challenges in both volumes, including those for sewing and crafting, conductive crafting, electronics, and e-textiles. It might be a good idea to ask youths whether they have any crafting experience—knitting, crocheting, weaving, etc.—because it might be useful for engaging in and extending many of the projects in this volume in creative ways, although such activities are not supported in these books. This section is meant to give you a sense of things that you'll need to have on hand, as well as general instructions for their use.

TOOLS

BASIC SEWING AND CRAFTING TOOLS

The ability to sew is crucial to many of the Design Challenges in this volume. Helpful guides throughout the book can be copied onto construction paper to help youths learn the basics of hand stitching, tying knots, threading a needle, and sewing a button, sequin, or other objects. In addition to sewing, the activities and Design Challenges contained in this book connect deeply to the traditions of crafting both in and out of school. For most of these tools, you only need a few per group, as they can be shared easily among four to eight youths.

(1) Sewing needles will be some of the most important tools for your e-textile Design Challenges; they come in a variety of lengths and eye sizes. Look for some that have larger eyes (like those labeled as "crewel" or "embroidery" needles), but note that they still must be small enough to fit through the e-textile components in your circuit. If you're worried about threading needles for larger groups, **(2) needle threaders** are inexpensive and can be used to help thread regular sewing needles, or try **(3) self-threading needles**. Although self-threading needles come in a variety of sizes and brands, not all self-threading needles will work with conductive thread. We recommend the Clover Self-Threading needles, which come in a five-pack. Note that the largest and smallest needles in this pack may prove difficult to use with e-textile components. **(4) Beeswax** (one or two for a large group) is also useful, particularly when working with conductive thread because the ends of the thread tend to fray.

(5) Straight pins, while not necessary for any of the Design Challenges in this volume, can be useful to help keep multiple layers of fabric in place while sewing.

Straight pins with pearl heads are easier to see if dropped or placed in a garment while sewing; they also are easier on the fingers. **(6) Embroidery hoops** (we suggest the 10" size) are frames made of two hoops and make sewing or embroidery easier by creating a taut, flat surface for stitching. **(7) Pincushions** hold sewing needles and straight pins when not in use. We recommend placing sewing needles in pincushions to help in setup and cleanup with larger groups. They also help to hold self-threading needles steady during threading.

(8) Fabric scissors (also called *dressmaker's shears*) typically have handles that bend upward so that the blades can sit flat along a surface while cutting. They are also sharper (and can be resharpened), but they also are more expensive than household paper scissors. For this reason, you'll want to keep these scissors clearly labeled and out of reach when working on paper-based projects. **(9) Embroidery scissors** are smaller and less expensive and are

particularly useful for cutting thread and more precise cuts.

(10) Tailor's chalk can easily mark and be easily brushed off most fabrics. Such a tool, or something like a fabric pencil or a water- or air-soluble pen, is useful when you want to sketch out sewing lines that you don't want to be visible on the final project. **(11) Retractable measuring tape** is useful to have in the toolbox to make measurements, and it retracts neatly into its shell to avoid the rolling-up tendency of classic dressmaker's tape or the inflexibility of a standard ruler. Note that there are versions made from both metal and fabric (which adds more flexibility around curved surfaces). **(12)** A **seam ripper** can make it easier to tear out knotted pieces of thread or misplaced stitching. **(13) Tweezers** can be useful for fine detail work in sewing and beadwork.

(14) A **mini-iron** is a small iron designed for use in interior spaces, corners, or small areas when you want to avoid objects that will melt under high heat. It can be useful as a way to press fabric before sewing or to affix iron-on adhesives to your T-shirt, backpack, or other item. A full size iron and ironing board also can be useful if you have the space.

In addition, you'll need at least one method to seal knots made with conductive thread. Because of the thread's thickness, knots in conductive thread can easily come undone over time. To prevent this, use **(15) clear nail polish**, **(16) fabric glue**, or a **(17) low-temperature glue gun with glue sticks**. Fabric glue and a low-temperature glue gun are also useful for affixing decorative elements to your garments and craft projects. (We recommend a low-temperature glue gun to prevent burns and melting plastic, but any type of glue gun will work.)

A few additional tools are useful for the instructor to have on hand to precut large amounts of fabric (and are not listed as supplies needed in the individual Design Challenges), including a **(18) gridded ruler**, which is a translucent, wider-than-usual ruler with markings to aid in the precise measuring and cutting of straight edges or sharp corners. It can be used to cut down felt or other fabrics to a specific size across a variety of projects. Be careful not to cut into the ruler, as it can be damaged easily. To aid cutting, you also can use larger metal rulers that won't be as easily damaged. **(19)** A **self-healing sewing mat** is marked out with centimeter or inch increments and is used as a protective surface for cutting with a rotary cutter or utility knife. **(20)** A **rotary cutter** is designed to be used in conjunction with a self-healing mat and has a straight edge for cutting large amounts of materials with a good deal of precision. Alternatively, **(21) pinking shears** have zigzag blades that cut a unique edge and reduce fraying. These shears can be used to create an attractive edge or to cut fabric that might easily fray (conductive or nonconductive woven fabrics) and can be useful when cutting large quantities of fabric.

Basic Sewing and Crafting Tools

BASIC ELECTRONICS TOOLS

There are a host of useful basic tools to have around to help with electronics. For most of these tools, except for the multimeter and alligator clips, it will be sufficient to have one or two of them for the entire group. Most of these supplies can be found at your local hardware or electronics supply store.

(1) Digital multimeters are handheld devices with a negative and a positive probe that measure electric current, voltage, and resistance to help determine whether a material or artifact is conductive or nonconductive. While it's possible to create many of these projects without multimeters, they help to make some of the invisible properties of electricity more tangible. We recommend getting digital multimeters with Continuity mode settings to aid in the debugging process.

(2) Diagonal wire cutters (also known as *side cutters*) easily cut copper wire, but they should not be used to cut harder metals. Some have spring-loaded handles to ease hand strain.

(3) Needlenose pliers are named for their long, thin shape and are useful for crafts or in electrical projects to bend wire, for fine detail work, or for bending the pins of two-pronged LEDs to make them sewable.

(4) Wire strippers are used to remove the plastic coating from insulated wires. Wire strippers typically have different gauge settings that can be used to strip wires of various widths.

(5) A **utility knife** is an all-purpose blade useful for cutting holes in thick material. We suggest that the instructor assist in using the utility knife for safety reasons.

(6) Alligator clips (also called *alligator test leads* and named for their resemblance to the jaws of an alligator) are electrical connectors attached to an electric cable for making a temporary connection to a battery or other component. The ones depicted here are vinyl-insulated, but noninsulated alligator clips will work well and may be easier to use when you're hooking up multiple clips to a single component. Use them with caution, though, as the teeth on the clips can damage electronics and also can slip off e-textile components.

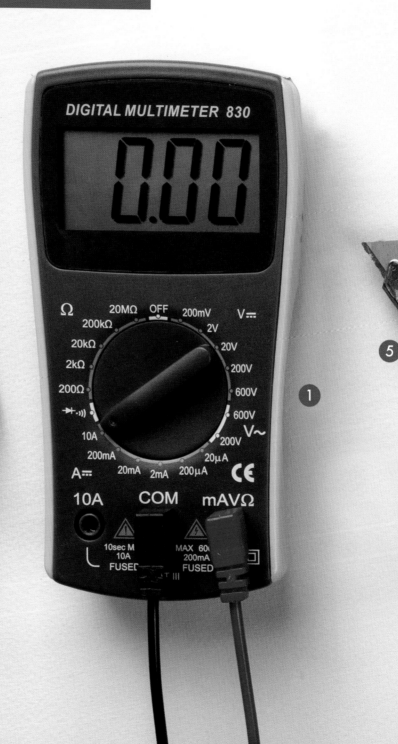

Basic Electronics Tools

MATERIALS

SEWING AND CRAFTING

More than accessories or decorative accents for these design challenges, crafting supplies allow for a good deal of personalization and adding meaning to the projects. While shopping, be sure to look around for other materials that might be meaningful to your youths or community, and consider using recycled goods in your designs as well. Here are a few suggestions for starter supplies to get the creativity flowing! Most of these supplies can be found at your local crafting supply store.

There are a host of everyday craft items, some of which you may already have on hand, including **(1) glitter**, **(2) feathers**, and **(3) paint** that could be used to embellish projects. We recommend having a large supply of **(4) googly eyes** (which can be affixed to almost any surface using your low-temperature glue gun) to instantly transform a project. **(5) Yarn** in a variety of colors can be cut to create "hair," to make ties or bows on clothing, or for many other possible uses in your projects. **(6) Assorted gems, rhinestones, and sequins** add extra light reflection and to embellish the work. **(7) Pipe cleaners** can be bent into various shapes to cast interesting shadows, twisted into a mustache, or cut and affixed to an e-puppet as hair.

(8) Assorted beads can be particularly useful in e-textile projects. **(9) Glass beads**, for example, can be used to insulate the conductive thread, prevent shorts, or embellish designs. Look for beads with larger holes so that they can be incorporated easily into projects without fraying the conductive thread. In addition, try to avoid bugles (small tubelike beads), as these can fray the thread easily. **(10) Indian glass beads** are larger and relatively inexpensive, and they come in a variety of shapes and colors. **(11) Puffy paint** (also called *dimensional fabric paint*) is useful both to insulate conductive thread to keep it from slowly corroding over time and to decorate T-shirts, backpacks, and other items.

Keep on hand **(12) assorted fabrics**, including quilting squares and scraps of fabrics. Look for a variety of patterns because youths like to cut out motifs to iron or glue onto designs. Also look for fabrics with a tight weave (to minimize stretch in the project, which will strain the sewn circuit) and fabrics that are medium in weight to allow for the needle to move in and out easily. To check the weave, pull on the fabric horizontally, vertically, and diagonally and look for fabrics that have little stretch in at least two of the three directions. **(13) Assorted colors of felt** (in 9" x 12" squares or larger bolts) are also useful for most projects. Because felt is a thicker

Sewing and Crafting

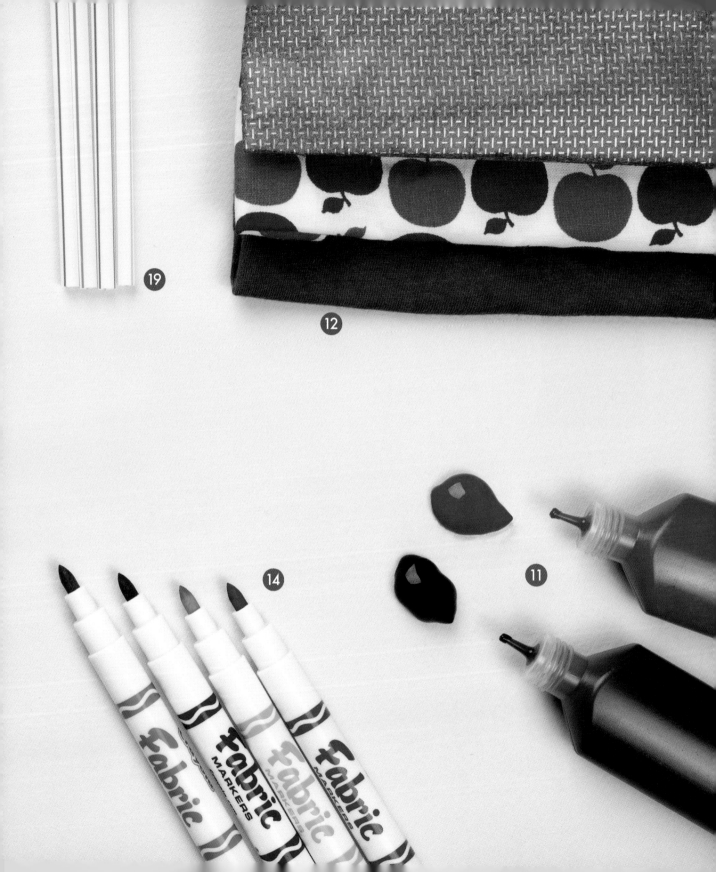

fabric and is not woven, it won't fray on the edges when cut. Felt is inexpensive and has some weight to it, but it allows a needle to pass through easily and allows for smooth sewing.

(14) Fabric markers leave permanent or semipermanent marks on fabric and are useful for drawing outlines before making cuts or for drawing designs into projects. They are easy to use and a great alternative to puffy paint or fabric glue, which take longer to dry.

(15) Sewing thread comes in a rainbow of colors and can be made from a variety of materials, including polyester, cotton, and viscose. While any thread that is suitable for hand-stitching will work, we recommend purchasing a polyester thread set in a variety of colors, as it's an all-purpose thread with a durable "give" and silky feel. Polyester thread also doesn't tangle easily.

(16) Assorted buttons can be a practical form of fastening, or they can be glued onto a creation to become an integral part of the design. Buttons come in a variety of shapes and sizes—be sure to gather a variety so that the color, size, shape, and quantity can be considered in the final design decisions. Due to the expense of these items, consider holding a button collection: Have youths bring in spare buttons from home over time for upcoming projects.

(17) Decorative duct tape, a new line of duct tape for crafters that retains the same properties as regular duct tape but comes in an array of colors and patterns. While not easy to sew through, duct tape is useful for personalizing projects and can also be functional. **(18) Brads** (paper fasteners) come in a variety of colors and sizes and can be added to your paper projects to create movement for arms and legs, among other uses. **(19) Bamboo skewers, plastic straws,** and **wooden sticks** are particularly useful in shadow puppet projects.

Throughout these design challenges, you'll see suggestions to include other everyday crafting items, including craft foam sheets, poster board, 8.5" x 11" sheets of cardstock, hole punches or dowels for making holes, colored plastic, as well as cotton cloths, cardboard, and wax paper needed to create a shadow puppet stage.

CONDUCTIVE CRAFTING

In DIY electronics, you can use the conductive properties of everyday materials as well as incorporate other specialty crafting items to inspire your electronic designs. While many of the things listed here are specialty items, just look around your environment to see if there are any items that are conductive and could be incorporated into your designs. Some of these items can be made (e.g., homemade Play-Doh) or picked up from your local general or craft store (e.g., magnets, metal fasteners, fine-steel wool, or aluminum foil, which can be ironed on fabric with fusible backing), but other items (e.g., conductive paints, ribbon, pens, or yarns) will need to be purchased through a special vendor. Even the antistatic foam that electronics are shipped in can be reused as a pressure sensor! For more ideas, look at KOBAKANT's web-based resource on "How to Get What You Want" (**www.kobakant.at/DIY**). Throughout this book, you will find shopping lists with suggested retailers to help you locate these and other specialty materials.

(1) **Paperclips** are one example of an everyday item that might be conductive and which can be bent into new shapes and creatively incorporated into your circuit designs. Use your multimeter's Continuity mode to test things out! (2) **Sewable metal snaps** can act as switches and typically are good conductors of electricity. It is important to look for snaps that are conductive (i.e., not covered in a protective coating)—take your multimeter with you to the store to help you check for this aspect. (3) **Sewable metal magnetic snaps** can be substituted for sewable metal snaps, but they offer a magnetic clasp instead of a simple snap. Note that magnets are also good conductors!

(4) **Conductive metal beads** are also useful, as they can be incorporated into e-textile designs for a switch, as well as for decorative purposes. Be careful, as not all metallic-looking beads are good conduc-

tors. (5) **Conductive thread** has many of the qualities of typical thread and can be used in hand sewing, but it also conducts electricity because it is plated with silver or stainless steel. Similar to wire or cables, conductive thread can carry current to power your e-textiles. It comes in both two-ply and four-ply. (6) **Conductive Velcro**® is similar to the regular product, but it has a conductive silver coating. Conductive Velcro can be sewn in or glued.

(7) **Conductive fabric tape** is a flexible fabric tape with conductive adhesive made from a blend of nickel-, copper-, and cobalt-coated nylon ripstop fabric. This tape is conductive on both sides (although not all conductive tapes are), making it easy to incorporate into e-textiles or other crafting projects. Other types of fabric tape made out of copper or aluminum are less flexible but are a little less expensive. (8) **Conductive fabric** is woven with

Conductive Crafting

conductive metal strands. There are a variety of conductive fabrics available that range in color, nonconductive materials (like bamboo), the conductive materials used (like silver, stainless steel, or copper), and their degree of stretchiness. Keep in mind that some of the fabrics will tarnish (making them resistant fairly quickly). For that reason, we recommend fabrics made with silver or stainless steel over copper taffeta, which will tarnish more quickly. Some retail companies, like LessEMF, sell a sample set of fabric swatches so that you can see and test various types. Keep in mind that most projects benefit from using a 1" square of fabric or smaller, so one piece of fabric will likely be enough for your entire group. For the purposes of the projects included in this volume, any of the conductive fabrics will work, but we suggest nonwoven fabrics (as they won't fray or whisker, causing shorts) or Lycra, which can be cut into small pieces and affixed using fabric glue.

If you're curious about the resistance of any these materials, you can measure it with your multimeter and calculate per meter (see the tips on using your multimeter in Continuity mode found in Design Challenge 1). In general, remember that the length of the thread or material will increase the resistance. Shorter threads or pieces of material have less resistance. Additionally, note that the greater the surface area of a material, the less resistance it will have, so thicker threads or wider strips of conductive fabric with more surface area will have less resistance than thinner ones. Note that conductive thread has more resistance than wire or cable, but that shouldn't present any problems at the size and scale of projects in these Design Challenges.

ELECTRONICS

Of the vast range of hardware options available to DIY and electronics hobbyists, we present a subset of materials that provide a good entry point into the domain of electronics. These include **(1) two-pin LEDs** (also referred to as *simple LEDs*) are small devices that light up when electric current passes through them. They are relatively inexpensive, produce a tremendous amount of light, and can last a very long time before burning out. Most LEDs are powered with about 3.3V and come in an assortment of colors and sizes. LEDs also can be incorporated into e-textile projects by bending the legs into two circles to make them sewable. To learn how to make your own DIY sewable LED, see the "DIY Sewable Electronics" section at the end of this chapter. **(2) Super Bright LEDs** are brighter than normal LEDs and useful in projects where you want to cast a shadow or illuminate a larger area.

You will encounter a variety of prefabricated circuits in everyday toys and materials, like electronic greeting cards. There are also a number of preassembled modules that can be used across a variety of projects, such as a **(3) recordable sound module**, which records sound and plays it back when a button is pressed. For early explorations, we recommend a 20-second recording module with a 9V battery connector. A **(4) miniature slide switch** can be used as a simple on/off switch in a project.

(5) Spools of insulated hook-up wire come in a variety of colors and sizes and can be cut into smaller pieces and incorporated in your projects or used for prototyping. Note that when purchasing wire, certain colors have connotations in the field of electronics. Red wire will typically denote the power (or positive connection to the battery), and black wire will typically indicate the ground (or negative connection to the battery). **(6) Electrical tape** provides an insulating barrier to any exposed wires, helping to prevent shorts. **(7) Flexible solar panels** are thin semiconductor wafers specially treated to form an electric field when struck by light. The solar panel can be used to charge a separate battery as well as run electricity directly from the solar panel through a circuit.

(8) 9V batteries (alkaline batteries) are energy sources that convert chemical energy to electricity. **(9)** A **9V battery snap connector** is a clip designed to attach to a 9V battery. There are two wires (red wire = positive; black wire = negative) that can attach easily to alligator clips or to other wires in your design. If your map connector has an unwanted plug at one end, simply use your wire cutters and strippers to expose the ends of the two wires and use them in your project.

In electronics, two-pin LEDs are normally paired with "resistors," electronic components designed to slow or oppose an electric current. In this case, resistors prevent the LED from being overwhelmed by the battery and burning out. However, throughout the projects in this volume, you

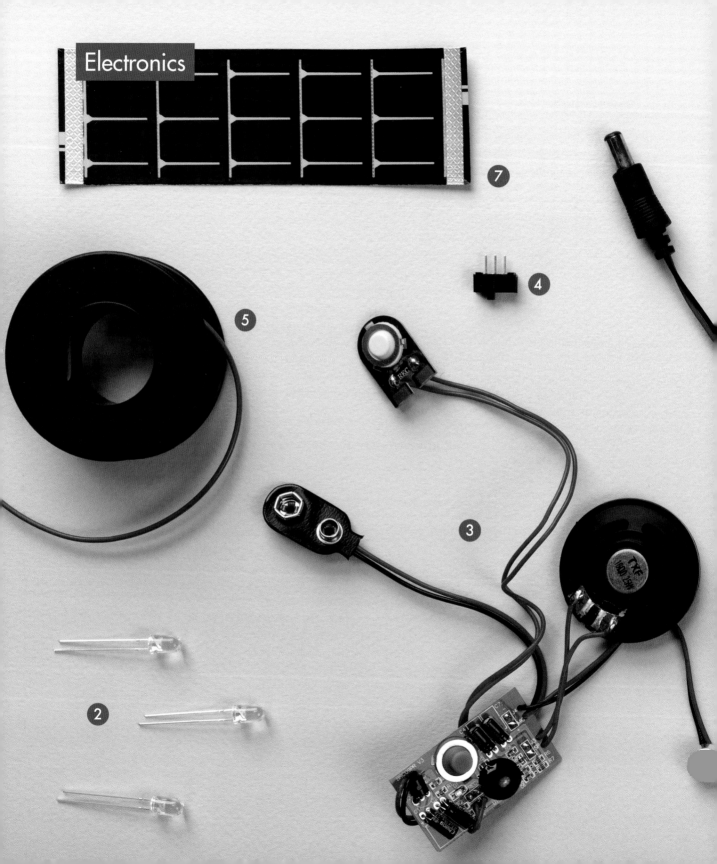

Electronics

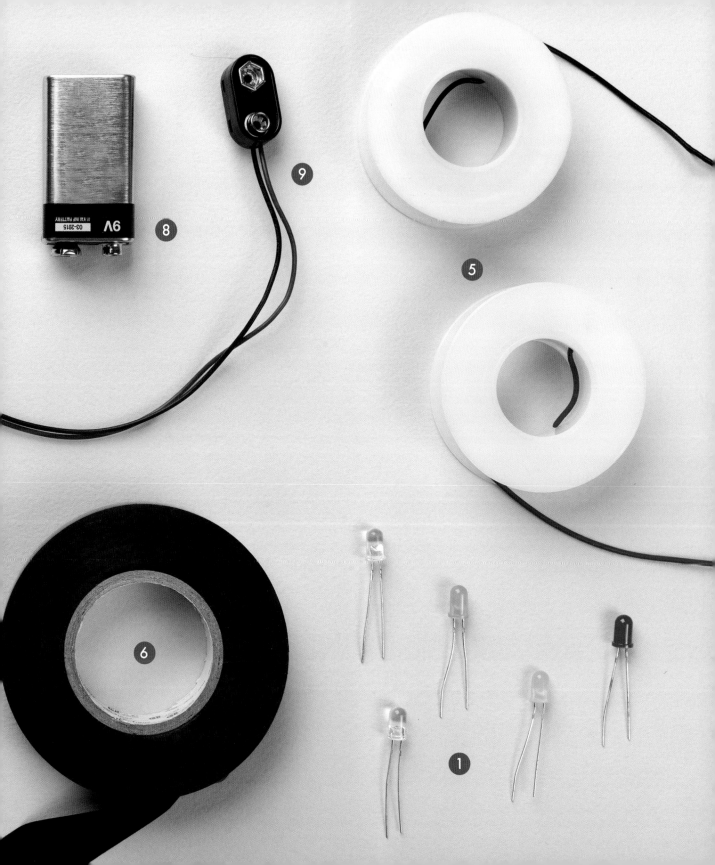

probably won't find a need for a resistor, as the LEDs recommended here often have a built-in resistor, and the conductive thread also poses enough resistance for two-pin LEDs (more so than wires), which is usually enough to prevent the LEDs from being overwhelmed by the battery.

Note It can actually be a good learning moment for your youths to overwhelm an LED on purpose. Unlike batteries, very little heat will be released, but you can expect a small amount of smoke and fumes when an LED is burned out. To check whether an LED has burnt out, you can use a 3V battery that you know is working and test your LED by pressing its two pins on the appropriate sides of the battery.

If you find a need for resistors in your circuit, use the following information to determine the resistor needed:

- Calculate the *supply voltage* for your energy source. *Voltage* is a measure representing the product of the current and resistance flowing through all or part of a circuit. You may have a voltage estimate offhand for your battery, such as if you're using a coin cell battery (3V) or 9V battery. If not, turn your multimeter to a setting to calculate the supply voltage (probably 20V in the DC range) and check the voltage that comes from your power source. Note that newer batteries will oftentimes have a higher voltage than their package indicates and, likewise, older batteries will have less voltage, so it's always useful to calculate this even if you have a rough estimate.

- Calculate the estimated *voltage drop* across the LED. You also can check the supplier's information or online resources for estimates of standard voltages by LED color or model. If you're unsure, you can use your multimeter to measure the amount of voltage needed in order to illuminate your LED(s) properly.

- Input the *desired LED current,* which is the amount of current that the LED uses when properly powered. 20 mega-amperes (mA) will work for most regular LEDs, and Super Bright LEDs can go from 30 mA up to several amps. Check the supplier's information if you are unsure what to input. If you or your youths are concerned about safety, you might find it useful to draw a continuum of "harm," with an LED on one end, a wall lamp in the middle, power lines on the opposite end, and lightning beyond the power lines. While an LED's current is relatively harmless, the current when playing with a wall lamp poses significantly more harm, and power lines or lightning even more so. While the activities in this book pose little harm beyond causing a small shock, you still may want to encourage youths to stay in the safe pool of microelectronics so that they don't try to apply what is learned here to higher-current electronics that plug into the wall.

- Now that you have all this information, input it into a resistor calculator to get the value of the resistor(s) that you will need to purchase. There are many available on the web if you Google "resistor calculator"; for example, see **www.hebeiltd .com.cn/?p=zz.led.resistor.calculator**.

EXPANDING YOUR DIY ELECTRONICS TOOLKIT

As mentioned previously, the collection of hardware here is a purposefully constrained set of components (emphasizing LEDs, speakers, switches, and various energy sources). This list is meant to serve as an introduction to electronics.

As the group's expertise and curiosity about electronics begins to grow, we recommend branching out to explore additional hardware such as different types of sensors (like tilt, light, bend, and temperature sensors), small motors, potentiometers, capacitors, and speakers, as well as more sophisticated tools like soldering irons. Your extended electronics journey can take many different forms, depending on the interests and abilities of the youths:

- Keep discarded electronic toys, computers, and other household electronics for them to disassemble and investigate (without being connected to the energy source, of course).

- Purchase small quantities of new types of hardware for them to explore when they finish projects early.

- Explore some of the other electronics toolkits available on the market (like Lego Mindstorms or Snap Circuits), as well as other learning resources that are featured in the back of this book.

E-TEXTILES

Electronic textiles, also known as e-textiles or soft circuits, are electronic circuits that use conductive fabrics, thread, and other flexible materials in conjunction with sewable electronic components, including LEDs, speakers, sewable battery holders, switches, and so on. Historically, e-textiles have been a highly specialized area of design, occupied almost exclusively by professional engineers and designers. However, the market recently has seen an emergence of new e-textile construction kits, like the LilyPad Arduino, fabrickit, and Aniomagic kits, as well as a growing collection of DIY guides on e-textiles (see Lewis and Lin, 2008; Pakhchyan 2008; Eng, 2009).

The *Soft Circuits* volume focuses on the LilyPad Arduino toolkit, which allows for easy integration of simple circuits (LEDs, sewable battery holders, etc.) into simple sewing craft projects, but it also introduces some of the computational possibilities of e-textiles with tools like the LilyPad Simple Board. All LilyPad Arduino products are manufactured by SparkFun Electronics (and can be purchased directly online at www .sparkfun.com) and a portion of the sales return to Leah Buechley, the creator of the LilyPad Arduino, to aid her in the continued development of and education through e-textiles.

The following materials provide the foundation for most e-textile projects: **(1) LilyPad LEDs**, unlike traditional LEDs, are mounted on easily sewable modules for fluid incorporation into fabric. They have labels that indicate the positive and negative ends. LilyPad LEDs are designed with a built-in resistor and can be purchased in an array of colors, including blue, pink, red, white, yellow, and green. **(2) 3V battery / coin cell battery** *(CR2032)* is a small, flat battery whose size (20 mm) and light weight makes it an ideal choice for discreet incorporation into circuits on wearables. Its front side is marked with a "+" and is positively charged and its back side is negatively charged. CR2032 batteries should power e-textile projects for weeks or months at a time. **Note:** To prevent these batteries from shorting out, do not allow them to touch each other or other conductive objects in storage. **(3) Sewable coin cell battery holders** are less expensive and have a neat pop-in, pop-out feature that makes changing 3V coin cell batteries easy. The feet of the holder have two small sew holes that allow it to be sewn into e-textiles or other garments. **(4) LilyPad coin cell battery holders** are similar to the sewable coin cell battery holder, but provide four large sew holes (two positive and two negative), instead of two. Only two out of the four holes need to be used to create the circuit; the other two can be sewn down to the fabric with nonconductive thread or for creating a separate circuit.

(5) The **LilyPad Button Board** sports a discrete momentary push-button switch (i.e., it closes the circuit when you push the button and opens it when you release the button) and two large sew holes that can be integrated easily into e-textile projects. **(6) LilyPad Slide Switches** can be used as a simple on/off switch in e-textile designs.

(7) The **LilyPad Arduino Simple Board** is a wearable, washable e-textile microcontroller that receives programs from the computer to control the behaviors of the electronic components in an e-textile. The LilyPad Simple Board has a built-in power supply socket for a rechargeable battery and an on/off switch; in addition, it has fewer petal connections than does the LilyPad Main Board. **(8)** The **LilyPad FTDI Basic Breakout Board** is a piece of e-textile-customized hardware that enables communication between a computer and the LilyPad Simple via a **(9) mini USB cable**—one side connects to the USB port and the other connects to your LilyPad pin.

(10) LilyPad LiPower is a sewable input unit, about the size of a quarter, that connects a rechargeable lithium polymer (LiPo) battery or another source of energy like a flexible solar panel to an e-textile circuit. Attach a rechargeable **(11) Single cell Lithium Polymer (LiPo) Ion Battery** (110 mA), flip the power switch, and you will have a 5V supply to power your project for approximately three hours.

(12) A LilyPad Buzzer is a small sound-emitting module that can produce a range of pitches. It can be embedded in your e-textiles projects and controlled by your LilyPad Arduino to create simple songs or sound effects that can be coordinated with your LEDs. It's even possible to create your own fabric or paper-based speaker with KOBAKANT's "fabric speaker" and related resources. The **(13) LilyPad LED Micro** is similar to LilyPad LEDs but without a built-in resistor.

Other LilyPad Arduino components are not required for the Design Challenges, but they may be interesting to explore or to have on hand for youths who finish their projects early. As you explore the SparkFun website and additional resources listed at the end of this book, you'll encounter an immense array of electronics that can be incorporated into your e-textile designs. For example, *LilyPad Micro LEDs* might be explored as a replacement for the LilyPad LEDs. LilyPad Micro LEDs still have sew holes, but they are smaller because they don't contain built-in resistors (which is why they cost less than their counterparts). However, LEDs with and without resistors function very differently and may cause unanticipated issues in your circuits—at the very least, play-test your circuits and avoid combining LEDs with and without resistors in the same circuit.

Another easy way to help youths get started with extended electronics explorations in e-textiles is to order the

ProtoSnap LilyPad Development Board, which includes a LilyPad Simple Board, LilyPad Button Switch, a LilyPad Slide Switch, five LilyPad White LEDs, a Lily-Pad red-green-blue (RGB) tricolor LED, a LilyPad Light Sensor, a LilyPad Temperature Sensor, a LilyPad Buzzer, and a LilyPad Vibe Board wired together on a single board (eliminating the need for alligator clips and the chance of mistaken connections). This makes it easy to explore the possibilities of the components before snapping the components apart and sewing them into a project. The prototype kits are also compatible with Modkit and come with a LilyPad FTDI Basic Breakout board, a LiPo battery, 60 inches of conductive thread, and a needle.

If the LilyPad Simple Boards are out of stock, they can be replaced with the LilyPad Arduino 328 Main Board. However, this is a more complex microcontroller (with a greater number of petal connections), and therefore you can expect some discrepancies between this LilyPad and the LilyPad Simple Board that we support. For example, the built-in LED is on a different petal than the two microcontrollers.

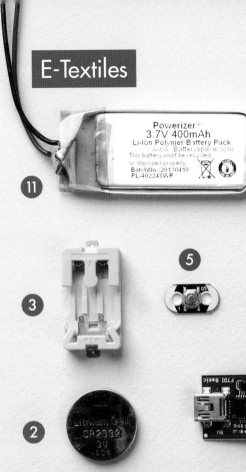

E-Textiles

11 — Powerizer
3.7V 400mAh
Li-Ion Polymer Battery Pack
www.Batteryspace.com
This battery must be recycled
or disposed properly.
BatchNo.:20130418
PL-402248WR

3

5

4 ON

2 Lithium Cell
CR2032
3V
.906

8 FTDI Basic
DTR RXI TXO 3V3 CTS GND
GND
5V TX RX BLK

6 VOLT +

10 LilyPad
Off
On
C B

7 a5/ 19   a4/ 18   a3/ 17
a2/ 16
B   G
11
On   Off
5   6   9   10
LilyPad Arduino

13   1

12 CCV084
B16 G
4510

9

ORGANIZING YOUR SPACE

Physical design materials like those described in the previous sections require organized spaces for storage, as well as some attention to how you organize the room(s) with stations for youths to freely visit over the course of the project. In the following sections, we make some recommendations on ways to organize these materials to save time during the setup and cleanup stages of each of the Design Challenges. These suggestions are based on what we have found useful in our own work.

STORING MATERIALS

As you begin to order and receive materials, it's important to think immediately about how to store materials that are not in use between projects. If you plan to make *Short Circuits* a regular part of your activities, we suggest dedicating at least one large cabinet or bookshelf to material storage, with several smaller but portable tackle or crafting boxes filled and ready to be distributed to the project tables (about one per group of three to eight youths). In addition, consider acquiring one or two expandable laundry bags to keep T-shirts and other consumable textile supplies, and plastic hardware and craft drawer cabinets to store and label tiny items for easy access. You also may find it useful to have a collection of expandable file folders so that each youth can have one to store in-progress projects, parts, and design notes.

Large Bookshelf/Locked Cabinet

We suggest using a large cabinet or open bookshelf to store folded scraps or bolts of fabric on a few of the shelves, and to stack boxes of electronic parts ordered from SparkFun or elsewhere on other shelves. Consider keeping specialty electronics in their boxes from the manufacturer to protect them until they are used. Fill the shelves with stackable nested storage bins to keep materials handy. **Note**: While a locked cabinet can help to ensure that the materials are stored safely when not in use, it also can prohibit youths from experimenting with and finding a use for materials that would not be used otherwise, which is something you might want to encourage. Finding a way to balance these two objectives is key to inviting youths to play with the materials in a sustainable way.

Hardware and Craft Cabinets

Hardware and craft cabinets are smaller cabinets with multiple small drawers or bins for sorting and storing materials. These cabinets can be stored in your larger cabinet or on a bookshelf and are not meant to be portable. Rather, they should be used for storing extra supplies or those that are less frequently used.

More expensive but portable hardware and craft cabinets are available on wheels and can be used to move between rooms as needed.

As your materials arrive in the mail, it's important to organize, clearly label, and store them so that they can be accessed easily. This is particularly important because many components may look alike (for example, LEDs can look similar but have different colors and unique levels of resistance), and some components may be used less frequently than others. This can make it difficult, particularly for novices, to recall which component is which over time. A clear sorting and labeling system for incoming materials will pay off over the course of the workshops.

Hardware and craft cabinets with multiple drawers in various sizes can be a simple way to prevent later problems and are relatively inexpensive (at around $30). The drawers then can be labeled so that it's clear to your participants about what goes where. We also suggest placing information packets from the manufacturer in the same drawer as the supplies. What may seem like irrelevant information may come in handy as the complexity of the projects grows over time. The biggest caveat is to avoid the urge to throw disparate supplies together in a single bin. Rather, create a storage system and encourage the youths to place materials back in their appropriate places at the end of the session.

Short Circuits Group Toolboxes

Small portable toolboxes are extremely useful to have prepacked for small groups of youths. We suggest creating one toolbox for every three to eight youths. Toolboxes allow for easy setup and cleanup for your workshops, since small groups can access what they need quickly, daily cleanup can be made simpler when everyone works to place group supplies back in his or her own toolbox.

You can find an array of toolboxes online and at your local crafting, arts, home improvement, and hardware stores. We suggest looking for larger toolboxes with handles, lift-out trays, small compartments (to store supplies like needles and LEDs), and places to store or hang oft-used tools, like scissors.

Your *Short Circuits* group toolboxes should be packed with your low-cost, highly used, and reusable items. For example, consider packing the following in each group toolbox:

- Multimeter
- Fabric scissors
- Four to five small embroidery scissors to cut thread
- Tape measure
- Pincushion
- Sewing needles
- Spool of conductive thread

- Multiple spools of colored (nonconductive) thread
- Small scraps of conductive Velcro and conductive fabric
- Spare LEDs

- Multiple sets of alligator clips
- Fabric glue (to seal knots)
- Fabric markers or fabric chalk
- Conductive tape (for quick repairs)

CREATING WORKSTATIONS

In addition to thinking through the general storage of materials, consider creating multiple stations in your space so that youths can access tools and materials efficiently as they create their projects. At each station, it's useful to cluster tools and materials that are typically used together to save time searching for materials.

Glue Gun Station

A glue gun is a useful tool for many of the activities in this volume. However, the tools and surfaces for the glue gun require some special safety attention and warrant having a special station set up in your space. At this station, you will want to consider covering the surfaces in some way to protect them from excess glue. Consider using scraps of cardboard, an old sheet, or another thick, heat-resistant material to protect the surface of the station. Include stands for the glue guns and a method to turn off and on (or unplug) the glue gun easily to avoid leaving glue guns on longer than needed. Depending on your need for glue guns in our Design Challenges, you should consider having one available for every 3 to 10 youths, if possible.

Cutting Station

Another useful station is a cutting station. Ideally, this station should include a large, self-healing cutting mat, fabric scissors, rotating cutting knife, measuring tape and/or ruler, and fabric. The large cutting mat can be used to measure and cut large amounts of material. Clearly label the scissors that are meant to cut fabric as opposed to paper, and keep them near this station. While this station is probably most likely to be used by the educator or group leader, it's helpful to have this station set up so that youths can have a central location to access fabric shears (which could be attached to the station by a long piece of yarn to help youths remember not to take them elsewhere or to use on paper).

Ironing Station

An iron and ironing board are useful for multiple projects but are especially helpful for creating a flat surface for sewing by pressing out creases in fabric. While this station will be used less often, it can be helpful to have irons or ironing boards placed away from general work areas to avoid accidental burns.

Technology Hub

Many of the activities in this volume require some access to an Internet-based computer. While ideally it's nice to have one computer or laptop per youth, most of the work will be conducted offline, crafting or using physical materials in some way. Therefore, you may want to experiment to see if your group can share a smaller number of computers in one central area. Youths will use the computers to share their work with online communities (like Instructables.com or others suggested at the Interconnections website), conduct research for their projects, and program their wearable computers (i.e., their LilyPad Arduino Simple Boards). Flexible access to this station is important to the success of many of the design projects.

In addition to computers, consider having one or more dedicated digital cameras with photo and video capabilities, as well as universal serial bus (USB) cord(s) or SD card slots to download material to the computer, at your technology hub. Encourage youths to document and share their work regularly within the local community and online to a much wider audience.

Using Modkit or Arduino software, the computers can be used to program and reprogram how wearable computers behave—as demonstrated in the Design Challenges featuring LilyPad Arduino Simple Boards. Programming environments like Modkit connect with the different boards via USB cables, so be sure to have materials like a LilyPad Arduino Simple, mini USB cables, and FTDI Basic Breakout Boards at the computers for groups to share.

Gallery Space

A gallery space to display and share projects in progress informally is useful to have readily available for larger, whole-group sharing and critique, as well as smaller informal share-outs during work sessions. Often, our educators would make use of the central projector and dry-erase boards for this purpose. However, this also could be a smaller station set up in the corner of a room.

A document projector can be useful to demonstrate sewing techniques or to share the details on particular projects or processes to larger groups that may be difficult to see otherwise. Our educators also would use document cameras or the cameras in their laptops frequently to project makeshift demonstrations and videos to the group (for how to tie knots, thread your needle, make a running stitch, etc.).

BRINGING YOUR CIRCUITS TO LIFE

Throughout the *Soft Circuits* Design Challenges, there are two tools: the LilyPad Arduino Simple Board and Modkit (a visual programming language used to program the LilyPad Arduino), which, used with an online community, help youths to turn their clothing and other creations into rich, dynamic artifacts and share their projects with the world. Modkit and the Interconnections website both are available for free and were designed with educational groups in mind. Modkit offers a free web-based environment and also has a low-cost desktop application for educators tailored for school settings. Modkit's Desktop application is described within the relevant Design Challenges. Take time to explore these tools to learn more about them and to figure out if there are any issues with account creation or restricted firewall access on your machines.

MODKIT MICRO

Modkit Micro (modkit.com) is a graphical programming environment that can be used with the LilyPad Arduino Simple, as well as other Arduino microcontrollers, via browser or desktop application options. Traditionally, programming languages for the LilyPad Arduino and other Arduino microcontrollers have been text-based (building upon the Wiring language). However, the text-based nature of the Arduino language makes it difficult for novices to program their devices successfully. Hoping to lower the barriers to programming, Modkit Micro's design was inspired by the visual programming environment Scratch (scratch.mit.edu/), which replaces text with easy-to-use blocks of code that can be snapped into place. Youths who have prior experience with Scratch (see also the *Script Changers: Digital Storytelling with Scratch* volume in this collection) will recognize similar blocks when they begin to use Modkit Micro.

Modkit Micro allows youths to program the LilyPad Simple to control the LEDs, Buzzers, and other LilyPad components in different ways. For example, using Modkit Micro, you can tell the LEDs to blink, to light in a particular pattern, or to turn on (or off) in the presence of light. Modkit Micro employs simple graphical blocks that can be dragged and dropped to make scripts (though Modkit lets you see the program in a text-based language if you want to compare the code to the graphic blocks). For more information on how to get started with Modkit Micro, consult the website. Additional information about how to use this software to program your LilyPad, as well as additional support materials, are found in the *Soft Circuits* Design Challenges 3 and 4.

As a bonus feature for those who purchased this book, Modkit has provided a special help area on their website (modkit.com/softcircuits). There, you can find instructions for the version of Modkit used here, additional guides, videos of others creating projects from this book using Modkit, and other features.

SHARING PROJECTS IN AN ONLINE COMMUNITY

Social networks like Instructables.com allow people to document and share projects that blend electronics, crafts, and textiles. Giving youths a few minutes to post their projects on such a shared community allows them to become part of the larger participatory culture and share their work beyond the local community. Images and videos are useful additions to any project post, so be sure to have a digital camera available (ideally with photo and video capture capabilities). There are several worksheets integrated throughout the book to help guide youths in generating ideas for the project posts.

SIMPLE CIRCUITS

Getting started in this volume requires a basic understanding of simple circuits, which are described here but also presented in greater depth throughout the Design Challenges in this volume. At its simplest, a circuit is a continuous loop through which electricity can travel. All circuits have a *power source*—in this volume, youths will use 9V batteries, 3V coin cell batteries, and rechargeable LiPo ion batteries. In addition, circuits may include *outputs* (such as lights or speakers) and *inputs* (such as switches or sensors). In designing a circuit, the goal is to guide the electricity out of the battery, through any components (like lights or switches), and then back to the battery.

One of the simplest circuits you can make consists only of a battery and a light, as shown here.

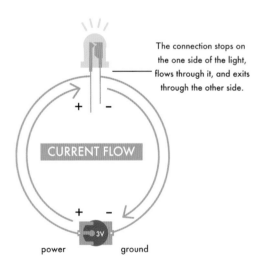

The connection stops on the one side of the light, flows through it, and exits through the other side.

Note Batteries and LEDs have a "positive" and a "negative" side. The positive side is also known as "+" or "power," and the negative side can also be called "−"or "ground."

In the figure shown here, the solid lines represent electrical connections between components made with some sort of wire,
alligator clips, or (in the case of an e-textile circuit) conductive thread. The arrows indicate the direction in which electricity is flowing through the circuit. You always should make connections from the positive end of one component to the positive end of another, and from negative to negative ends. If positive and negative connections ever touch or cross, this will result in a *short circuit.* To remind yourself and the youths of these rules, teach them the mantra, "positive to positive and negative to negative."

If your circuit looks like this:

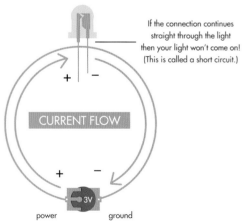

If the connection continues straight through the light then your light won't come on! (This is called a short circuit.)

then your light will not turn on. This is another example of a short circuit. It occurs because the wire between the positive and negative legs of the LED makes it easier for the electrical current to cross there, rather than moving through the LED itself. This is a common mistake when sewing a circuit in e-textiles.

E-TEXTILE CIRCUITS

Here is an example of this same circuit with LilyPad components and conductive thread.

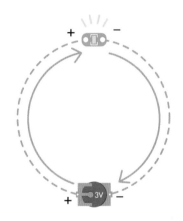

The LED is now a sewable LilyPad LED, and the wire is depicted in the figure as dotted lines where conductive thread would be sewn into the circuit.

Adding a Switch

In the simple e-textile circuit pictured above, you can turn the light on or off only by inserting and removing the battery from its holder. Adding a switch provides more control, and the battery can stay in its holder.

Here's how a switch works: a switch is simply any break in the circuit that can open and close.

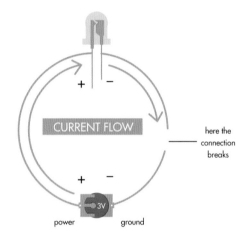

In this picture, the LED won't light up because there is a break in the circuit that prevents electricity from flowing all the way through the circuit and back to the battery. Adding a switch at that spot is similar to closing and opening the break in the circuit (and turning on the light) when you either push a button or slide a switch from "off" to "on."

If you were to sew a circuit with a button switch into fabric, it would look like this when you are not pressing the button

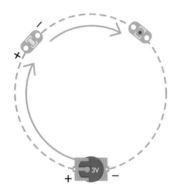

And it would look like this when the button is pressed:

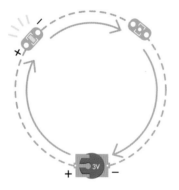

Note Switches don't have positive or negative sides, so it doesn't matter in which direction you place one within your circuit.

BEYOND THE BASICS

You can experiment with more complicated circuits by adding more lights and different kinds of switches. To add more lights, you'll need to arrange them "in parallel." For example, this could mean that the first light's positive end is connected to the second light's positive end. Likewise, the first light's negative end should be connected to the second light's negative end. Alternatively, all the lights could be in parallel to the circuit's energy source, as also depicted here. In this way, you can include several LEDs in your design. For more information on placing circuits in parallel, see later Design Challenges in this book.

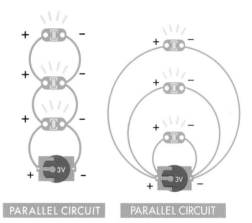

PARALLEL CIRCUIT   PARALLEL CIRCUIT

ESSENTIAL STITCH CRAFT

The types of e-textile Design Challenges found in both *Short Circuits* and *Soft Circuits* require basic hand-stitching skills. This section of the book contains various methods for threading needles (both traditional and self-threading), tying secure knots, and basic sewing stitches. We provide some diversity here in the techniques, as we've found that different tips resonate with different people. Once you find techniques that work for your group, feel free to ignore the rest. It's essential to take a few minutes to practice these basic techniques with youths to be sure that most, if not all, are able to sew independently. These sections can be shared with youths, but similar materials and information appear throughout the Design Challenges.

THREADING A NEEDLE

HOW TO DOUBLE-THREAD A TRADITIONAL NEEDLE

1. Cut a piece of thread about two to three feet in length.

2. Use one hand to pinch the thread very close to the end and put the short bristle of thread on the eye of the needle.

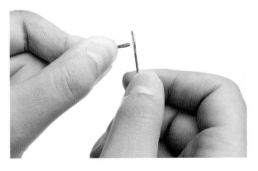

3. Pull the loose end through the eye of the needle until both ends of the thread meet and are equal in length.

4. If you have a problem threading the needle, beeswax could be used on the thread to help keep it from fraying, or try using a needle threader (see additional tips on using a needle threader later in this chapter).

5. If the thread is still fraying, trim off the frayed thread at a 45-degree angle and try again.

HOW TO DOUBLE-THREAD A CLOVER SELF-THREADING NEEDLE

Self-threading needles add an extra expense to a project but can save a lot of time, especially if you or any members of your group have poor eyesight, or if you are working with large groups. We recommend Clover self-threading needles, especially when working with conductive thread, as not all brands work well with that thread. When using self-threading needles, the thread pulls down over a bridge at the top of the needle (depicted visually here in three steps) and is not threaded through the eye of the needle.

1. Place your pincushion on a hard surface. Then put the self-threading needle in the pincushion pointing straight up to steady it.

2. Cut a piece of thread to about two to three feet in length.

3. Find the approximate center of the piece of thread.

4. Pinch the thread with your thumbs and forefingers in two places about an inch apart from one another (similarly to how you might floss your teeth).

5. Place the thread over the top notch of the needle (the "bridge" of the needle), as shown in the picture.

6. Pull down firmly on the thread, and it should snap down into the eye of the needle.

7. Move the thread back and forth within the eye to make sure all of the thread went through the passage (it should move freely back and forth). If not, remove the thread and try again. If it's stuck badly on the needle, you may need to cut your thread and begin again.

Important notes: Do not pull the thread any further down than the first eye! The second eye is not intended for use. Remember that self-threading needles are more delicate and should not be forced through the fabric or your e-textile components, as this could break the eye of the needle.

THREADING A NEEDLE WITH CONDUCTIVE THREAD

Some conductive thread tends to fray easily. Before pulling the thread through the eye of the needle, try pulling the thread taut and snip off the end at a 45-degree angle to give it a sharper point. Use a small amount of water, beeswax, or saliva to dampen the end of the thread, bringing the end of the thread to a point. Then take the needle in one hand, feed the thread slowly through the eye of the needle with the other hand, and pull the thread through.

USING A NEEDLE THREADER

You can use a needle threader to help pull the thread through a small needle eye. This can be used for conductive and non-conductive thread, but it is particularly useful for four-ply thread, which is the thickest of the conductive threads that we recommend.

1. Insert the wire of the threader completely through the eye of the needle.
2. Feed the thread through the wire loop.

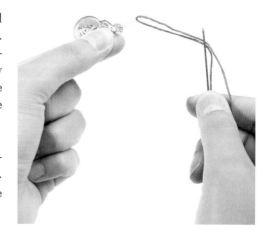

3. Then pull the needle threader back out the eye of the needle, bringing the conductive thread with it.

4. Even out the two ends of the thread so they are of equal length and prepare to tie your knot.

TYING KNOTS

Youths will need to learn how to tie knots at the start and end of their stitching lines. In e-textiles, you will need to tie knots more frequently than you would in a regular sewing or crafting project, so these techniques are particularly important to the group's productivity. We list several techniques here for tying knots, but you might want to use one technique and stick to it, as switching between techniques can add confusion for novices.

TYING BEGINNING KNOTS

Quilter's Trick

This tip comes from a quilting instructor and is consistent and very easy!

1. Once your needle is threaded, double up the thread by pulling the two ends of the thread together so that they are equal lengths to create the appearance of one thread.

2. Lay the needle and thread on the table in front of you to create a circle, with the ends of the thread facing the tip of the needle.

3. Pick up the threads and pull them toward the tip of your needle, overlapping the two just a bit.

4. Leaving a small tail at the ends of the threads, begin coiling the threads as a single unit around the needle (and toward the tip) two to three times (the more you wrap, the larger the knot will be).

5. Pinch and hold the wrapped thread in place with one hand, then gently pull the coiled thread over the needle eye and continue down the length of the thread.

6. You have a knot!

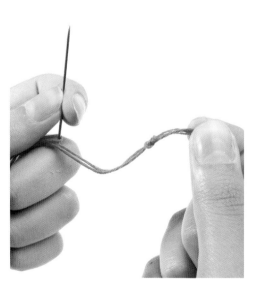

7. Trim the tail of the knot to leave about a 1/8- to 1/4-inch length of thread. Tails that are too long can cause problems with sewing and could cause shorts in conductive thread, while tails that are too short may cause your knot to come undone.

8. Remember to secure your knot with nail polish, fabric glue, or a low-temperature glue gun to keep it from unraveling (see later in this section).

Tying a Traditional Roll Knot

1. Once your needle is threaded, double up the thread by pulling the two ends of the thread together to be equal lengths to create the appearance of one thread.

2. Wrap the thread around your left index finger, crossing the threads in the middle of the index finger to make an X, with the tail of the thread facing your hand (this is where the knot will be).

3. Cover the X with your left thumb.

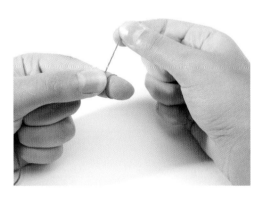

4. Then roll the thread between your thumb and forefinger until it rolls off the end of your finger.

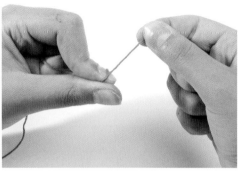

5. Continue to roll the thread and use your middle finger to steady and tighten the knot while sliding it down to the end of the thread. Pull the thread tight with your right hand.

6. You have a knot!

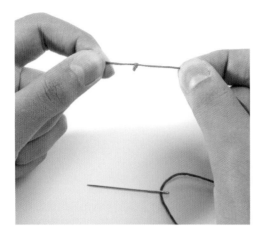

7. Trim the tail of the knot to leave about a 1/8- to 1/4-inch length of thread. Tails that are too long can cause problems with sewing and could cause shorts in conductive thread, while tails that are too short may cause your knot to come undone.

8. Remember to secure your knot with nail polish, fabric glue, or a low-temperature glue gun to keep it from unraveling (see later in this section).

Tying a Circle Knot

We have developed this technique (based on the traditional roll knot) during our workshops and have found it to be easier for younger participants.

1. Once your needle is threaded, lay your threaded needle on the table in front of you in a straight line. **Note** that the images depicted here are of a single-threaded needle, not a double-threaded needle as we recommend. The same knotting technique can be used in both cases.

2. Take the tail of the thread(s) and create a small circle.

3. Move the tail of the thread(s) through the inside of the circle. Although doing this once will work, if it's repeated two or three times to coil the thread around the circle, you'll create a bigger knot that is less likely to pull through your fabric.

4. Pull the needle and thread with one hand and pull the tail to close the circle with your other hand.

5. You have a knot!

6. Trim the tail of the knot to leave about a 1/8- to 1/4-inch length of thread. Tails that are too long can cause problems with sewing and could cause shorts in conductive thread, while tails that are too short may cause your knot to come undone.

7. Remember to secure your knot with nail polish, fabric glue, or a low-temperature glue gun to keep it from unraveling (see later in this section).

ENDING KNOTS

For Double-Threaded Needles Only (Like Those Suggested Previously):

1. Stop sewing so you have a few inches of thread left before running out.

2. Cut the thread right below the eye of the needle (or if you have long threads, give yourself at least a couple inches of thread from the fabric to work with).

3. There are now two threads.

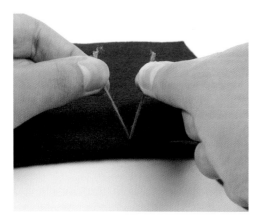

4. Make an X with the threads.

5. Bring one of the threads down and wrap it around the other thread, and pull the threads tight (similar to the first steps in tying your shoe).

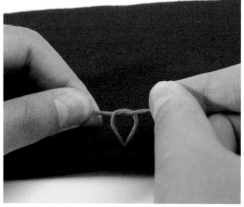

6. Repeat the last two steps.

7. Now you have a knot very close to the fabric!

8. Trim the tail of the knot to leave about a 1/8- to 1/4-inch length of thread. Tails that are too long can cause problems with sewing and could cause shorts in conductive thread, while tails that are too short may cause your knot to come undone.

9. Remember to secure your knot with nail polish, fabric glue, or a low-temperature glue gun to keep it from unraveling (see later in this section).

For Either Double- or Single-Threaded Needles:

1. Take your needle and slip it under an existing stitch to form a loop.

2. Guide your needle through the loop and tighten.

3. Repeat steps 1 and 2 two or three more times.

4. Now you have a knot very close to the fabric!

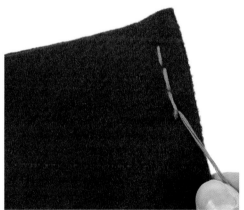

5. Trim the tail of the knot to leave about a 1/8- to 1/4-inch length of thread. Tails that are too long can cause problems with sewing and could cause shorts in conductive thread, while tails that are too short may cause your knot to come undone.

6. Remember to secure your knot with nail polish, fabric glue, or a low-temperature glue gun to keep it from unraveling (see later in this section).

SECURING KNOTS

Conductive thread knots are known to come undone. Here are a couple of suggestions to keep your knot tied and to help prevent your stitches from pulling out. You can use clear nail polish, fabric glue, or a low-temperature glue gun to do this.

Securing Beginning Knots: Glue or Polish

After you tie the *beginning knot* in your threaded needle (but before you start sewing), put a dab of clear nail polish or fabric glue on it.

Blow it dry, and now it's ready to start stitching beneath your fabric. Remember to start your stitching on the opposite side of the fabric from your components to help prevent shorts!

Securing Ending Knots: Glue or Polish

For the ending knot, put just a dab of nail polish on the knot. Don't soak the thread or materials with nail polish, as it could damage it.

Securing Knots: Glue Gun

After the beginning knot is sewn in (on the backside of the fabric), put a dot of hot glue on it. Repeat the same on the end knot (on the backside of the fabric).

Note When using clear nail polish, limit the quantity. Youths mistakenly seem to believe that more is better, but it's not in this case. If saturation happens, the following bad outcomes will result:

- The material will become stiff and difficult to sew through.
- The conductive thread will harden, lowering its conductivity.
- If the electronics sew hole is coated with nail polish, the polish will act as an insulator on the metal, and a solid connection (thread to metal) won't be made.

STITCHES

Basic Running Stitch

The running stitch is an excellent stitch to use with novices and is particularly good to use when crafting soft circuits because it can be removed easily (as opposed to backstitching or other more decorative stitching techniques). To get started, perform the following steps:

1. Stick your needle through the fabric from back to front (this will hide the knot).

2. Pull the thread through until the knot is firm against the backside of your fabric.

3. Now, move your needle about 1/8 inch along the path that you'll be sewing and bring your needle through the fabric again, but from front to back.

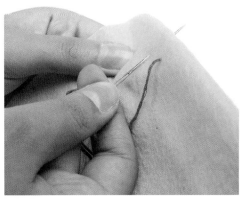

4. You've just made your first stitch!

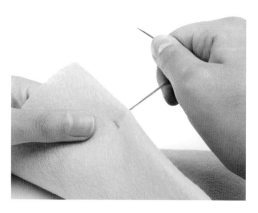

5. Repeat by bringing your needle from back to front, then front to back. Make sure to pull your thread taut each time you move your needle through the fabric to avoid unwanted lengths of thread, which can tangle or cause shorts when working with conductive thread.

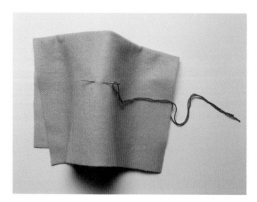

6. Keep stitches even and close to one another to prevent stitches from being snagged or touching another thread, either of which may cause a short when working with conductive thread.

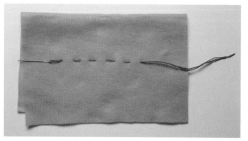

Other Stitches

There are a variety of other stitches that you can explore as your group gains more comfort with hand sewing, including the backstitch. However, we suggest that you refrain from introducing these techniques until the group becomes more familiar with hand sewing and e-textiles, as these techniques become more likely to tangle the thread and are more difficult to undo when you've made a mistake.

Stitching Tips

Youths may struggle at first with sewing, especially with conductive thread. No worries—if they're patient, they'll get used to the thread's behavior quickly. For instance, if the thread gets into a knot, they should not pull it tight, but patiently untangle it using a needle to pull the knot apart.

If stitching continues to be difficult for youths, try one or more of the following:

- Use fabric chalk to mark the dotted path that your needle should follow. It should brush off easily, but if not, wash your fabric with some water. Fabric markers (a more permanent mark) also can be used to sketch the path and even provide dots for even stitches between components.

- Keep stitches relatively close together. This will help the design to hold up better over time.

- For speed, slip your needle in and out of the fabric several times before pulling the thread through. Also try folding the fabric accordion-style to make it even easier to make multiple stitches at once. This is a more advanced technique, but it might be useful to introduce to your group early in the process.

- Use the "Running Stitch Practice" worksheet (found in Design Challenge 2 of this volume) to practice your stitching techniques by connecting the dots with nonconductive thread. Youths then can add their own dots and stitches to complete the diagram. As an extra challenge beads, buttons, and sequins can be incorporated into the design to help the youths think about using the thread to fasten physical objects to paper or fabric using nonconductive thread.

ESSENTIAL E-TEXTILES TIPS

The following list includes more advanced e-textiles tips than youths will need at first. We recommend that you return to this section once you have started working on your first project—most of this information will make little sense out of context. In addition, there are many more hints throughout each of the Design Challenges.

CUTTING CONDUCTIVE THREAD, CONDUCTIVE FABRIC, AND OTHER CONDUCTIVE MATERIALS

Always try to cut these materials in a spot that's away from your fabric or project, as small conductive "whiskers" will be released that could cause invisible problems in the circuit later.

CREATING SOLID CONNECTIONS

When you arrive at a component in your soft circuit, be sure to sew the thread through each sew hole *two to three times*, if possible, to ensure a solid connection between the petal and the conductive thread. A loose or dangling connection means that you've not completed the loop in your circuit. You should add these extra loops to the hardware only (rather than stitching through the fabric); extra stitches through the fabric will hold the hardware in place more securely, but if the stitches need to be removed during troubleshooting, they can cause more problems. If you find loose connections, consider using your glue gun to secure them better.

USING GLASS BEADS, PUFFY PAINT, AND OTHER MATERIALS TO INSULATE CONDUCTIVE THREAD

If your design requires you to cross the positive (Power) or negative (Ground) stitching lines, there are ways to avoid creating a short circuit:

1. Use rounded glass beads to insulate the conductive thread and raise the connection a safe distance above the other line. Avoid sharp-edged glass beads, particularly bugles, as they tend to fray the conductive thread. You also can use glass beads to help insulate the thread to prevent it from slowly tarnishing over time.

2. Other materials will insulate the thread as well, including puffy paint (remember to allow for drying time), hot glue, or other beads made from wood or plastic.

SHORT ON TIME TO SEW?

Instead of sewing the entire circuit, youths can use hot glue to run conductive thread between electric components if they don't have enough time to sew everything. If this method is chosen, it's important to sew the components in place first to get a solid connection. BONUS! The glue from the glue gun can help to insulate the thread as well. See also the additional stitching tips given previously to help speed up the hand-sewing process.

GETTING CREATIVE!

Think outside the box! One quick hint for youths is that stitched lines of conductive thread don't need to be straight to be functional. Once you've designed the layout for your circuit, you can connect your components by sewing interesting patterns or shapes. The Silly Bandz craze (involving rubber-band bracelets formed into shapes like hearts, stars, bones, etc.), taught us that there are lots of ways to create a loop other than a simple circle. Experiment with fun and curving shapes as you sew your conductive thread!

TROUBLESHOOTING TIPS

Each Design Challenge contains a list of specific debugging tips—things to look for if your circuits don't work. The following list is a general "quick list" checklist that you might want to bookmark for reference for all your simple circuit projects.

- *Check the battery power:* Take out the battery and straddle it with an LED, matching the positive leg to the positive side (printed side of a 3V battery)

and the negative leg to the negative side.

- *Check for polarity:* Make sure that the (+) sides of the LEDs are oriented toward the (+) end of the battery holder. Similarly, make sure that the (−) sides of the LEDs are connected to the (−) end of the battery holder.

- *Check for crossed lines:* Make sure that no two lines are touching in the design, as this will cause a short.

- *Check for solid connections*: Make sure that the conductive thread has been sewn around the component two or more times and the component is not dangling from the project.

- *Check the LEDs:* Make sure that none of the LEDs have been sewn through in a way that connects the positive to the negative end of the LED.

- *Check for frayed stitches:* Make sure that none of the stitching has been cut accidentally or has frayed. If you're unsure and have a multimeter, check the continuity of the lines. It will beep if there is a continuous connection between any two points in your circuit using the two probes. If it doesn't beep and you still have a problem, then look for a shorted or frayed conductive thread line.

- *Check for any loose strands of conductive thread:* Be sure to check the back of the project! Affix any dangling pieces (your glue gun is an easy way to tie things down) so that they are out of the way and not touching other conductive components.

- *Check your parallel circuits:* If you used more than one LED, are the LEDs sewn in parallel? (If not, the 3V battery will not have enough power to light more than one LED.)

- *Check your LED color choices:* Have you mixed the colors of your LEDs? Are only some LEDs (like the red LEDs) illuminating? If so, don't worry; your circuit is probably working, but your battery just doesn't have enough voltage to light all the LEDs in the current design. Consider removing some LEDs (such as those at the higher end of the light spectrum, like whites, blues, and greens) from your project.

ESSENTIAL DIY ELECTRONICS

In this section, we describe some essential techniques for your electronic equipment. These sections can be shared with youths, but similar materials and information appear as tips throughout the Design Challenges. In addition, this section contains how-tos for creating your own sewable electronics, which can be modded (modified) for use in various projects.

MULTIMETER BASICS

Your multimeter can be used to measure a variety of invisible properties of electronics, including *resistance, current*, and *voltage*. You also can use your multimeter to help debug the stitching in your project to find unintentional breaks in your circuit. Here are just a few benefits of the multimeter; but see the additional tips presented throughout the Design Challenges.

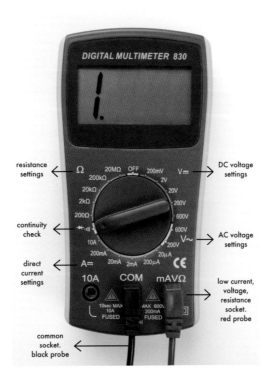

How to Measure Resistance in Materials (Using the Continuity Setting)

Are you wondering whether a material or object is conductive enough to use in your circuit? You can use your digital multimeter to check. Set the multimeter to Continuity mode (look for the image that looks like sound coming from a speaker if you're using the SparkFun Digital Multimeter recommended in this book). Now touch the probes together. The multimeter should emit a high-pitched tone. This shows that a very small amount of current is flowing successfully, with little or no resistance between probes. In testing a new material, touch the two probes to the surface. If current can flow between the negative and positive probes, you'll hear the multimeter emit a tone, indicating that the material has a low resistance and can be incorporated easily into your circuit. Note that the numbers on your meter show the degree of resistance in the material (some materials will have more than others). See also the "How Do I Use a Multimeter?" worksheet found in Design Challenge 1.

How to Test for Continuity in a Conductive Thread Line

At times, you might wonder whether the stitching has been cut or broken between two points in your circuit. You can use your digital multimeter to check. To get started, set the multimeter to Continuity mode. Place one probe at one end of a thread line and the other probe at the other end; you should hear a tone indicating that they are connected. If it does not emit a tone, then you can begin to trace the route by moving the probes along it to check if there are breaks, frays, or shorts in the thread line.

Measuring Voltage of a Battery

You also may be wondering whether your battery has enough power to light the LEDs or run the other components in your circuit. To find out, you'll need to measure its voltage. For example, to measure voltage on a LiPo battery, perform the following steps:

- Pull out your digital multimeter and make sure the black probe is plugged into the COM (common) jack and the red probe is plugged into mAVΩ.

- Set the multimeter to 20V in the DC range (DC is a straight line, while AC is the wavy line).

- Squeeze the probes with a little pressure against the positive and negative plastic terminals of the LiPo battery. The black probe is customarily connected to the ground or negative (–)

side of the battery and the red probe to the positive or (+) side of the battery.

- The reading on the multimeter will tell you the remaining voltage on your battery.

Remember, if the battery loses too much of its voltage, it will be unable to light your LEDs or power your other components!

Measuring Current

Sometimes you may wish to know how much current is flowing through your circuit or through one of your circuit's components. To measure current, you must put your multimeter in *series* with your circuit, as follows:

- First, make sure the multimeter's black probe is plugged into the COM (common) jack and the red probe is plugged into mAVΩ.

- Set the multimeter to 20mA (or 200mA if you're expecting a stronger current).

- Disconnect your circuit at the point where you wish to measure the current (near the battery for measuring the current flowing through the whole circuit, and past a component if you have a circuit wired in parallel and you wish to measure the current flowing through that component). Close the newly made gap in the circuit with one probe from the multimeter on each side of the gap. (You may wish to use alligator clips to

connect the multimeter probes to your circuit to hold the probes in place.)

Note that measuring current through an e-textile circuit that has already been sewn down may be prohibitively difficult due to the necessity of disconnecting the circuit. Instead, consider measuring current on an incomplete sewn circuit.

TESTING YOUR COIN CELL (3V) BATTERIES AND LEDS

Testing Your 3V Battery

You can test your 3V coin cell battery quickly to see if it has been shorted by taking a two-pin LED (that you know to be working) and holding it directly on the 3V battery. Make sure that you place the longer of the two pins on the positive (printed) side of the battery and the shorter of the two on the negative side of the battery. If the LED illuminates, you have a working battery! It's important to note that it takes different levels of voltage to light different colors; for example, a red LED takes less voltage to light than does a blue LED. This is because the amount of voltage needed to light an LED depends on the light's wavelength. So be careful to test the battery with the appropriate LED(s) for your project.

Testing an LED with Your Coin Cell Battery

Similarly, there are several reasons that you may want to check your two-pin LEDs, including to check what color your LEDs are and to see if the LED is burned out (in case it was overloaded at some point). Grab a 3V coin cell battery that you know to be working and hold the LED's pins on either side of the battery to see whether your LED is working and what color it is. Make sure that you place the longer of the two pins against the positive (printed) side of the battery and the shorter pin against the negative side of the battery.

Note This is one of the simplest circuits you can make: a great activity to share with youths!

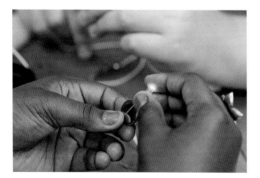

DIY SEWABLE ELECTRONICS

MAKING DIY SEWABLE LEDS

Creating your own sewable LEDs from standard two-pin LEDs is quite easy and cost effective. Here are a few simple steps to guide your process:

1. Bend the positive leg (i.e., the longer leg) out 90 degrees at a right angle.

2. Curl the leg around needlenose pliers to form a spiral-like loop that you can sew through.

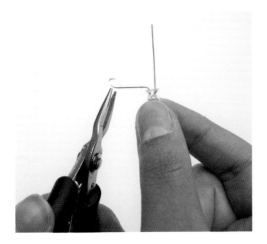

polarity with a flat spot on the negative leg side of the LED bulb.

3. Bend the second leg (i.e., the shorter negative leg) out 90 degrees in the other direction.

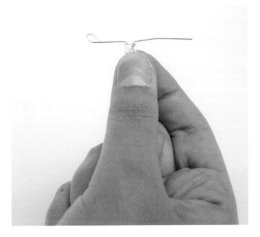

4. Consider bending this leg into either a triangle or square shape to distinguish it from the positive leg. Alternatively, you can use a permanent marker to mark the positive loop (as seen in the photo), and some LEDs indicate the

What If You Mix Up the Two Pins After They Are Bent?

Use your alligator clips to create a simple circuit, connecting your LED to your 3V battery in its holder. If it doesn't light, then try switching sides. Then use a permanent marker to mark the positive leg of the LED so you don't mix them up again.

Are These DIY Sewable LEDs Hand-Washable Too?

Yes, they are!

Are You Ready for More DIY Sewable Electronics?

In the companion volume of this book collection, *Soft Circuits,* we provide two additional ideas for creating sewable electronics: a DIY switch for turning a circuit on and off, and a DIY battery holder. Look for these two optional e-fashion crafting ideas in Design Challenge 3 of *Soft Circuits*: ElectriciTee!

DESIGN CHALLENGE OVERVIEWS

CONTENTS

DESIGN CHALLENGE 1: INTRODUCTION TO THE ELECTRONIC CIRCUIT

Total Time: 105 minutes

The goal of this challenge is to familiarize youths with the notion that all systems are made up of components, that each component has a specific set of behaviors, and that the way that a system functions depends on the interconnections among its components. In this challenge, they will be introduced to the idea of electronic circuits as systems and will learn to identify the system's components (e.g., load, energy source, and wire), behaviors (e.g., conductor versus resistor), intended goals (e.g., to turn on a light-emitting diode [LED]), and an overall function that depends on the system's interconnections (i.e., the interactions among the components and their behaviors in the system). Youths will experiment to create a simple electronic circuit in order to light up an LED. In addition, youths will learn how balancing feedback loops can help them make the most of limited resources in their circuits.

DESIGN CHALLENGE 2: IT'S ALIVE! MAKING E-PUPPETS

Total time: 320–350 minutes

Building on the systems thinking concepts introduced in Design Challenge 1 (i.e., systems have components, behaviors, and goals), youths will probe more deeply into a system's interconnections in the creation of a simple switch for an electronic puppet (e-puppet). Through this process, youths uncover ways to preserve limited resources by identifying potential leverage points—that is, places to intervene productively by changing a component of the system with the result of changing the overall goal of the system. In addition, youths will learn about character development and aspects of storytelling in ways that support them in beginning to think about stories as systems, too.

DESIGN CHALLENGE 3: SPEAKING STORIES

Total time: 160 minutes

This challenge encourages youths to see a story not as a collection of settings, characters, and plot elements, but as a study of relationships. Youths explore the interconnections between the goal or resolution of a story, its structure, and the behaviors of its components through small-group brainstorming, game play, and collaboration. The idea of story-as-system is contrasted with the incorporation of a recording/playing device (part of an electronic system) into one of the activities. Comparisons between stories and circuits as systems help youths to recognize that systems can exist anywhere.

DESIGN CHALLENGE 4: DIY FLASHLIGHTS AND SHADOW PUPPETS

Total time: 265 minutes

The goal of this fourth challenge is for youths to learn about how a system's structure can determine specific component behaviors and larger system dynamics or interconnections. Youths experiment with different circuit structures and battery voltages to discover how circuits can be structured in series and parallel formations. They apply this understanding toward the design and development of flashlights made from inexpensive materials, and then they use their creations to put on a shadow puppet show.

DESIGN CHALLENGE 1 INTRODUCTION TO THE ELECTRONIC CIRCUIT

Total time: 105 minutes

OVERVIEW

The goal of this challenge is to familiarize youths with the notion that all systems are made up of of components, that each component has a specific set of behaviors, and that the way that a system functions depends on the interconnections among its components. In this challenge, they will be introduced to the idea of electronic circuits as systems and will learn to identify the system's components (e.g., load, energy source, and wire), behaviors (e.g., conductor versus resistor), intended goals (e.g., to turn on a light-emitting diode [LED]), and an overall function that depends on the system's interconnections (i.e., the interactions among the components and their behaviors in the system). Youths will experiment to create a simple electronic circuit in order to light up an LED. In addition, youths will learn how balancing feedback loops can help them make the most of limited resources in their circuits. **Note**: This first challenge is duplicated in both books on circuitry: this book and *Soft Circuits: Crafting e-Fashion with DIY Electronics*.

PRODUCT

Construct and diagram a simple circuit.

TARGETED SYSTEMS THINKING CONCEPTS

An electronic circuit is one example of a system made up of a collection of components (each with unique behaviors) that work together to send power to an object. For a circuit to work, components must be set up in a particular way (structure), which determines their specific behaviors and interconnections with other components that make up the overall functioning of the system. Circuits are structured in particular ways to meet an explicit goal (for example, to light an LED). In doing so, circuits use the energy in a battery as a limited resource. Discerning the circuit's current state and using processes to move the circuit toward a desired goal state involve the process of balancing feedback loops.

PARTS

PART 1: LIGHT ME!

Youths will be challenged to illuminate an LED by tinkering with different arrangements of a battery, conductive fabric, and alligator clips. A discussion about the components, behaviors, goals, and interconnections within a circuit will help them see a circuit as an example of a system. A "human circuit role play" helps them model their understanding through embodied play, and a reflection activity follows.

Time: 50 minutes

PART 2: LEARNING ABOUT CONDUCTIVITY AND RESISTANCE

Youths will use multimeters on a variety of objects to learn how electric current passes through material. They will work together to guess which materials act as conductors and which act as insulators, learning about conductivity and resistance in the process. Finally, they will build circuits with little to no resistance to learn about limited energy resources, short circuits, and balancing feedback loops.

Time: 55 minutes

KEY DEFINITIONS

SYSTEMS THINKING

Identifying a system. Identifying a system and distinguishing it from other kinds of things that aren't systems. Specifically, a system is a collection of two or more *components* and processes that interconnect to *function* as a whole. Speed and comfort in a car for example are created by the interactions of the car's parts and thus are "greater than the sum" of all separate parts of the car. The way a system works is not the result of a single part but is produced by the *interaction* among the components and/or individual agents within it. A key way to differentiate things that are systems from things that aren't is to consider whether the overall way something works in the world will change if you remove one part of it.

Identify the way a system is functioning. The *function* of a system describes the overall behavior of the system—what it's doing or where it's going over time. A system's function might emerge naturally based on interconnections among components, or it might be the result of an intentional design (in which case, we also might refer to the function of a system as its *goal*). Regardless, the function of a system is the result of the dynamics that occur among components' interconnected behaviors.

Identifying components. Identifying the parts of a system that contribute to its functioning. Components have certain qualities and/or behaviors that determine how they interconnect with other components, as well as define their role in the system. Without being able to effectively identify the parts of a system, it's hard to understand how a system is actually functioning and how it might be changed.

Identifying behaviors. Identifying the specific actions, roles, or behaviors that a component of a system displays under various conditions. Being able to identify behaviors becomes important when we change systems, as often a component will look the same after the change, but its behavior will be different.

Identifying interconnections. Identifying the different ways that a system's parts, or *components,* interact with each other through their *behaviors,* and through those interactions, change the behaviors of other components.

Perceiving dynamics. Perceiving a system's dynamics involves looking at a higher level at how the system works. Dynamics in a system are often characterized by circles—patterns that "feed back" on another. These are called feedback loops. Understanding dynamics gives insights into the mechanisms and relationships that are at the core of a system and can be leveraged to create systemic changes.

Designing a system. Creating a system through engaging in an iterative design process, one that entails iterative cycles of feedback, troubleshooting, and testing. One of the most effective means of developing systems thinking is to regularly create and iterate on the design of systems, and doing so in a way that creates opportunities for students to think about generic systems models that apply across multiple domains and settings.

Distinguishing the goal of a system. The goal of the system is what a system that was intentionally designed is intended to do. Sometimes this might be the same as the functioning of the system ... other times the goal and the *function* are not aligned. A given system might have multiple goals or purposes that are at play simultaneously, and come into conflict. Being able to understand system purpose or goal gives a sense of the ideal state of a system from a particular perspective.

Balancing feedback loops. Relationships where two or more elements of a system keep each other in balance, with one (or more) elements leading to increase, and one (or more) elements leading to decrease. These processes keep a system at the desired state of equilibrium, the system goal. Usually, balancing feedback processes stabilize systems by limiting or preventing certain processes from happening. Having a sense of how balancing feedback loops operate can give a person a sense of what will make a system stable.

Limited resources. In any system, it is important to understand which resources are finite (i.e., will run out at a certain point). Keeping in mind which resources are limited helps people make decisions about how best to maximize resources.

CIRCUITRY

Conductor. A material through which electric current flows easily.

Conductivity. The degree to which a material conducts electricity.

Electronic circuit/circuit. The unbroken path(s) capable of carrying an electric current (i.e., a "loop").

Electric current. A flow of electric charge through a medium (e.g., wire, conductive fabric, or LED).

Current flow. The rate at which an electric charge passes through a point in the circuit.

Load. A device (like a lightbulb or motor) that requires electric current passing through it to give it power.

Resistance. A measure of how difficult it is to "push" current through a circuit. A *resistor* is a component in a circuit that limits, but doesn't stop, the flow of electric current.

Short circuit (or "short"). A low-resistance connection between the two sides of the battery, causing the energy of a battery to drain or terminate completely.

COMMON CORE STATE STANDARDS	NEXT GENERATION SCIENCE STANDARDS
• W.6–12.2 (anchor standard)	• 3-PS2–3
• W.6–8.3	• MS-PS2–3
• RST.6–8.4	• 4-PS3–2
• RST 6–8.7	• 3–5-ETS1–1
• RST.11–12.9	• 3–5-ETS1–2
• SL.6–12.4 (anchor standard)	• MS-ETS1–2

MATERIALS OVERVIEW

For each youth, you will need to create ahead of time a Circuit Kit that consists of a zip-closed bag filled with the following system components:

- A 3V or "coin cell" battery
- 2 alligator clips
- 1 piece of conductive fabric (to be cut in half)
- 1 LED light, either a two-pronged LED or a LilyPad Arduino[1] LED

For each group, you will need to create a Conductivity Kit, which is a container filled with the following:

- A variety of conductive and nonconductive materials, such as paper clips, conductive fabric, buttons, pencils, fabric, tinsel, coins, etc.

ADDITIONAL MATERIALS
- Digital projector
- Scissors
- Design journals (1 per youth)
- Multimeters (1 per group)
- Extra 3V batteries

- Sticky notes or 3" x 5" note cards with tape
- Graphite pencils
- Paper
- Distilled water
- Salt
- Conductive fabric
- Conductive thread

HANDOUTS

- "System of the Electronic Circuit"
- "An Electronic Circuit: An Example of a System"
- "How Do I Use a Multimeter?"
- "Tracing Current Flow"

OVERALL CHALLENGE PREPARATION

- Familiarize yourself with how a circuit works and is connected by referring to the "An Electronic Circuit: A System" worksheet, as well as additional resources on circuits and electricity in Appendix B.
- Familiarize yourself with how a battery works by using some of the additional resources in Appendix B.
- Familiarize yourself with the multimeter using the "How Do I Use a Multimeter?" handout.
- Create a sample connected LED circuit (see "Part 1: Light Me!").
- Prepare the sticky notes or 3" x 5" cards for the Human Circuit Role Play activity (see "Part 2: Learning about Conductivity").
- Prepare a Circuit Kit for each youth.
- Prepare a Conductivity Kit for each group.

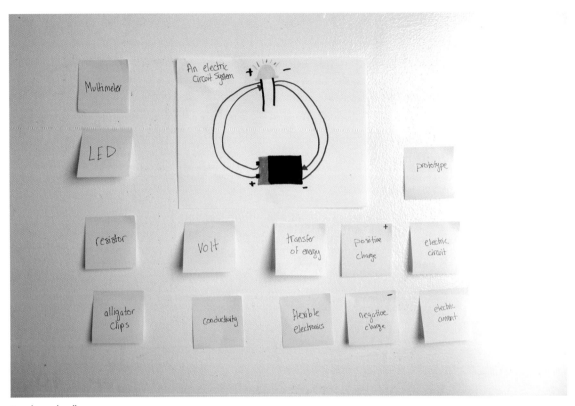

Sample word wall.

- Setting up a word wall can be helpful for integrating essential vocabulary into the activities in each challenge. Refer to the vocabulary often, and keep the word wall highly visible and clutter free. You can add new vocabulary in each unit to the terms already in use from previous challenges.
- Want to learn more about electronics? Check the list of great, novice-friendly resources featured in Appendix B.

PART 1: LIGHT ME!

Youths will be challenged to illuminate an LED by tinkering with different arrangements of a battery, conductive fabric, and alligator clips. A discussion about the components, behaviors, goals, and interconnections within a circuit will help them see circuits as an example of a system. A "human circuit role play" helps them to model their understanding through embodied play, followed by a reflection activity.

Time: 40–50 minutes

STUFF TO HAVE HANDY

- Circuit Kits (prepared in advance by the instructor; 1 per youth)
- Scissors
- Index cards and tape or sticky notes
- Pencils

HANDOUTS

- "An Electronic Circuit: A System"
- "System of the Electronic Circuit"

IMAGINE AND CREATE: LIGHT UP AN LED—10 MINUTES

Sending electricity to an object requires a power source and an uninterrupted circuit path, or *loop,* through conductive material. Usually, though, these requirements are invisible to youths in their everyday experiences with electric objects; for example, few young people know that electrical energy flows in two directions in a power cord, or why batteries have a positive (+) and negative (–) side.

This first activity makes the behaviors of components and interconnections in an electonic circuit more visible and gives youths an opportunity to test their assumptions about what is going on "behind the scenes" in any electricity-powered object.

1. Explain to youths that the first thing they are going to do is try to light an LED. Each youth (or each group) will receive a set of components that can help achieve this goal.

2. Before distributing the kits and allowing youths to experiment with the materials individually or in small groups, introduce each component in the Circuit Kit by holding it up for everyone to see. Build on youths' prior knowledge by asking if anyone is familiar with these components. Investigate their prior experience with circuitry concepts by asking if anyone has any guesses about what they might need to know to get the LED to illuminate.

	Alligator clip	An electrical connector (named for its resemblance to the jaws of an alligator) that gets attached to an electric cable to make a temporary connection to a battery or other component. Also called *alligator test leads*. SparkFun—PRT-11037
	3V battery (also called a *coin cell battery*)	An energy source in which chemical energy is converted into electricity. We recommend using the common CR2032 type battery for e-textile projects (20 mm), which should power e-textile projects for weeks at a time. SparkFun—PRT-00338

	Conductive fabric	A fabric woven with conductive metal strands. A variety of conductive fabrics are available that vary in their conductive materials (like silver or copper) and their degree of stretchiness. RIPSTOP: SparkFun—DEV-10056
	LED	An LED is a small device that lights up when an electric current passes through it. The positive end of the LED is the longer of the two legs. These LEDs also can be used in all e-textile projects by bending the legs in two circles with needle-nose pliers. LEDs are available in many colors. Electric Stitches: 5 mm White Clear LED

3. Hand out a Circuit Kit to each youth and challenge him or her to discover a way to light up the LED, working individually or collaboratively. The goal is for youths to discover that some configurations work, and others do not.

Note   At first, avoid telling youths that their solutions need to take the shape of an uninterrupted circuit or loop, or that they'll need to incorporate all components into their design. Allow them to experiment with finding a solution themselves.

As the youths are working, keep in mind that some of them might know and understand the idea of batteries having "positive" and "negative" sides, although others might not know what that means. Likewise, some youths will understand that "positive goes with positive and negative goes with negative," but again, they might not understand why. These are ideas you can emphasize as they experiment with their circuits.

Depending on how open-ended you want the discovery process to be, you can give youths a hint about the LEDs and tell them that one side is positive and the other is negative (and tell them which is which). This could make the task more straightforward, but it also might keep them from testing other conjectures and ideas.

VOICES FROM THE FIELD

Have youth experiment with other ways to connect alligator clips. Many have a misconception that the clips need to be directly connected to the battery holder only, not thinking of the other conductive and insulating parts of the alligator clip. For instance, if the plastic sleeve is removed from the clip, another alligator clip can be easily attached, allowing another circuit to build off of the +/− lines' clips.

—DIANE GLOSSON, RESEARCH ASSISTANT AT INDIANA UNIVERSITY

4. After a few minutes, turn off the room lights to see if anyone has a glowing light. If some of the circuits don't function, ask the following guiding questions to allow youths to troubleshoot their circuits:

- Does the circuit make a *complete loop?*

- Are the *connections tight* between components?

- Is the *battery connected on both sides* to the LED?

- Have they connected *negative to negative* (e.g., battery to LED) and *positive to positive?*

IMPORTANT TIPS FOR THIS ACTIVITY:

- If you are using two-pronged LEDs, keep in mind that the longer leg of the LED is the positive end (and, likewise, the shorter leg is the negative). Because youths might bend the legs of the LEDs in this exercise and later may have difficulty telling the positive and negative ends of the LED from one another, you may want to have them *mark the positive ends of the LED with a permanent marker* at the beginning of the exercise. Alternatively, you can look at the LED in this illustration. Most LEDs have one flat side to their base; the flat side is the negative side.

- If youths are having trouble incorporating the conductive fabric, you might give them a hint to use their scissors (i.e., the conductive fabric can be cut in half, with one piece used to connect to the positive side of the battery and the second piece used to connect to the negative side).

- It is also possible to create a working circuit *without* the conductive fabric.

- If some youths finish early or have prior knowledge of circuits, you can challenge them by giving them additional LEDs and more alligator clips to create more complex circuits in series or parallel configurations (see "Design Challenge 4: DIY Flashlights and Shadow Puppets" in this book or the "e-Textile Cuff" challenge in the *Soft Circuits: Crafting e-Fashion with DIY Electronics* for more detail).

- Youths may try to use the alligator clips to "clip" the 3V battery, but this would short out the 3V [connecting the (+) and (−) sides of the battery]. The same thing would happen if they decide to "wrap" the battery in conductive fabric. Have extra batteries on hand, and warn youths that *a warm or hot battery is a sign of a short!*

- If you're unsure of whether a 3V battery is still good, use a two-pronged (non-Lily-Pad) LED to test your battery by placing the negative leg of the LED on the (−) side of the battery and the positive leg of the LED on the (+) side to see if it lights up. If not, then the battery is shorted or is no longer working. In addition, this trick is useful to test whether the LED is blown, or what color it shows when illuminated.

Youth testing an LED.

SHARE: WHAT MAKES A WORKING CIRCUIT?—15 MINUTES

There are three goals to this discussion:

- First, it should serve to highlight some of the key vocabulary in becoming a systems thinker and how each applies to the system of an electronic circuit, including *components, behaviors, goals*, and *interconnections.*

- Second, we want to make sure that all youths understand that an *electronic circuit* is an unbroken path loop of interconnected components. *Electric current* can then *flow* through the circuit to power the *load* (in this case, the LED).

- Third, this is a good opportunity to start directing youths to think about circuits as a kind of *system.*

These goals can be accomplished simultaneously; in this first discussion, you can use some of the systems thinking vocabulary as you talk about how the circuit works. Specifically, you can talk about the circuit as a system, talk about the goal of the system (to light the LED), the components of the system, and identify what the behaviors of those components are and how they interconnect in order to conduct electricity (and light the LED) effectively.

1. Pass out the "An Electronic Circuit: A System" worksheet, introducing the concepts of flow and pointing out the loop or unbroken path in the electronic circuit, which makes the circuit capable of carrying an electric current. Also, point out the direction of the current flow and the positive and negative orientations of the battery and LED. *Some groups have adopted the mantra "positive to positive and negative to negative" to help youths remember the orientation of the components needed in a successful circuit.*

2. Introduce a system as something that can be described as having smaller parts, or *components,* that work together to achieve a goal. Present each component and show how all the components work together, Alternatively, if you think that some youths have a good grasp of these ideas based on their play and experimentation, you can have them present their circuit and explain what they have discovered.

3. The following questions could be used to facilitate the discussion:

- What are the components in this system that you created? *(Answer: Battery, conductive fabric, alligator clips, and LED.)*

- What are the behaviors of the different components in the system? *(Answer: The battery provides power, the conductive fabric and alligator clips carry electricity between the different components, and the LED produces light.)*

- What is the goal of this system? *(Answer: The goal of this circuit is to allow the energy from the battery to flow to the LED and give it power so that it lights up.)*

- What is happening to light the LED? *(Answer: Energy is flowing from the battery along the path of alligator clips and through the LED, which allows it to light up.)*

- This system works by routing electricity along a path. How does that energy move through the system? *(Answer: Batteries have one negative and positive side. When a circuit makes a closed loop, the battery's current flows through the conductive wires or thread to reach the load or LED, flowing through the device to give it power. The current flows toward the opposite side of the power source; i.e., the negative side of the battery.)*

- What are the interconnections in this system? *(Answer: The battery is connected to the alligator clips and conductive fabric through its behavior of providing electricity and their behavior of conducting or carrying electricity. The clips and LED are connected through the clips' behavior of conducting electricity and the LED's behavior of converting electricity into light.)*

- Can the components be connected in *any* way, or are there particular interconnections that are optimal? *(Answer: All components must be connected in a circular configuration so that the electric current has a path to flow along. If the parts are not connected and there is an opening in any part of the circuit, then the LED won't light up.)*

REFLECT: DOCUMENT YOUTHS THINKING—10 MINUTES

As a final activity, which can be used as an assessment, pass out the "System of the Electronic Circuit" worksheet. Ask youths to fill this out individually.

RESEARCH: WHAT'S GOING ON INSIDE THE CIRCUIT?—5 MINUTES

To further youths' understanding of how batteries and electronic circuits work, show one or more of the videos listed in Appendix B as an introduction to how electricity is generated within a battery and how current flows through a circuit.

One important difference between electronic circuits with lightbulbs (depicted in most of these videos) and those with LEDs is that like batteries, LEDs have positive and negative sides that must correspond with the direction of the electric current.

PLAY: HUMAN CIRCUIT ROLE PLAY—10 MINUTES (OPTIONAL)

In this activity, groups of youths will model an electrical system, where each group member takes on the role of one component in a circuit. The goal of "acting out" the circuit is to embody the various pieces of the system and begin reasoning about its specific behaviors. This is also a collaborative activity for youths to make meaning collectively and talk through any misunderstandings they have from the previous activity.

1. Divide the class into teams of 6–8 members who will create a human circuit. Have sticky notes (or 3" x 5" note cards) ready with each component of the circuit, including (1) the power (i.e., battery); (2) the load (i.e., LEDs or other components in the circuit that use electricity); and (3) the path or the connection between components or parts (i.e., the alligator clips, wires, conductive fabric, etc.). *Alternatively, you could have youths generate names of the components.*

2. Have participants label themselves as part of the system by placing the corresponding sticky notes or note cards on their shirts. *Optional: You might consider adding new components to the system that the youths are modeling, like a switch that interrupts the energy path (turning the circuit off and on) to prepare them for upcoming challenges.*

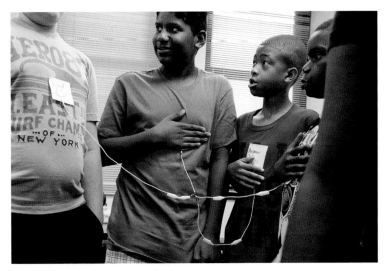

Youth acting out the "human circuit role play."

3. Have each youth verbalize the interpretation of his or her modeled component, clearly stating what it does in the circuit, and where that person thinks he or she should be within the circuit (e.g., next to other components). It is helpful to have a knowledgeable adult or peer to help each youth think through the new system components, the purpose of the circuit, and the end goal of a working circuit. Guide this verbalization with some focused questions, such as the following:

- What are the various components in the system? *(Answer: LEDs, battery, alligator clips, conductive fabric.)*
- What will the load (in this case, the LED) do when the circuit is complete? *(Answer: Light up.)*
- What is the structure of your circuit? *(Answer: An uninterrupted loop.)*
- What direction is electricity moving in? Is there any directionality of the components (i.e, are youths incorporating the positive and negative portions of the battery into their design and if so, how)? *(Answer: Yes, the current is moving from the positive end of the battery through the LED and returning to the negative side of the battery.)*

4. After the teams have created a complete circuit, they can present their circuits to the class. Each youth then can name his or her part and what it does.

VOICES FROM THE FIELD

Systems thinking took on a whole new meaning today, requiring me to step out of my comfort zone and teach a method of thinking that was still new to me. However, I was really surprised at how easy this concept was to apply. The students easily grasped the idea of seeing the electrical circuit as a system. They could discuss the components, the interconnections, the purpose, and the intended outcome of a circuit. They even constructed a human model of a circuit. Each student was able to explain the component they represented and describe the interrelationships in the system.

—LORI BELL, NATIONAL WRITING PROJECT

WHAT TO EXPECT

The "System of the Electronic Circuit" worksheet is primarily designed to ensure that youths grasp the fundamentals of both creating a working electronic circuit and understanding it as a system, which will be essential for the remaining Design Challenges in this book. If they don't understand key concepts, such as the conditions for and directionality of the current flow, they will face repeated frustration. This is also an opportunity to get them thinking about how systems differ from other kinds of cause-and-effect relationships.

The final question on the worksheet, "Explain how this circuit functions as a system," is intentionally broad, for the purpose of providing youths with an opportunity to apply their experience building the circuit to explaining what they understand conceptually about systems. We don't recommend scoring this final question for anything other than effort, as youths have few resources to answer it accurately at this point. Because it is an exploratory item, it might be worth having a whole-class discussion about this question once everyone has had a chance to complete the worksheet.

	Novice	Expert
Circuitry concepts	• Does not label parts of the electronic circuit diagram or does so inaccurately • Does not recognize the negative and positive sides of the LED and battery in the diagram • Does not connect the negative side of battery to the negative side of the LED (and likewise with the positive sides) • Does not use key vocabulary like *load, current,* and *circuit* • Does not incorporate conductive fabric or does so in a decorative/ nonfunctional way • Does not create a working circuit • Does not accurately indicate the direction of the current flow	• Labels all parts of the electronic circuit diagram accurately • Labels the negative and positive sides of the LED and battery in the diagram • Connects the negative side of the battery to the negative side of the LED (and likewise with positive sides) • Is able to use key vocabulary, like *load, current,* and *circuit* • Is able to incorporate conductive fabric into diagram in a functioning/ nondecorative fashion • Creates a working circuit (with only purposeful breaks or interruptions that would serve as switches) • Accurately indicates the direction of the current flow
Systems thinking concepts	• Unsure how to answer or does not give any answer • Describes a circuit simply as a collection of parts, with little attention given to how individual parts of the circuit contribute to the overall goal (i.e., lighting the LED) • Explanation does not acknowledge the relationship between the orientation of circuit parts [i.e., the (–) of the LED is not connected to the (–) of the battery] and the current flow in the circuit	• Can explain that a circuit is a system because it has multiple elements whose behaviors interconnect to make it work, and more specifically, that it is the way these elements interact with each other that causes the system to work (i.e., the LED to light up) • Can provide details about how a current flow is achieved through the proper orientation of circuit parts (i.e., the (–) of the LED is connected to the (–) of the battery)

DESIGN CHALLENGE 1, PART 1

AN ELECTRONIC CIRCUIT: A SYSTEM

This diagram depicts an electronic circuit and the direction of the current flow. In any working electronic circuit, it's important to have an unbroken path or loop, which makes the circuit capable of carrying an electric current to power the load (in this case, the LED). Notice the direction of the current flow and the positive and negative orientations of the battery and LED. It might be helpful to say out loud "positive to positive and negative to negative" to help you remember the orientation of the components needed in a working circuit.

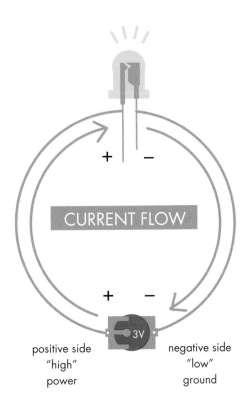

positive side   negative side
"high"   "low"
power   ground

DESIGN CHALLENGE 1, PART 1

SYSTEM OF THE ELECTRONIC CIRCUIT

Components of the system: Draw the diagram of your electronic circuit in the space below. Be sure to label your diagram with all of the components.

Current flow: Indicate in your diagram where the positive side (+) and negative side (−) is in the battery and LED. Use arrows to indicate the direction that the current flows.

> **COMPONENTS TO LABEL:**
>
> - 3V battery
> - LED
> - Conductive fabric
> - Alligator clips

Explain how this circuit functions as a system.

PART 2: LEARNING ABOUT CONDUCTIVITY AND RESISTANCE

Youths will use multimeters on a variety of objects to learn how electric current passes through material. They will work together to guess which materials act as conductors and which act as insulators, learning about conductivity and resistance in the process. Finally, they will build circuits with little to no resistance in order to learn about limited energy resources, short circuits, and balancing feedback loops.

Time: 55 minutes

STUFF TO HAVE HANDY

- Conductivity Kits (prepared in advance by the instructor; 1 per group)
- Multimeters (1 per group)
- Journals
- Graphite pencils
- Paper
- Distilled water
- Salt
- Conductive fabric
- Conductive thread
- *Optional:* Circuit Kits (prepared in advance by the instructor; 1 per youth)
- *Optional:* Scissors
- *Optional:* Extra 3V batteries

HANDOUTS

- "How Do I Use a Multimeter?"
- "Tracing Current Flow"

IMAGINE AND PLAY: CONDUCTORS VERSUS INSULATORS—15 MINUTES

In this series of activities, youths will learn more about how to determine which materials in their everyday environment are good conductors and which are good insulators.

1. Have youths visualize a very hot summer day in a playground. Tell them to imagine sitting down on the top of a shiny metal slide that's been exposed to the sun all afternoon. The slide is very hot and burns the underside of their legs, so they climb down the ladder and move to the plastic slide next to it. The plastic slide is hot, but it doesn't burn like the metal slide does.

- Why did one slide get hotter than the other, and what does that say about the materials from which they're made? The answer is that metal is an example of a *conductor,* a material that lets heat and electricity pass through it.

- Plastic, on the other hand, is a good *insulator,* a material that does not let heat and electricity go through it easily.

2. Ask youths if they have a sense of what kinds of materials might be conductive, and why. Do the same for the kinds of materials that might be insulating, and why. Document these initial conjectures on the board.

3. Show youths the multimeter and explain that it is a tool used for measuring multiple characteristics of electrics, especially voltage and current. Show how to use the (+) and (–) probes of the multimeter in Continuity mode (which shows the amount of electricity that can pass through a circuit) to discover which objects make better conductors and which make better insulators. Objects that make good conductors will cause the multimeter to beep, while the multimeter won't make a sound when it touches insulators.

	Multimeter	A handheld device with a negative and a positive probe, designed to measure electric current, voltage, and resistance, and to help determine whether a material or artifact is conductive or not conductive. SparkFun—TOL-09141
	Continuity mode	An electrical test used to determine the presence and location of a broken connection, as well as whether a particular material will be conductive. To set a multimeter to Continuity mode, turn the dial to the icon that looks like sound coming out of a speaker and place the black and red plugs on the probes in the holes as shown in the picture to the left.

Note We used the SparkFun digital multimeter in Continuity mode (not all multimeters have a Continuity mode, so look carefully at the device you are purchasing to make sure it has one). In addition, the Continuity mode might look different on your device.

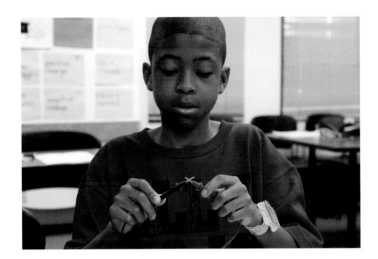

4. Tell youths that the goal for the next 10 minutes is to predict whether a particular material is conductive, and then to test it. Suggest that they draw a graphic organizer in their journals with three columns labeled "Component," "Prediction," and "Outcome." Youths can use labels like "C" for conductivity materials and "NC" for nonconductive materials.

Sample Table

Component	Prediction	Outcome
Tinsel	*Conductive*	*Nonconductive*
Conductive Fabric	*Conductive*	*Conductive*
Paper Clip	*Nonconductive*	*Conductive*
Rubber Bouncy Ball	*Nonconductive*	*Nonconductive*

5. Distribute Conductivity Kits, multimeters, and "How Do I Use a Multimeter?" handouts to groups.

6. Tell youths to set the multimeter to Continuity mode and explain that they are listening for a beep. Ask youths to think about why some materials might be conductive while others aren't.

Note If you prefer, youths can work together in pairs to complete the activity.

IMPORTANT TIPS FOR THIS ACTIVITY:

- Some common conductors are metals, like copper, aluminum, gold, and silver.

- Some common insulators are glass, air, plastic, rubber, and wood.

- Pencils are interesting to test because some parts (the lead) are conductive, and some parts (the wood) are not.

SHARE: WHAT MAKES A WORKING CIRCUIT? — 10 MINUTES

Once youths are finished testing everything in their kits (and perhaps everything in the room!), you can bring the whole group back together for a quick debrief about what they found. If you kept a list of initial conjectures on the board, this is a good time to return to those conjectures to see how things panned out.

1. The following questions could be used to facilitate the discussion:
   - Was anyone surprised or confused to discover that some fabrics are conductive (like the conductive fabrics in the kit), while others are not (like their own clothing)?
   - Did anyone find that in some objects, a portion of it is conductive (like the metal on an alligator clip) while other parts aren't (like the plastic covering)?

2. Explain that multimeters measure the degree of *resistance* in a circuit, which is the measure of how much a material keeps electricity from passing through it. All materials contain some resistance.

3. If the idea of resistance is a little unclear, a water analogy can be helpful: resistance is like a garden hose filled with sand. When the hose is turned on, the sand slows down the flow of water in the hose. We can say that the hose with sand has more resistance to water flow than does a clear hose. Now, if we want to get more water out of the hose, we would need to turn up the water pressure at the faucet. The same is true with electricity—materials with low resistance (i.e., conductors) let electricity flow easily, while materials with higher resistance (i.e., insulators) require more energy to make the electricity flow.

4. This makes it sound like conductivity is always a good thing in circuits. However, that's not always the case. The next part of the discussion will highlight why you need some resistance in your circuit to balance the system.

IMAGINE AND PLAY: DEGREES OF RESISTANCE — 10 MINUTES

What might not be readily apparent when youths simply test for conductivity is that every material has some degree of resistance, and that its resistance builds the farther that the current needs to travel (for example, a longer wire presents more resistance than a shorter wire). In this activity, youths will become familiar with measuring the degree of resistance.

1. Gather some materials in which youths can measure the degree of resistance readily, including one or more of the following:

    - A graphite pencil, to shade a large rectangular area on paper
    - Distilled water, to which you gradually add salt
    - A long strip of conductive fabric
    - A long piece of conductive thread

2. Explain to youths that the goal of the activity is to measure the maximum and minimum degree of resistance presented by one or more of these materials.

3. Have youths set the multimeter to Continuity mode and explain that they aren't just listening for a beep now—they also should be looking at the numbers shown on the meter.

4. For measuring materials like the graphite pencil on paper, the conductive fabric, or conductive thread, have youths start with the probes near one another (or touching) and then gradually move the two probes apart. They will find that the degree of resistance increases as the two probes move farther and farther apart.

5. For measuring materials like water with salt, youths should measure several times. For each measurement, place the probes in the same location, but stir in a bit more salt before each new measurement. Youths will find that salt decreases the resistance in the water (making it more conductive over time).

6. All in all, youths should discover that materials present a degree of resistance depending on the type of material and the length or area of the material. *In addition, they should realize that a material with high resistance is a poor conductor of electrical current.*

MOD THIS ACTIVITY: USE A HOMEMADE POTENTIOMETER

In fact, what youths learned about the difference in resistance across various materials in the activity just completed mirrors what happens in components called "potentiometers," which control the amount of resistance in a circuit (used to dim lights, for example). Have youths connect the homemade potentiometers that they just created to a simple circuit (i.e., a battery/battery holder, alligator clips, and LED) to control the brightness of the LED.

IMAGINE: TRACING FLOW, LIMITED RESISTANCE, AND BALANCING FEEDBACK LOOPS—10 MINUTES

One final important activity is for youths to think about the limited resource of energy and, in particular, how that energy source functions as a part of a system and needs to be in balance with other elements. The energy source—generated though the 3V battery in this case—is a crucial component of a system; indeed, without energy, the system of a circuit would not work (in the language of systems thinking, it couldn't achieve its goal).

1. What is the function of conductive and resistive materials in a circuit? Both are useful, but for different reasons. *(Answer: Conductive materials allow the circuit to flow freely, while resistive materials can be used to control the flow or stop it altogether.)*

2. Explain that batteries and other components like LEDs need to be part of a balanced circuit system. *Balancing feedback loops* are processes that are put in place to help move a system toward its goals or keep a system at a desired state of equilibrium. Usually, balancing feedback processes stabilize systems by limiting or preventing certain processes from happening. In electronic circuits, one way that we can balance the system is to think more deeply about conductivity and resistance (and we'll explore other ways in the remaining Design Challenges in this book).

3. Ask a couple of questions before you get started:
   - When a circuit is built using materials that have too much resistance, what happens? *(Answer: The circuit fails to power the load or achieve the intended goal; e.g., to light the LED.)*
   - When a circuit is built using materials that have too little resistance, what happens? *(Answer: If the circuit fails to meet any resistance, the current will be returned to the battery, causing it to short or die.)*

   Add youths' conjectures to the board. You will be investigating these questions more deeply in the next exercise on short circuits.

4. Project the "Tracing Current Flow" handout or distribute it to youths in groups. Ask the following questions:
   - What is different about Figure A and Figure B? Which of these represents a balanced system? What is going to happen to the LED and the 3V battery in both diagrams? Which circuit presents a greater degree of resistance? *(Answer: Three possible differences between the two figures are that the circuit in*

Figure B bypasses the LED, that the LED will not light up, and that the circuit poses too little resistance and the battery will short out (dispensing all of its energy at once and get hot). Figure A is the only system in balance, with a minimal amount of resistance posed by the LED so that the current isn't returned directly to the battery.)

- Are the path of the circuit and the lighting of the LED interconnected, and if so, why? (*Answer: Yes, they are related. In Figure B, the circuit bypasses the LED rather than flowing through it. This means that the energy from the battery is rapidly flowing through the circuit without meeting any resistance to limit the flow. And, equally important, no energy is flowing through the LED to power it.*)

- What do you think will happen in circuits A and B)? Is that problematic? Why or why not? (*Answer: The battery will be shorted in Figure B, and you'll need a new battery. In Figure A, the LED will turn on.*)

PLAY AND RESEARCH: LIMITED RESOURCES AND SHORT CIRCUITS—10 MINUTES

In this activity, youths will learn about what causes a short circuit, as well as certain signs or symptoms that can commonly occur when a short is draining the battery. At this point, you might want to search for videos or other resources to support this under-standing. There are also activities you can try. For example, you may want youths to put together a circuit like the configuration in Figure B by hooking up an alligator clip to the positive and negative sides of the battery or just using a paper clip and connecting it to the positive and negative sides of the battery. What happens? What youths should experience is that the battery starts to get hot. They should discover then that if they try to use this battery to light their LED, the battery no longer has power: it has been shorted out. Warn youths that a "warm battery" is a sign of the battery being shorted. The goal is for them to understand first that the stored energy in the battery has run out. This is an experience that they are doubtless familiar with in their everyday experiences with batteries, but they may be less familiar with *why* and *how* a battery has drained.

Here's a short explanation of what is happening: Basically, a battery is made of a limited amount of chemicals that produce electricity. When an uninterrupted loop of conductive material is made in an electronic circuit, the current begins to flow. The presence of other components on the circuit (such as an LED) creates some resistance in the circuit and causes the chemical reactions to occur at a regular speed, thus pro-longing the life of the battery. However, when the circuit has no or very little resistance, the energy from the battery is released more rapidly. It's useful to think about the battery as a limited resource, like water stored in a bathtub. Having some resistance in the circuit is like limiting the exit of water in the tub to a small trickle. Sticking with the water analogy, having little to no resistance is like having a wide open drain in the tub, which empties it almost immediately.

If a battery is shorted, it means that the positive and negative sides of the battery are connected through something with low resistance (like a wire), which causes a large amount of current to flow through the connection in a very short amount of time. This makes the battery discharge all of its energy, which is why the battery "dies." This large current through the battery also causes a rapid buildup of heat, which, for larger batteries, could even start a fire.

DESIGN CHALLENGE 1, PART 2

HOW DO I USE A MULTIMETER?

The multimeter tool is used to test and measure multiple characteristics of electronics (hence, *multi* and *meter*). Testing for continuity determines if an electrical path can be established between two points. This is handy when you want to check if your connections are secure in a circuit, or when you want to test various materials to see if a current can pass through them.

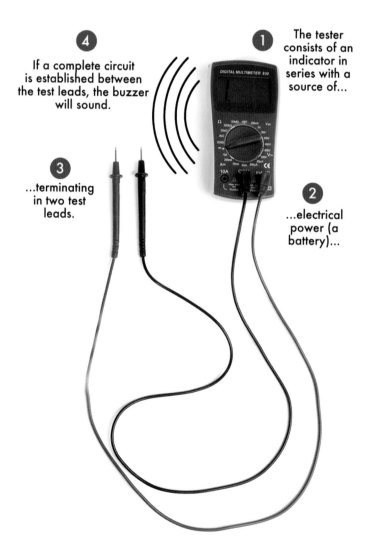

1 The tester consists of an indicator in series with a source of...

2 ...electrical power (a battery)...

3 ...terminating in two test leads.

4 If a complete circuit is established between the test leads, the buzzer will sound.

DESIGN CHALLENGE 1, PART 2

TRACING CURRENT FLOW

These two diagrams depict two similar but slightly different circuits. Use your finger to trace the path of each circuit. What is different about Figure A and Figure B? What is going to happen to the LED and the 3V battery in both diagrams? Which of these diagrams represents a balanced system?

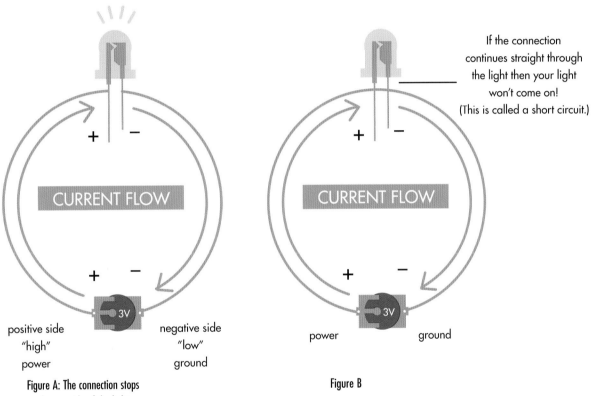

If the connection continues straight through the light then your light won't come on! (This is called a short circuit.)

positive side "high" power

negative side "low" ground

power

ground

Figure A: The connection stops on the one side of the light, flows through it, and exits at the other side.

Figure B

USING A MULTIMETER IN CONTINUITY MODE

Step 1: Turn Your Project Off

You can only test continuity when the device you're testing is not powered. Continuity works by poking a little voltage into the circuit and seeing how much current flows—the test is safe for your device, but if there is already voltage in the circuit, you'll get an incorrect reading, so always turn it off before you begin.

Step 2: Plug in Your Test Leads

Plug the black probe into COM and the red probe into mAVΩ.

Step 3: Configure Your Testing Mode

Turn the multimeter dial to the symbol depicted here with propagation waves around it (like sound coming from a speaker). (Note that this is not a universal symbol, and your multimeter may have a different symbol or settings.)

Step 4: Test Your Multimeter

Touch the tips of the probes together to ensure that your multimeter works. The display should change to a three-digit number (its displaying resistance), and it should emit a beep.

A beep means that power is flowing freely between the probes.

If there is no beep, resistance in the line is keeping the current from reaching the other side.

Step 5: Test a Component, Circuit, or Object for Continuity

Squeeze the probes with a little pressure against some objects—pencils, paper clips, glass, rubber bouncy balls, *anything!* Materials with low resistance (causing the multimeter to beep) are conductive.

Continuity is nondirectional, so it doesn't matter which probe you use on which end of the object that you're testing.

DESIGN CHALLENGE 2
IT'S ALIVE! MAKING E-PUPPETS

Total time: 320–350 minutes

OVERVIEW

Building on the systems thinking concepts introduced in Design Challenge 1 (i.e., systems have components, behaviors, and goals), youths will probe more deeply into a system's interconnections in the creation of a simple switch for an electric puppet (e-puppet). Through this process, youths uncover ways to preserve limited resources by identifying potential leverage points, that is, places to intervene productively by changing a component of the system with the result of changing the overall goal of the system. In addition, youths also learn about character development and aspects of storytelling in ways that support them in beginning to think about stories as systems, too.

PRODUCT

Youths will design a unique character, a short storyline, and a simple hand-sewn circuit to create an e-puppet. This e-puppet will have a working circuit and a handmade switch, which can be activated by some gesture or interactions with the e-puppet. The e-puppet then can be shared and posted to an online community. Consult our website at **digitalis .nwp.org/gnl** for suggestions but you may want to consider Instructables.com, DIY.org, or another venue for your sharing your work.

TARGETED SYSTEMS THINKING CONCEPTS

Switches rapidly change a system's dynamics or interconnections. A switch can act as a leverage point in an electronic circuit—a point where one intervenes to change or create the conditions that change the function of the system. The placement of the switch in the system acts as a balancing mechanism to preserve limited resources and help to meet the system's goal of conserving energy, creating what's called a *balancing feedback loop*.

PARTS

PART 1: SWITCH IT UP!

This Design Challenge introduces a new component to change a system's dynamics or interconnections: namely, a switch. With the capacity to open and close a circuit easily, a switch acts as a powerful leverage point in a system. This follows directly from the idea that ended Design Challenge 1: the notion that energy is a limited resource, and systems should be designed to preserve it. The placement of the switch in the system acts as a balancing mechanism, creating what we call a *balancing feedback loop* to help meet the system's goal of conserving energy.

Time: 30 minutes

PART 2: PLANNING AND DESIGN TIME

It's time to start planning the designs for an e-puppet! In this process, youths will explore creative ideas for their switches and circuit designs and plan the character design, story ideas, and circuit layout for their own e-puppet design.

Time: 50 minutes

PART 3: BRINGING IT TO LIFE!

In this activity, youths will bring the plans that they created during the design time to life. We suggest breaking this part into two phases: "Creating Form and Function" and "Bringing the Character to Life." First, youths create the shape of their puppet and integrate the circuitry components to ensure that they function. Then they complete the creation of their puppet through adding imagery and decorative elements in support of their story.

Time: 150–180 minutes

PART 4: WRAP IT UP

The goal of Part 4 is to have youths share and reflect on their e-puppetry projects. They will have an opportunity to share their projects with their local peer group, as well as a distributed online community called Interconnections. Finally, youths will reflect on their e-puppet experience and connect it to the core systems thinking concepts in this Design Challenge.

Time: 90 minutes

KEY DEFINITIONS

SYSTEMS THINKING

Balancing feedback loops. Relationships where two or more elements of a system keep each other in balance, with one (or more) elements leading to increase, and one (or more) elements leading to decrease. These processes keep a system at the desired state of equilibrium, the system goal. Usually, balancing feedback processes stabilize systems by limiting or preventing certain processes from happening. Having a sense of how balancing feedback loops operate can give a person a sense of what will make a system stable.

Identifying a system. Identifying a system and distinguishing it from other kinds of things that aren't systems. Specifically, a system is a collection of two or more components and processes that interconnect to function as a whole. Speed and comfort in a car for example are created by the interactions of the car's parts and thus are "greater than the sum" of all separate parts of the car. The way a system works is not the result of a single part but is produced by the *interaction* among the components and/or individual agents within it. A key way to differentiate things that are systems from things that aren't is to consider whether the overall way something works in the world will change if you remove one part of it.

Identify the way a system is functioning. The function of a system describes the overall behavior of the system—what it is doing or where it's going over time. A system's function might emerge naturally based on interconnections among components, or it might be the result of an intentional design (in which case, we might also refer to the function of a system as its goal). Regardless, the function of a system is the result of the dynamics that occur among components' interconnected behaviors.

Identifying components. Identifying the parts of a system that contribute to its functioning. *Components* have certain qualities and/or *behaviors* that determine how they *interconnect* with other components, as well as define their role in the system. Without being able to effectively identify the parts of a system, it's hard to understand how a system is actually *functioning* and how it might be changed.

Identifying behaviors. Identifying the specific actions, roles, or behaviors that a component of a system displays under various conditions. Being able to identify behaviors becomes important when we change systems, as often a component will look the same after the change, but its behavior will be different.

Identifying interconnections. Identifying the different ways that a system's parts, or *components*, interact with each other through their *behaviors*, and through those interactions, change the behaviors of other components.

Perceiving dynamics. Perceiving a system's dynamics involves looking at a higher level at how the system works. Dynamics in a system are often characterized by circles—patterns that "feed back" on another. These are called feedback loops. Understanding dynamics gives insights into the mechanisms and relationships that are at the core of a system and can be leveraged to create systemic changes.

Designing a system. Creating a system through engaging in an iterative design process, one that entails iterative cycles of feedback, troubleshooting, and testing. One of the most effective means of developing systems thinking is to regularly create and iterate on the design of systems, and doing so in a way that creates opportunities for youths to think about generic systems models that apply across multiple domains and settings.

Distinguishing the goal of a system. The goal of the system is what a system that was intentionally designed is intended to do. Sometimes this might be the same as the functioning of the system ... other times the goal and the *function* are not aligned. A given system might have multiple goals or purposes that are at play simultaneously, and come into conflict. Being able to understand system purpose or goal gives a sense of the ideal state of a system from a particular perspective.

Limited resources. In any system, it is important to understand which resources are finite (i.e., will run out at a certain point). Keeping in mind which resources are limited helps people make decisions about how best to maximize resources.

Leverage points. Particular places within a system where a small shift in one thing can produce big changes in everything. Leverage points are difficult to find because they often lie far away from either the problem or the obvious solution. It is because of the multitude of cause and effect relationships, feedback loops, and system structures that a seemingly small change can be amplified, often in unexpected ways. Not every place in a system is a leverage point—sometimes changing one thing in a system will produce only small effects not felt throughout the system. Leverage points are important since they let us know where to focus our energies when we try to change systems.

CIRCUITRY

Electronic circuit/circuit. An unbroken path capable of carrying an electric current (i.e., a *loop*).

Current. Flow of electric charge through a medium; e.g., wire, conductive fabric, or a light-emitting diode (LED).

Current flow/flow. The rate at which an electric charge passes through a point in the circuit.

Debugging. The iterative process of identifying and removing errors from hardware or software designs.

e-Textiles. Everyday textiles and clothes that have electronic components embedded in them; also known as *electronic textiles* or *smart textiles*.

Switch. A component that controls the flow of current by opening and closing a circuit.

STORYTELLING

Character. A real or imaginary person represented in a story

Character traits. The distinguishing features or specific qualities of a character that affect its actions

COMMON CORE STATE STANDARDS	NEXT GENERATION SCIENCE STANDARDS
• W.6–8.3	• 3-PS2–3
• RST.6–8.3	• MS-PS2–3
• RST.6–8.4	• 4-PS3–2
	• 4-PS3–4
	• MS-PS3–2
	• 3–5-ETS1–1
	• 3–5-ETS1–2
	• 3–5-ETS1–3
	• MS-ETS1–2
	• MS-ETS1–4

MATERIALS OVERVIEW

For each youth, you need to create an e-Puppet Kit that consists of a zip-closed bag filled of the following system components:

- 3 alligator clips
- A 2-inch piece of conductive tape or conductive fabric (to create a switch)
- A 3V battery[1]
- A 3V sewable battery holder[1]
- 1 LilyPad LED[2]

ADDITIONAL MATERIALS

- Extra switch materials, which could include LilyPad Button Boards, LilyPad Slide Switches, conductive Velcro, conductive tape, conductive fabric, or other conductive materials

- Planning materials like paper, colored pencils, markers, and/or crayons

- Fabric markers or sewing chalk

- Conductive thread

- Regular thread

- Needles

- 2 pieces of felt for each youth (12" x 12" squares, preferably in light colors)

- Decorative materials like yarn, "googly" eyes, assorted buttons, fabric markers, pipe cleaners, or other materials

- Glass beads (for decoration and insulating conductive thread)

- Either clear nail polish, fabric glue, or a low-temperature glue gun/glue sticks (to secure knots)

- Fabric scissors

- Computer with Internet access (ideally 1 per youth)

- Digital projector

- Digital camera(s) with photo and video capabilities, as well as universal serial bus (USB) cord(s) to download material to the computer

- Optional: Scanner

- *The Girl Effect* videos, available from **girleffect.org**

HANDOUTS

- "Switch Diagram"

- "Switch It Up!"

- "Planning Your e-Puppet"

- "Sample e-Puppet Circuit Diagram"

- "Running Stitch Practice" (preferably copied onto construction paper)

- "Tracing Current Flow" (from Design Challenge 1, Part 2)

- "Posting Your e-Puppet"

- "Self-Reflection on e-Puppets"

OVERALL CHALLENGE PREPARATION

- Familiarize yourself with the "Switch Diagram" handout.

- Develop a demonstration version of an e-puppet that includes a switch.

- Prepare an e-Puppet Kit for each youth.

- Create individual or a class Interconnections login account and test the firewalls in your computer lab to make sure you can access the website for the wrap-up activities.

- Setting up a word wall can be helpful for integrating essential vocabulary into the activities in each challenge. Refer to the vocabulary often and keep the word wall highly visible and clutter free. You can add new vocabulary in each unit to the terms already in use from previous Design Challenges.

VOICES FROM THE FIELD

The *Short Circuits* curriculum is designed to teach systems thinking in a cross-curricular way. Therefore, the puppets could be made the first week of school and used throughout the year to teach dialogue, persuasion, narratives, conflict resolution, story elements, and many other literacy concepts.

—LORI BELL, NATIONAL WRITING PROJECT

PART 1: SWITCH IT UP!

This exercise introduces a new component to change a system's dynamics or interconnections: namely, a switch. With the capacity to open and close a circuit easily, a switch acts as a powerful leverage point in a system. This follows directly from the idea that ended Design Challenge 1: the notion that energy is a limited resource, and systems should be designed to preserve it. The placement of the switch into the system acts as a balancing mechanism, creating what we call a balancing feedback loop to help meet the system's goal of conserving energy.

Time: 30 minutes

STUFF TO HAVE HANDY

- Extra switch materials (e.g., LilyPad Button Boards, LilyPad Slide Switches, conductive Velcro, conductive tape, conductive fabric, or other conductive materials)

- e-Puppet Kits (prepared in advance by the instructor; 1 per youth)

- Computer with Internet connection

- Digital projector

- *The Girl Effect* videos, available from **girleffect.org**

HANDOUTS

- "Switch Diagram"

- "Switch It Up!"

VOICES FROM THE FIELD

The lesson began with a review of circuits from the day before. We also had the youths write definitions to key concepts in both systems thinking and the context [in which] it was being taught, electronic circuits. The youths seemed to have a good grasp on systems thinking concepts; however, many youths, and one group in particular, kept referring to the systems thinking vocabulary in terms of electrical circuits. It was then that we redefined systems to the youths and made sure that they knew that even though an electrical circuit is a system, a system is not an electrical system. To make this point even more relevant to the youths, we had them name a system that they were familiar with. The youths were all able to name a system, the components, the interconnections, and the purpose of the system.

—LORI BELL, NATIONAL WRITING PROJECT

IMAGINE AND PLAY: WHAT IS A SWITCH?—15 MINUTES

A switch is just one of the many ways that limited resources—such as energy—can be preserved in a circuit; it is also something that youths already should be familiar with. A switch in the home—on a light, a television, etc.—functions the same way that the switch will work in this challenge: it interrupts or breaks the electronic circuit to stop the flow of current. The system can only function when the switch is in the closed position to complete the circuit.

1. Start a conversation by talking about energy. What is it? Where does it come from? Is it an unlimited resource? If these concepts seem too abstract for your group, narrow the conversation to talk about the energy in a battery—is it unlimited? Then pose a question: how can we make sure that we are using the energy in a battery only when we *want* to, so that we're not using it up when we're not around, sleeping, etc.? (*Answer: to preserve limited resources (i.e., energy), you have to stop the current flow through the circuit. You can do this by removing a battery, of course ... But is there another way—maybe a better way?*)

2. This should bring up the idea of a switch—a way to control when energy flows through a circuit. Explain that youths will explore several different ways to create a switch, eventually choosing one switch to use in their e-puppet during this Design Challenge.

3. Introduce a formal definition: A *switch* is a component that controls current flow by opening and closing a circuit (like a gate). A *closed switch* completes the circuit so that electric current can flow through it, and an *open switch* creates a break in the circuit and stops the current. We need switches because, as you learned in Design Challenge 1, energy is a limited resource, so we should design systems that preserve it.

4. Distribute the e-Puppet Kits and extra switch materials (e.g., LilyPad Button Boards, LilyPad Slide Switches, conductive Velcro, conductive tape, conductive fabric, or other conductive materials). Introduce new circuit parts as needed, pointing out how to identify the positive and negative ends of the components. Let youths know that the metal petals on the LilyPad parts need to come into firm contact with the alligator clips and/or conductive thread.

	Alligator clips	An electrical connector (named for its resemblance to the jaws of an alligator) attached to an electric cable for making a temporary connection to a battery or other component. Also called *alligator test leads*. SparkFun—PRT-11037
	3V battery (also called *coin cell battery*)	An energy source in which chemical energy is converted into electricity. We recommend using the common CR2032 type battery for e-textile projects (20 mm), which should power e-textile projects for weeks at a time. SparkFun—PRT-00338
	LilyPad LED	An LED is small device that lights up when an electric current passes through it and is frequently used as an indicator lamp in many everyday devices. LilyPad LEDs are designed with a built-in resistor and can be purchased in an array of colors, including blue, pink, red, white, yellow, and green. Note that the LED petals are labeled to indicate the positive and negative ends. LilyPad LEDs: SparkFun—e.g., DEV-10081 (soldina)
	3V sewable battery holder	A battery holder for the common CR2032 type 3V battery. The holder has a neat pop-in, pop-out feature that makes changing the battery easy. The feet of the holder have two small holes that allow it to be sewn into e-textiles or other garments. SparkFun—DEV-08822

	Conductive fabric	A fabric woven with conductive metal strands. There are a variety of conductive fabrics available that vary in the conductive materials used (like silver or copper) and in their degree of stretchiness. RIPSTOP: SparkFun—DEV-10056
	Conductive tape	Flexible conductive fabric tape with conductive adhesive made from a blend of nickel-, copper-, and cobalt-coated nylon ripstop fabric. This tape is conductive on both sides, making it easy to incorporate into e-textile or other crafting projects. LESS EMF—Tape: Nickel/copper/cobalt fabric Cat. #A225
	Conductive Velcro	Similar to Velcro, but with a conductive silver coating. Conductive Velcro can be sewn or glued, but no adhesive is supplied. LESS EMF— 1" hook and loop fastener Cat. #A207
	LilyPad Button Board (also called a *momentary push button* Switch)	This board has a very discrete button and two large sew holes that can be integrated easily into e-textile projects. The button closes when you push it and opens when you release it (which is why it's called a "momentary push button"). SparkFun—DEV-08776
	LilyPad Slide Switch	This is a simple slide switch that can be used as an on/off switch in e-textile designs. There are two large sew holes that make it easy to integrate the switch into your project. SparkFun—DEV-09350

5. Have youths try to recreate the simple circuit they made in Design Challenge 1, Part 1, but this time have them add a switch of their choosing. Remember, the primary goal of the circuit is to illuminate the LED, as before, but by adding this mechanism, we create a secondary goal: preserving energy. Challenge youths to play with the materials and find as many ways to create a switch as possible with a range of materials. Possible solutions include:

   • Remove the battery or disconnect the alligator clips … the simplest switch possible in this system!

   • Incorporate prefabricated switches, like the LilyPad Button Board or LilyPad Slide Switch.

   • Design a switch from conductive materials—fabric, Velcro, or tape—attached to the alligator clips (this solution will be important for understanding how to create a switch in the e-puppet design).

   • Create a homemade switch from everyday materials like paper clips or other common conductive materials. (For example, one youth created a fishing scenario on his T-shirt, where a dangling paperclip bent into the shape of a fishhook completed a circuit whenever it came into contact with a fish's mouth, illuminating a LED in the fish's eye to indicate that it had been "caught.")

6. At some point, have youths play with the placement of their switch in the circuit. Does it matter where the switch goes? Does it always have the same behavior and interact with the other components in the same way? *(Answer: Yes, it's the same. The directionality of the switch and location of the switch in the circuit does not matter.)*

REFLECT AND SHARE—WHAT DO YOU KNOW ABOUT SWITCHES?—15 MINUTES

In this activity, youths take a closer look at switches and begin to use diagramming to demonstrate their understanding.

1. Once each group has created a working circuit that incorporates at least one solution for the switch, have them diagram their working circuit using the "Switch It Up!" handout. Remember to emphasize that the diagrams should not just show the components and their unique behaviors (e.g., batteries power the circuit, LEDs can produce light, switches can complete or break the circuit, etc.). They also should mention the ways that the components are interconnected and their resulting interactions (e.g., the LED will turn on when the switch is closed).

2. Have volunteers share some of the solutions that they found, collecting ideas that were similar or different. In the discussion, help the youths to think about how the switches are actually working (how they are breaking off or connecting the circuit). Note that switches don't have to be made the same way, or even located at the same point of the circuit, so long as they are interrupting (and connecting) the flow of energy.

3. At this point, youths should have a fairly firm grasp on how a circuit functions, so this discussion can be used to expand that understanding to incorporate a switch. This is also an opportunity to continue to emphasize systems vocabulary as a way of conceptualizing the circuit. Specifically, whereas the goal in Design Challenge 1 was to get youths thinking about the components, behaviors, and goals of circuits, in this challenge, you can encourage them to focus on the new (and sometimes competing) goals in the system, as well as the interconnections between components and how the system's goals can be accomplished only through the interactions among its components (and the ways their behaviors affect each other).

4. The focus on switches also should serve to highlight potential leverage points and an introduction to the mechanisms and processes keeping the system in balance

(i.e., using the switch to create balancing feedback loops). The following questions could be used to facilitate the discussion:

- We incorporated a new component when the light turned on. What is this component called? *(Answer: A switch.)*

- How would you define it? From the perspective of a circuit, what do you think happened when you turned the switch on and off? Can you explain what was happening to the energy when the LED was off versus when it was on? *(Answer: A switch is a component that controls the current flow by opening and closing a circuit. When the circuit is interrupted by the switch, the current flow is stopped and the battery's energy is conserved.)*

- What are some different ways to create a switch? *(See Step 5 in the previous section.)*

- How does a switch change the way a system works? [*Answer: Now there is a new component that interacts with other components and changes the system. Whereas before, the connection from the battery to the light and from the light to the battery was continuous, now the behavior of the switch (i.e., that it can interrupt the flow of energy between the battery and the light) changes the connection from the light to battery (i.e., it interrupts it), and thus changes the behavior of the battery (i.e., the flow of energy out of the battery stops).*]

- What is the goal of the system? *(Answer: There are two competing goals in this system. The first goal is to light the LED. The second goal of the system, however, is to preserve the battery's limited energy.)*

5. Pass out the "Switch Diagram" handout or project it for all to see. In the discussion, try to highlight some ways of drawing and representing circuits so that youths can use similar ones later in their planning. For example, in the diagram, youths will see a gatelike drawing as a switch, although they may have chosen to draw a simple oval to represent the LilyPad Button Board. Both are ways of representing the system, but the gate is a more conventional way to diagram a switch.

IMPORTANT TIP FOR THIS ACTIVITY:

Unlike LEDs, switches have no polarity. This means that there is no "negative to negative, positive to positive" rule that governs the direction of the switch in a circuit; the behavior of the switch is the same regardless of the way it is positioned. LilyPad prefabricated switches often are marked on one end with an "S" for switch and (–) for ground, although *ground* shouldn't be confused with *negative*.

RESEARCH: WHAT'S A LEVERAGE POINT?—10 MINUTES

Now that youths have an understanding of what a switch is and how it works from a circuitry perspective, it's time to help them think about how the switch operates from a system perspective. On one hand, a switch can simply be thought of as another component of the system that interacts with other components to change the goal of the system. However, because adding the switch makes such a significant change to the overall goal of the system, we say that it isn't *only* another component—in fact, it represents a leverage point in the system. There are often several leverage points in a system, and in everyday problem solving, locating a leverage point can make all the difference in creating productive vs. ineffective solutions.

1. Begin by showing the two *Girl Effects* videos. Although the two videos are similar, they provide slightly different information about how the "girl effect" might work, which will be productive for youths trying to learn about leverage points for the first time. Note that the second video specifically talks about pregnancy and HIV, although there is no detail about either and no images (the video consists entirely of text). If these are topics that you are not permitted to discuss in your class, you might want to show only the first video (which uses those terms, but only very briefly).

2. After watching "The Big Picture" video, ask youths what the creators of the video are proposing—what do they think the world should do (or where do they think people should focus their energies) if their goal is to help do something about global poverty? (*Answer: Focus on adolescent girls: they propose that if the fate of girls in poverty changes, then the fate of their village can change, which affects the entire country, which in turn affects the world*).

3. Watch the second video, "The Girl Effect." Again, ask what the creators of the video are proposing. (*Answer: the same thing as for Step 2.*) Ask youths to explain why the creators of the movie think that girls are so important—why might girls cause such a big change in the outcome for so many people?

4. Now ask youths to think about the "system" that is being described in the two videos. You might want to do this as a whole-class activity on the board. Begin by brainstorming the components of the system observed in the two videos. Then ask youths to think about how those components might be connected. (Note that this is also a good opportunity to model for youths how one might represent a system, particularly one that doesn't merely include components, but also represents interconnections.)

5. Now focus on the girl in the system, who should be one of the components. Inform youths that when there is a part of the system that has a big effect on the entire system when it is changed, we call that component a *leverage point.* You might want to give them a specific definition (included here).

Leverage points: Particular places within a system where a small shift in one thing can produce big changes in everything. Leverage points are difficult to find because they often lie far away from either the problem or the obvious solution. It is because of the multitude of cause and effect relationships, feedback loops, and system structures that a seemingly small change can be amplified, often in unexpected ways. Not every place in a system is a leverage point—sometimes changing one thing in a system will produce only small effects not felt throughout the system. Leverage points are important since they let us know where to focus our energies when we try to change systems.

6. Ask youths why focusing on 12-year-old girls might be a leverage point in this system. You might want to explain that not all solutions to problems are equal, and that some use leverage points and some do not. Explain that in "The Girl Effect," if the video had proposed that the solution to the issue of girls in poverty was only to provide free medicine to adult women who had contracted HIV as a result of living in poverty when they were young (certainly a good thing to do), that wouldn't necessarily prevent more women from getting into poverty. On the other hand, the solution that it proposes—of making sure that girls when they are very young (at age 12) get healthcare and stay in school—leads to a snowball effect in which a whole life may turn out differently, benefiting generations.

7. Now bring out the "Switch Diagram" handout from earlier and look at it as a group. Ask youths what they think the leverage point is in this system. Note that there really isn't one right answer to this question—needless to say, removing the battery from the system would dramatically change the goal of the system and cause it not to work at all. But the switch doesn't destroy the system—it merely changes it. The important point to focus on here isn't whether youths identify the switch as a leverage point; rather, they should explain why whatever component they've identified is likely to change the way that the system works based on interconnections with other components in the system.

WHAT TO EXPECT

Hopefully, the introduction of the idea of the switch will be incorporated easily into youths' understanding of how a circuit works. If not, that is an indication that learners are still working on their understanding of how a circuit functions. With respect to systems thinking concepts and vocabulary, the introduction of a new component should hopefully focus youths' thinking on the interconnections among components. Specifically, asking them to think about how the introduction of a new component changes the behavior of the system should help them to focus on how the behavior of one component affects the behavior of another component. The focus on switches also should serve to highlight new goals, potential leverage points, and the process by which a system works to remain in balance (i.e., through various balancing feedback loops).

	Novice	Expert
Circuitry concepts	• Struggles to understand how energy flows through a circuit • Struggles to explain why or how a circuit has to be completed • Struggles to explain how a switch operates and can be incorporated into a circuit in order to function • Understands that a switch closes and opens an otherwise complete circuit, but struggles to understand that there is a continuous flow of energy from the battery in a complete circuit and that a switch serves to interrupt and reestablish that flow to conserve the battery's energy • Is unable to create a circuit diagram involving an LED, a battery, and a switch and name the behaviors of each component	• Can explain how energy flows through a circuit and how and why a circuit has to flow in a closed loop • Understands that there has to be a continuous flow of energy through a circuit and can explain how and why a switch should be incorporated into a circuit to conserve energy and interrupt the flow • Is able to understand and create a diagram of a working circuit in various shapes and configurations (not just a simple circle) • Is able to create a circuit diagram involving an LED, a battery, and a switch and name the behaviors of each component
Systems thinking concepts	• Struggles to think about a circuit conceptually as a system of interrelated parts, and finds difficulty understanding when aspects of circuitry are described or referred to in terms of systems thinking vocabulary • Aspects of circuits are primarily discussed causally (e.g., the LED works because it's connected to the battery), and therefore cannot offer an explanation detailing how a switch functions to conserve energy • Can list components of a system, but struggles to explain how their behaviors are interconnected • Has difficulty identifying the goals of the system • Has difficulty talking about the system as having limited resources that need to be preserved • Has difficulty identifying potential leverage points in the system	• Demonstrates the ability to think about a circuit conceptually and clearly understands (and can explain) that a circuit is a system because it has multiple components that work together to achieve a goal, and more specifically, that it is the way these components interact with each other that causes the system to work (i.e., the LED to light up) • Can offer an explanation of how adding the component of a switch changes the behavior of other components (and, to a lesser extent, the overall goal of the system) • Easily identifies the goals of the system • Can talk about the system as having limited resources that need to be preserved • Can identify potential leverage points and explain how and why they change the system through interconnections with other components

DESIGN CHALLENGE 2, PART 1

SWITCH DIAGRAM

This diagram depicts an electronic circuit with a switch in both the off and on position. Consider if the circuit were controlling water instead of electric current: the switch would act as a valve or faucet to control the water flow out of the faucet.

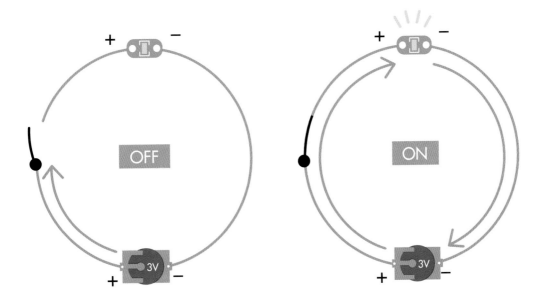

DESIGN CHALLENGE 2, PART 1

SWITCH IT UP!

Components of the system: Draw the diagram of your electronic circuit in the space below. Be sure to label your diagram with all of the components.

Current flow: Indicate in your diagram where the positive side (+) and negative side (−) are in the battery and LED. Use arrows to indicate the direction that the current flows.

> **COMPONENTS TO LABEL:**
>
> - 3V battery
> - LED
> - Switch
> - Alligator clips

Name and explain some of the interconnections in this system.

PART 2: PLANNING AND DESIGN TIME

It's time to start planning the designs for an e-puppet! In the process, youths will explore creative ideas for their switches and circuit designs and plan the character design, story ideas, and circuit layout for their own e-puppet design.

Time: 50 minutes

STUFF TO HAVE HANDY

- The e-puppet model that you created during prep time
- Planning materials, like paper, colored pencils, markers, and/or crayons
- Extra switch materials (e.g., LilyPad Button Boards, LilyPad Slide Switches, conductive Velcro, conductive tape, conductive fabric, or other conductive materials)
- e-Puppet Kits (1 per youth)

HANDOUTS

- "Planning Your e-Puppet"
- "Sample e-Puppet Circuit Diagram"

RESEARCH: PUPPETS, CREATIVE CIRCUITS, AND SWITCHES—10 MINUTES

Now that youths have investigated ways that various switches can be made, build on that understanding by having them think creatively about how to apply switches to the e-puppet. This is a time to give youths the big picture for the e-puppet by sharing your own model, as well as highlighting the interconnections between the puppet's behavior, its character, and the electronic circuit, before youths begin to plan an e-puppet of their own.

1. Show your e-puppet model to your class. In this demonstration, you want to make sure that two things come across: first, that the LED lights up *when you want it to*, and second, that the LED lights up *for a reason* (this latter notion incorporates the idea of character development).

2. In addition, you should talk about how the e-puppet has a different circuit layout than the diagrams that youths have been making and creating. For example, ask the group why the circuit in the puppet works. Doesn't it need to be in a loop?

[Answer: It still works because it makes a closed path or circuit (in this case, when the two hands of the puppet touch).]

3. Create a sample diagram on the board of the e-puppet circuit and compare it to those created in the last part of the activity and in Design Challenge 1. Facilitate a discussion and challenge youths to come up with other creative circuit designs.

4. If youths are having trouble understanding how the sample e-puppet circuit will work, have them build a human circuit as they did in Design Challenge 1, but this time in the configuration depicted in the "Sample e-Puppet Diagram" handout. Label each youth/component in the circuit as needed and have them close the loop by standing hand in hand in a circle.

IMAGINE AND CREATE: CHARACTER CREATION—20 MINUTES

It's time to brainstorm about the character design and circuit integration in youths' e-puppets. The goal of these activities is to come up with a uniquely designed character and to think about ideas for how the LED can be integrated meaningfully into the e-puppet to support the character designed.

1. Pass out copies of the "Planning Your e-Puppet" and the "Sample e-Puppet Circuit Diagram" handouts so that youths have a rough sense of the design for a hand puppet. Note that other customized designs can be made: objects or imaginary creatures of all kinds can be made into "puppets" that interact with each other.

2. Next, get youths started thinking about aspects of character creation: narrative and aesthetic.

    *   The *narrative* aspect involves the conceptualization of who the character is (e.g., his/her/its personality and character traits—motivation, likes, dislikes, actions, sense of the story in which he or she takes part, and so on).

    *   The *aesthetic* aspect involves imagining what the puppet will look like and how this will affect the action that he/she/it must take in order to activate the LED (as an example, perhaps the LED will light up when the puppet puts its hands together or touches its head).

    *   These two aspects of design should be intertwined, and you might ask youths to brainstorm both aspects at the same time. The goal is for each youth to develop the character of an imaginary creature, as well as a sketch of its appearance.

3. Now pass out paper and drawing supplies and let youths get started sketching their own puppets. **Note**: Make sure that the outline they draw is made a little bigger than their hands.

IS THE GROUP HAVING TROUBLE GETTING STARTED?

Try placing youths in small groups and ask each group member to draw a simple shape. Then have them pass the paper to their left and, when each has a different paper, add one feature to the creature. Pass drawings again to the left, and each adds something else to the one they're now holding, and so on. Continue this process, and after a few minutes, stop and have youths look at the character that they are now holding. Have them describe the characters and imagine character traits for each. Ask volunteers to share some of their group's best characters with the whole group. **Note**: Another imagination starter might be to pass out picture books. Ask youths to choose one of the book's characters and imagine how to make it into a puppet—what character traits would it have?

4. Conduct a discussion about the role that a circuit could play in their character designs. Could the LED be the light on Rudolph's nose? A princess's glowing heart? A pirate's eye? Could the shape of the circuit be used in some creative way? Could it make an action happen that highlights an essential character trait? Could the lines of the circuit be the pattern on the puppet's T-shirt? The skull and crossbones of the pirate's hat? The character's arms?

> Characters do things. They feel things. They hear things. They say things. ... characters act.
>
> —READ/WRITE/THINK, 2003 NCTE[3]

MOD THIS PROJECT

This project has been done successfully with other materials—like cardstock or cardboard instead of felt, or sock puppets instead of hand puppets (see example project photos with alternative materials). Note that different materials bring forward different challenges when sewing, so you might want to experiment before choosing one base material over another. Alternatively, you can use other electronic components like regular LEDs, wire, aluminum foil, and/or conductive tape in the designs.

IMAGINE AND CREATE: CIRCUIT DESIGN—20 MINUTES

Have youths integrate a circuit into their design plans. This is far from a trivial point, for both substantive and logistical reasons. Conceptually, some youths will struggle with figuring out how to build a circuit in this shape and to incorporate a switch. The planning will take some trial and error.

1. Have youths create a drawing of the circuit on a real-size sketch of the puppet. You might want to provide the "Planning Your e-Puppet" handout for them to sketch on or to use as a reference as they draw on other paper.

2. Next, have youths create a prototype of the circuit using alligator clips, batteries, and LEDs, and laying the prototype onto their puppet design to test their planned circuit.

3. Before moving on to the next step, youths should demonstrate that they have drawn a circuit that works, and, equally important, *that their diagram accurately represents the working circuit that they have designed.*

4. Have youths share their circuit designs with a peer to see if there are potential problems in their designs and to brainstorm any additional ideas.

IMPORTANT TIPS FOR THIS ACTIVITY:

- Note that a circuit needs to make a closed loop, but the *shape* of the loop can be very creative. The Silly Bandz craze (featuring rubber-band bracelets formed into shapes like hearts, stars, bones, etc.), shows that there are lots of ways to create a loop other than a circle. Suggest that youths think about a rubber band that could take on any shape (e.g., animals, letters, dinosaurs, etc.); so long as it's a single loop without crossing over itself, it will work as a circuit.

- Threads must not touch, or they will cause a short circuit. If the circuit *needs* to cross over itself (as in a figure-eight design) or intersect in any other way (like in a cross or X pattern), youths can use glass beads or other insulating materials to insulate the circuit at the crossover point to prevent a short.

- Logistically, youths will want to think about the actual arrangement of the components of their system relative to the shape and size of the puppet. For example, spreading out the battery, LED, and switch means a lot of sewing and more opportunity for something to come loose or touch something unintentionally, causing the battery to short.

- Youths also will want to avoid sewing too close to the edge of the material, as well as think about which components should be hidden on the inside of the puppet and which should be sewn on the outside.

- Likewise, youths need to make sure that the location of the battery doesn't interfere with their ability to work the puppet and make the switch connect.

SHARE AND ITERATE: INTRODUCING THEIR CHARACTERS—20 MINUTES

The goal of this next part of the activity is for youths to share their designs and perhaps generate ideas to elaborate on their earlier character ideas. Encourage youths to borrow and mod ideas from their peers. **Note:** This activity works best with the whole group.

1. Discuss the characters that the youths just planned. The following prompts could be used to facilitate the discussion:

   • Tell us about the character that you have chosen to create. What's its name?

   • Tell us about the character's traits and actions.

   • In your e-puppet, how will the switch work? Tell us more about the switch diagram.

   • What action will the puppet do that causes the LED to turn on?

   • What are some small tweaks that could help to refine your character/the group's characters further, or to turn on and off the LED better? Could the switch be better integrated or could the switch diagram better support the proposed character?

2. As youths share their designs, encourage them to give "warm" and "cool" feedback to each other (see "Approach to Conversation and Critique" in the Introduction).

   • This activity generally begins with a few minutes of warm feedback—comments about how the work presented seemed to meet the desired goals.

   • Then it moves on to a few minutes of cool feedback, sometimes phrased in the form of reflective questions. Cool feedback may include possible disconnects, gaps, or problems in attaining the goal.

   • Often, ideas or suggestions for strengthening the work are presented during this time.

3. Did the feedback activity give the youths any additional ideas for their e-puppets? If so, perhaps they want to sketch, make notes, or iterate on their designs.

4. Another way to support youths in developing ideas together is to have them generate "Yes, and …" feedback for each other, as opposed to "Yes, but …" or negative feedback. This type of feedback (also explained in the Introduction) reserves judgment and focuses on elaborating on the original idea as generated by the youths.

WHAT TO EXPECT

The drawings and diagrams that youths create to model the circuit for their puppets will be rich with information about what they understand—particularly about circuits, but also about character development.

	Novice	Expert
Circuitry concepts	• Struggles to explain why or how a circuit has to be completed • Does not recognize the negative and positive sides of the LED and battery in the diagram • Does not connect the negative side of the battery to the negative side of the LED (and likewise with the positive) • Does not sketch a working circuit diagram, or the circuit lacks a switch • Is unable to understand and create a diagram of a working circuit in various shapes and configurations (uses just a simple circle)	• Can explain how energy flows through a circuit, and how and why a circuit has to flow in a closed loop • Labels all parts of the diagram accurately, including the positive and negative sides of the LED and battery • Connects the negative side of battery to the negative side of LED (and likewise with the positive) • Is able to create a circuit diagram involving an LED, a battery, and a switch • Is able to understand and create a diagram of a working circuit in various shapes and configurations (not just a simple circle)
Storytelling concepts	• The *who* of the character is not clearly conceptualized (e.g., has one or more problems with articulating his or her personality and character traits like motivation, likes, dislikes, and actions, as well as a sense of the story in which he or she takes part) • Does not have a well-developed aesthetic for the character, involving imagining what the puppet will look like, and how this will affect the action that he/she/it will do in order to activate the LED • Has not thoughtfully intertwined the two abovementioned aspects of character design	• Has clearly conceptualized *who the character is* (e.g., his or her personality and character traits like motivation, likes, dislikes, and actions, as well as a sense of the story in which he or she takes part) • Has a well-developed aesthetic for the character, involving imagining what the puppet will look like, and how this will affect the action that he/she/it will do in order to activate the LED • Has thoughtfully intertwined the two abovementioned aspects of character design

DESIGN CHALLENGE 2, PART 2

PLANNING YOUR E-PUPPET

This is a sample pattern to help you design your e-puppet. You can enlarge it to fit the size of your fabric, adjust the arms and head, and/or change its basic shape as needed to match your puppet's character and personality. You can also use this worksheet to plan your puppet's circuitry. This puppet pattern should be large enough to fit your hand, so you will need to draw it larger than shown here.

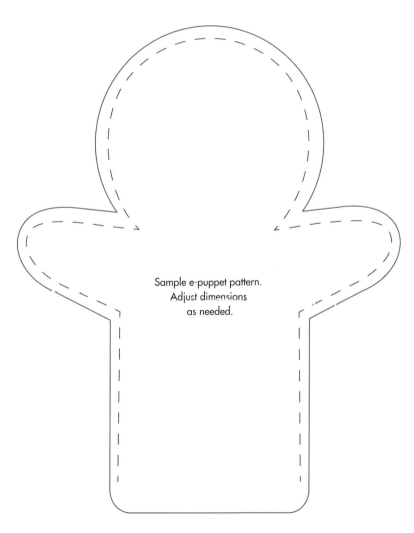

Sample e-puppet pattern.
Adjust dimensions
as needed.

DESIGN CHALLENGE 2, PART 2

SAMPLE E-PUPPET CIRCUIT DIAGRAM

This diagram depicts a sample e-puppet circuit layout with a switch on the hands of the puppet. When the hands touch, the circuit closes and lights the LED.

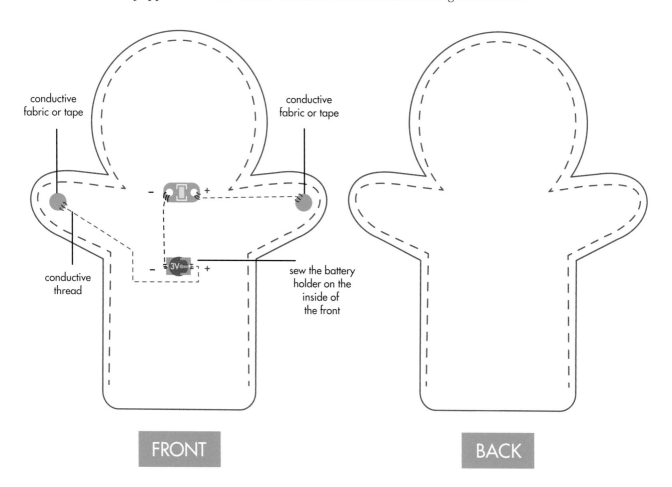

TO GET STARTED MAKING YOUR E-PUPPET:

1. Cut out the shape of the puppet, cutting through both sheets of felt at the same time to create two identical shapes. Choose one piece to be the front, and put the back of the puppet aside for now.

2. Lay out all your circuit components on the front side of the felt design, including the LED, the 3V battery in its holder, and your switch materials. You may want to secure your switch materials by sewing them in place with nonconductive thread or by using the adhesive on the conductive tape.

3. Think through which components should be on the front of the puppet (like the conductive pads on the hands of the puppet), and which should be hidden on the inside (like the battery holder).

4. Prepare to sew with the conductive thread by double-threading your needle and knotting the thread at the end. Place nail polish or fabric glue on the knot before sewing, both to avoid getting it on the metal petals of the circuit parts and to insulate them. *Secure your knots every time you thread your needle!*

5. Whenever you get to an end knot, place the knot on the opposite side of the circuit parts and then secure it again with clear nail polish, fabric glue, or low-temperature hot glue. This will help prevent insulating the metal pads of the circuit parts as well. A little goes a long way—there's no need to go overboard!

6. Begin progressively sewing down the components and stitching the connections. In the design in the sample puppet circuit, there are three *separate* lines that require stitching:

   - From the left hand's conductive material to the positive end of the battery

   - From the negative side of the battery to the negative side of the LED

   - From the positive end of the LED to the right hand's conductive material

7. Start by stitching (three times!) through the left hand's conductive material, and then continue to stitch to the positive end of the battery holder. Stitch through the battery holder (three times!), knot, and cut your thread. Remember to place your end knot on the opposite side of the fabric as your component and to secure the knot with clear nail polish, fabric glue, or low-temperature hot glue.

8. Tie another knot in your needle's thread and secure it before you start sewing. Now it's time to sew down the second line: Sew through the negative side of the battery holder (three times!) and continue your running stitch to the negative side of the LED and sew (three times!) through the sew hole in the LED. Knot your thread on the opposite side of the fabric, secure your knot, and cut the excess thread.

9. Now it's time for the final line: Begin by double-threading and tying another knot in your needle's thread. Then sew through the positive end of the LED (three times!) and continue sewing to the right hand's conductive material. Sew through the conductive material (three times!) and then knot your thread on the opposite side of the fabric, secure the knot, and cut the excess thread.

10. Double-check all knots to make sure that they're secure and there are no long tails coming off your knots that could cause shorts. Trim those that are too long, but be careful not to cut them too short!

11. Double-check to make sure all your components are attached securely to the felt and have solid connections with the conductive thread—take out your stitching or repair your stitching as needed.

12. Double-check to make sure that you don't have any loose needlework hanging off the back—if you find any loose threads, secure them in a way that won't cause any shorts in your circuit.

13. Test the circuit with your hand to see if it works. If it doesn't, see if you can find a way to make changes to your project's design that will fix the problem. Use the multimeter if needed to check to make sure there aren't any breaks in your circuit.

14. Congratulations—your e-puppet circuit is finished!

PART 3: BRINGING IT TO LIFE!

In this activity, youths will bring the plans that they created during the design exercise to life. We suggest breaking this part into two phases: "Creating Form and Function" and "Bringing the Character to Life." First, youths create the shape of their puppets and integrate the circuitry components to ensure that they function. Then they complete the creation of their puppet through the addition of imagery and decorative elements to support their story.

Time: 150–180 minutes

STUFF TO HAVE HANDY

- Regular thread
- Needles
- e-Puppet Kits (1 per youth)
- Pens or fabric markers
- Conductive thread
- Extra switch materials (e.g., LilyPad Button Boards, LilyPad Slide Switches, conductive Velcro, conductive tape, conductive fabric, or other conductive materials)
- 2 pieces of felt for each youth (12" x 12" squares suggested)
- Decorative materials like yarn, "googly" eyes, assorted buttons, fabric markers, glass beads, pipe cleaners, or other materials
- Fabric glue
- Low-temperature glue guns and sticks
- Clear nail polish, fabric glue, or glue gun (optional)
- Fabric scissors
- Construction paper

HANDOUTS

- "Running Stitch Practice"
- "Sample e-Puppet Circuit Diagram" *(from Part 2)*
- Optional: "Tracing Current Flow" *(from Design Challenge 1, Part 2)*

CREATE (PART 1): MAKING YOUR PUPPET—ABOUT 90 MINUTES

During this phase, youths stitch their circuits into fabric for eventual inclusion in their e-puppets. The puppets can take any form, so encourage participants to get creative! Refer back to the "Planning Your e-Puppet" and "Sample e-Puppet Circuit Diagram" handouts used in Part 2 (as well as youths' earlier plans) for a basic puppet template to follow.

1. Before they get started, have youths practice threading their needle and tying knots.

2. Youths can use the "Running Stitch Practice" worksheet to practice proper stitching techniques by connecting the dots with nonconductive thread, then adding their own dots and stitches to complete the diagram. **Note:** We suggest you print this practice sheet on construction paper, as the weight and texture is slightly better for sewing.

3. Once they have successfully completed their practice worksheets, give each youth two pieces of felt for the front and back of the puppet. Have them place the pieces on top of one another.

4. Based on their earlier plans from Part 2, "Planning and Design Time," have youths sketch the shape of their puppets with a pen or fabric marker. Make sure that they leave extra room around the edges so that when they glue the two pieces of fabric together in the next part of the activity, they still will leave enough room for their hands to fit inside.

5. Each youth now should cut out the shape of the puppet, cutting through both sheets of felt at the same time to create two identical shapes. For now, youths should choose one piece to be the front and put the back of the puppet aside.

6. Make sure that everyone has an e-Puppet Kit, including an LED, a 3V battery in a holder, and switch materials. Have the youths lay out their components on their felt designs using either their designs from the previous part of this challenge or the "Sample e-Puppet Circuit Diagram" handout.

7. Help youths to think through which components should be on the front of the puppet (e.g., the conductive pads on the hands of the puppet), and which should be hidden on the inside (e.g., the battery holder).

8. **CRITICAL STEP**: Have each youth prepare to sew with the conductive thread by threading the needle and knotting the thread. Whenever someone knots the thread, it's important to use clear nail polish, fabric glue, or low-temperature hot glue to hold the knots. Have youths use the nail polish or the fabric glue on the knot before sewing to avoid getting it on the metal petals of the circuit parts (and insulating them). Then encourage youths to create their end knots on the opposite side of the circuit parts and then secure clear nail polish, fabric glue, or low-temperature hot glue to hold the knots. This will help prevent insulating the metal pads of the circuit parts as well. Remind them that a little goes a long way—no need to go overboard!

	Conductive thread	Similar to wire, conductive thread can carry current to power your e-textiles. Most conductive threads are plated with silver or stainless steel and can be used for hand-sewing. Note that the thread has more resistance than wire, but it shouldn't present any problems at the size and scale of projects in these Design Challenges. We recommend two-ply or four-ply conductive thread. Conductive Thread— 60 g (stainless steel): SparkFun—DEV-11791

9. Ask youths what would happen if they made very large stitches, or if they didn't loop through the component several times at the end. (*Answer: The components would fall off or not make a solid connection with the thread.*) This is also true for the conductive fabric or tape, which needs to have a firm connection with the conductive thread: Remember that the circuit must be a *complete loop* to work.

10. Ask youths what will happen if they don't cut the thread between components. (*Answer: They'll create a short in their circuit. See "Tracing Current Flow" from Design Challenge 1, Part 2.*)

11. **CRITICAL STEP**: Have youths progressively sew down the components and stitch the connections. In this design, there are three *separate* lines that require stitching:

   • From the left hand's conductive material to the positive end of the battery

   • From the negative side of the battery to the negative side of the LED

   • From the positive end of the LED to the right hand's conductive material

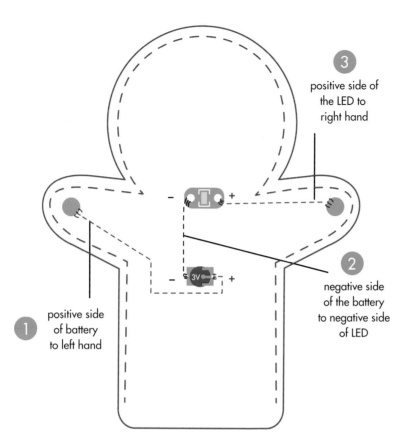

positive side of
the LED to
right hand

3

negative side
of the battery
to negative side
of LED

2

positive side
of battery
to left hand

1

12. **CRITICAL STEP:** Whenever youths reach a component in the circuit (e.g., either an LED, battery holder, or the snaps/Velcro), they need to stitch through the component *several times* to create solid connections with the conductive thread. They also will need to knot and cut the thread when they get to the end of one of the stitching lines (avoiding long tails).

13. Consider starting the process as a group and completing the first stitching line together as a way of modeling the activity.

14. When youths run into trouble, let them know that an essential skill of anyone who works with technology—physical or digital—is the ability to *debug,* the act of iteratively identifying and removing errors from a design. Chances are that they likely will need to iterate on their designs. That's good—in fact, it's one of the goals of this challenge! Be sure to leave time for this type of learning. This project does not require a lot of stitching, but youths should be prepared to cut out their mistakes and try again as needed.

15. The debugging steps contain possible solutions to common problems, though try to avoid supplying the answer right away—errors in youths' designs are often fueled by conceptual misconceptions that can be best rectified through iterative testing and experimentation.

16. Congratulations—the e-puppet's circuit is finished! Have youths test the circuit on their hand to see if it works.

IMPORTANT TIPS FOR THIS ACTIVITY:

- Before stitching, make sure that youths' puppets can actually *perform* the action required to make the switch connect. For example, if the arms have to touch, it is important that the puppet is large enough for each youth's hand to be inserted into the puppet and that the arms are long enough to touch each other to complete the circuit.

- The "Sample e-Puppet Diagram" handout illustrates just one possible solution for how to create an e-puppet, and many other variations of this model can be successful. Encourage youths to experiment, but check in with them often during the design process to avoid time-consuming (and possibly confusing) mistakes.

- Some youths may struggle at hand-sewing with the conductive thread at first. But their difficulty should lessen as they gain experience in the thread behavior. For instance, when the thread knots, don't pull it tight. Rather, patiently untangle it, using a needle if necessary to gently pull apart the knot.

- An easy technique for starting a conductive stitch with youths is to tie a knot at the end of the double-threaded needle, trim the end, and immediately put nail polish on it. Holding it in their fingers, blow it dry, and then start to sew with the knot underneath the fabric on the side opposite the electric component; this will allow the youths to make clean connections between the conductive thread and the sew hole on the component to ensure connectivity for a closed circuit.

- When tying off an end knot, do the same as the beginning stitch by finishing on the side of the fabric opposite the electric component. This will keep the nail polish away from the conductive hole on the part.

- **Having trouble?** Refer to this book's Toolkit for troubleshooting guidance and additional techniques for working with conductive thread.

DEBUGGING STEPS:

- Check to make sure that no two lines are crossed in the design, as this will cause a short.

- Make sure that the (+) sides of the LEDs are oriented toward the (+) end of the battery holder.

- Make sure that the (−) sides of the LEDs are connected to the (−) end of the battery holder.

- Check to make sure that each component has a solid connection (i.e., the conductive thread has been sewn around the component two or more times) and is not dangling from the cuff.

- Check to make sure that none of the LEDs have been sewn through from the positive to the negative end.

- Check to make sure that none of the stitching has been cut accidentally or has frayed. If there are any questions about whether the stitching is still good in a particular spot, use the multimeter in Continuity mode (but remember to remove the battery before doing so!).

- Check the back of the puppet to make sure that there are no long tails on the knots or any threads that make unnecessary loops. Affix with hot glue any dangling pieces so that they are out of the way and not touching other conductive components.

VOICES FROM THE FIELD

"Iteration" became a word that came naturally for the children, each time their e-Puppet did not work as they troubleshoot the problem together with their partners, and also with the facilitators.

—VERILY TAN, INDIANA UNIVERSITY

CREATE (PART 2): BRINGING THE CHARACTER TO LIFE—ABOUT 60–90 MINUTES

During this phase, youths finish assembling their puppets and use decorative materials to display their puppets' characters.

1. Once the circuit is completed from the previous part of the challenge, have youths place the second sheet of fabric behind the first.

2. The puppet then can be constructed by attaching the front and back together around the edge by sewing with regular thread or with fabric or hot glue. **Note:** Be careful not to glue the bottom of the design, so that there can be an opening for someone's hand to go in.

3. Have youths test the puppet again. Does it work the way it was supposed to? If not, help them make the necessary adjustments.

4. Once the puppet works (yay!) then distribute the decorative elements of the circuit to each table and allow youths to embellish their puppets. Remind them to use their earlier character development plans.

IMPORTANT TIPS FOR THIS ACTIVITY:

- Avoid passing out decorative materials until youths have integrated their circuits into their puppets. We've found that the actual puppet creation can take a very long time, with many youths becoming so engrossed in creating and designing their puppets that they have difficulty completing the circuitry in a timely manner.

- The silver in the conductive thread can corrode slowly over time. Some youths might want to cover the circuits with puffy paint—it not only insulates the thread and ensures the conductivity of the project over time, but hiding the stitches can add another design element.

Example projects using felt:

Examples with alternative materials:

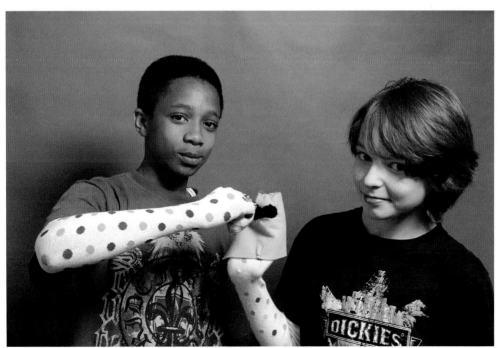

DESIGN CHALLENGE 2, PART 3

RUNNING STITCH PRACTICE

Practice your running stitch by connecting the dots with *nonconductive thread.* Then add your own dots and stitches to complete the diagram.

RUNNING STITCHES GO OVER & UNDER THE FABRIC

1. Double thread the needle and knot it at the end.
   Push the needle through the underside of the paper and by the #1 •
   Connect the dotted line by sewing in and out of the dots, making sure to stay on the line.

2. Continue to connect the dots. Using the thread to make a line.

3. Use your running stitch to complete the picture by connecting the robot's shoulders, ending at Point 1.

PART 4: SHARE AND PUBLISH!

The goal of this part is to have youths share and reflect on their e-puppetry projects. They will have an opportunity to share their projects with their local peer group as well as a distributed online community called Interconnections. Finally, youths will reflect on their e-puppet experience and connect it to the core systems thinking concepts in this challenge.

Time: 90 minutes

STUFF TO HAVE HANDY

• Youths' earlier design plans for their e-puppet characters

• Their finished e-puppets

• Pencils

• Computers with a high-speed Internet connection (1 per youth is ideal)

• Digital camera(s) with photo and video capabilities and USB cord(s) to download material to the computer

• *Optional:* Scanner

HANDOUTS

• "Posting Your e-Puppet"

• "Self-Reflection on e-Puppets"

PUBLISH: POSTING TO THE WEB—60 MINUTES

Today, young people are becoming both consumers and avid producers of online media. The goal of this part of the activity is to give youths the opportunity to post their e-puppets to an online e-textiles community, such as the ones suggested at the Interconnections website (**digitalis.nwp.org/gnl**). Joining such an online community allows people to document and share projects that blend electrics and textiles. This is ideal for posting e-textile projects like those found in this book. Giving them a few minutes to do this allows youths to post their work and become part of the larger participatory culture.

1. If you haven't already done so, create login usernames and passwords for youths (or allow time for them to create their own logins), and test the firewalls in your computer lab to make sure that you can access the website.

2. Allow youths time to visit the chosen website and briefly explore the projects posted there, leaving comments or "liking" projects as they go (login required for comments and "likes"). It might be useful to make note as they explore about what makes a good post (for example, a vivid picture, great text accompanying the post, an outstanding title, etc.).

3. After they've taken time to view other users' offerings, distribute the "Posting Your e-Puppets" worksheet. Ask youths to complete the worksheet before they post their projects on the chosen website. Remind them to refer to their notes about what makes a good post as they work on their own writing.

GIVE YOUR PROJECT A NAME:

What will you call your e-puppet? Give it a unique and inspiring name! The name is also the title of your post.

WRITE A PROJECT DESCRIPTION:

1. What inspired you?

2. Describe the materials you used to create your e-puppet, including all the circuit components.

3. Describe how your e-puppet works and any other details you think are important for others to know about.

PHOTO SHOOT PLANNING:

1. What should the photo(s) look like online? Sketch or write a description of what they should look like. (Example: "Photo 1 should be the e-puppet with the LEDs turned on; Photo 2 should be the e-puppet laid flat.") Should there be a video of the e-puppet in action for the site? If so, what should the video show?

2. Have small groups of youths take turns taking pictures and/or videos of their finished projects. Scanning some of the planning materials would make interesting additions to the posts as well. Remind them to refer to their notes about what they thought makes a good post as they work on their own pictures and video.

3. Once they have drafted ideas for their posts, have youths log in to the website to post their projects. It might be useful to have all the youths in your group use a single login to post projects, so you have the ability to edit projects or content if needed.

4. Encourage youths to do the following:

- Give their project a unique name/title.

- Tag the project with "Short Circuits," "e-puppet," or another unique tag for your group.

- Write a compelling project description.

- Link to other web materials (like their videos that would need to be posted on YouTube before creating their Interconnections submission).

IMPORTANT TIPS FOR THIS ACTIVITY:

- In order for videos to be posted on Interconnections, they need to be hosted on a site like YouTube or Vimeo (http://vimeo.com), with a link that will be copied to Interconnections.

- What makes a good post? Encourage youths to photograph their work up close, with few distractions in the background. Encourage them to write a clever title and catchy text that is both informative and to the point. Encourage them to think of their audience when describing their project, how it works, and what they used to put it together.

- In a few days, check to see if there are any comments on any of your group's posts. In addition, encourage youths to comment on each other's work—reading and responding are important aspects of becoming part of an online community!

REFLECT AND SHARE: LET'S TALK!—30 MINUTES

As a final activity, which can be used as an assessment, distribute the "Self-Reflection on e-Puppets" worksheet. Ask youths to fill these out individually and to take some time to think about what they now know and understand about circuits and systems as a consequence of designing and crafting an e-puppet.

1. What is the purpose or goal of the circuit in your puppet, and how do the components and behaviors of the circuit work together to accomplish that goal? You can explain in words, pictures, or both.

2. Draw a diagram of your e-puppet, and make sure that you label where your switch fits in.

3. How does the switch work? What makes the switch a potential leverage point in your system?

4. What would happen to the system if you didn't have a switch?

5. Are there parts of what you made that if you took them away, that action would dramatically change the character you created, not just the circuit?

After the worksheets are completed and projects are posted, bring youths together to share their thoughts. This is an opportunity for them to move away from the specifics of their puppet design to start thinking more generally about circuits and the extent to which they are examples of systems. You might start the discussion by reviewing the questions on the worksheet, or you can use the following questions:

- Ask volunteers (or everyone) to share their e-puppet projects again (including their design plans, e-puppets, their actions, and their character traits). The presentations can be based on whatever criteria seem most interesting, but looking for contrasts is often particularly useful. For example, you might select youths whose puppets look quite different but have the same function, or select youths who have incorporated the switch into their designs in very different ways.

- Encourage youths to explain how they constructed their e-puppets, including:
  - The location of the circuitry components
  - How the switch was created
  - The name and personality of their characters
  - Any broader narrative or storyline that they created around it
  - How the components fit together to work as a system

- Encourage the use of essential vocabulary that was introduced in Part 1:
  - What was the goal of their e-puppet?
  - How do the components of the e-puppet work together to accomplish that goal? What components make up the system?
  - What are their respective behaviors?
  - How do the components of the circuits interconnect?
  - How does the behavior of one component affect the behavior of another component?
  - Where were the leverage points of the system?

- Encourage youths to think about the "system" of their e-puppet characters. Each youth should address the following questions:

  - Do you think that your fictional character can be thought about as a system?

  - If so, what components are working together to help create that system?

WHAT TO EXPECT

This final discussion brings together all the ideas that youths have covered in Design Challenges 1 and 2, so there's a lot of room to see growth (and potentially, to identify misconceptions). The big idea that we want youths to understand is that the e-puppet is a system that is composed of the circuit (which is also a system) and its own elements (of which the circuit is one). Look particularly for the ways that they are talking about interconnections between components and, of course, for their accurate use of vocabulary as well. Specifically, asking youths to think about how the introduction of a new component changes the behavior of a system should help them to focus on how the behavior of one element affects the behavior of another element. The focus on switches also should serve to highlight new goals, potential leverage points, and the process by which a system works to remain in balance (i.e., through various balancing feedback loops).

	Novice	Expert
Circuitry concepts	• Struggles to understand how energy flows through a circuit • Struggles to explain why or how a circuit has to be completed • Struggles to explain how a switch operates and can be incorporated into a circuit in order to function • Understands that a switch closes and opens an otherwise complete circuit, but struggles to understand that there is a continuous flow of energy from the battery in a complete circuit and that a switch serves to interrupt and reestablish that flow to conserve the battery's energy • Is unable to create a circuit diagram involving an LED, a battery, and a switch and name the behaviors of each component	• Can explain how energy flows through a circuit, and how and why a circuit has to flow in a closed loop • Understands that there has to be a continuous flow of energy through a circuit, and can explain how and why a switch should be incorporated into a circuit to conserve energy and interrupt the flow • Is able to understand and create a diagram of a working circuit in various shapes and configurations (not just a simple circle) • Is able to create a circuit diagram involving an LED, a battery, and a switch and name the behaviors of each component
Systems thinking concepts	• Struggles to think about a circuit conceptually as a system of interrelated parts and finds difficulty understanding when aspects of a circuit are described or referred to in terms of systems thinking vocabulary • Aspects of circuits are discussed causally (e.g., the LED works because it's connected to the battery) and therefore cannot offer an explanation detailing how a switch functions to conserve energy • Can list components of a system, but struggles to explain how their behaviors are interconnected • Has difficulty identifying the goals of the system • Has difficulty talking about the system as having limited resources that need to be preserved • Has difficulty identifying potential leverage points and balancing mechanisms in the system and does not describe the process by which a system works to remain in balance (i.e., through various balancing feedback loops)	• Demonstrates the ability to think about a circuit conceptually and clearly understands (and can explain) that a circuit is a system because it has multiple components that work together to achieve a goal, and more specifically, that it is the way these elements interact with each other that causes the system to work (i.e., the LED to light up) • Can offer an explanation of how adding the component of a switch changes the behavior of other components (and, to a lesser extent, the overall goal of the system) • Easily identifies the goals of the system • Can talk about the system as having limited resources that need to be preserved • Can identify potential leverage points and balancing mechanisms in the system and describe the process at which a system works to remain in balance (i.e., through various balancing feedback loops)

DESIGN CHALLENGE 2, PART 4

POSTING YOUR E-PUPPET

Use this worksheet to help plan what you will say about your e-puppet online.

GIVE YOUR PROJECT A NAME:

1. What will you call your e-puppet? Give it a unique and inspiring name!

WRITE A PROJECT DESCRIPTION:

2. What inspired you?

3. Tell about the character you designed, including its traits and actions (and the storyline you created, if you had one).

4. Describe how your e-puppet works and why.

PHOTO SHOOT PLANNING:

What should the photo(s) look like online? Sketch them out or write down a description of what they should look like, below. (Example: "Photo 1 should be the e-puppet with the LEDs turned on; Photo 2 should be the e-puppet laid flat.") Should there be a video of the e-puppet in action? If so, what should the video show?

DESIGN CHALLENGE 2, PART 4

SELF-REFLECTION ON MY E-PUPPET

1. What is the purpose or goal of the circuit in your puppet, and how do the components and behaviors of the circuit work together in order to accomplish that goal? You can explain in words, pictures, or both.

2. Draw a diagram of your e-puppet, and make sure that you label where your switch fits in.

3. How does the switch work? What makes the switch a potential leverage point in your system?

4. What would happen to the system if you didn't have a switch?

5. Are there parts of what you made that if you took them away, that action would dramatically change the character you created, not just the circuit?

Total time: 160 minutes

OVERVIEW

This Design Challenge encourages youths to see a story not as a collection of settings, characters, and plot elements, but as a study of relationships. They explore the interconnections between the goal or resolution of a story, its structure, and the behaviors of its components through small-group brainstorming, game play, and collaboration. The idea of story-as-system is contrasted with the incorporation of a recording/playing device (part of an electronic system) into one of the activities. Comparisons between stories and circuits as systems help youths to recognize that systems can exist anywhere.

PRODUCT

Youths will work together in small groups to create poster-size storyboards composed of nine panels and a sound speaker with an original recorded audio sample.

TARGETED SYSTEMS THINKING CONCEPTS

Stories are systems composed of components (e.g., the characters, actions, plot elements, settings, etc.) with distinct behaviors working together within a certain structure that then functions to achieve a goal.

PARTS

PART 1: WHAT'S THE STORY?

Youths are given a set of story components (two characters, a prop, a setting, and an event) and a goal/resolution and are asked to devise a coherent narrative structure from the relationships among the components. Retaining the same components, they then must create a new story that reaches a different outcome, which emphasizes the relationship between a story's structure and its goal. Ultimately, they transcribe one of their stories onto a nine-panel storyboard.

Time: 70 minutes

PART 2: MAKING CONNECTIONS

Youths use their prior circuitry knowledge to incorporate a recordable sound module into their storyboards. In this activity, they are challenged to make sense of a new electronic system based on the experience garnered from previous Design Challenges. Youths freely explore ways to enhance the communication of their stories through the interconnections between visual and aural media. They also are given an opportunity to iterate on their storyboards based on feedback received in Part 1.

Time: 60 minutes

PART 3: STORIES AS SYSTEMS

Youths present and reflect on their recorded sound modules and their storyboards. In the process, they draw parallels between story generation and the systems concepts explored in previous Design Challenges. Exploring the form that systems can take across domain contexts attunes youths to think more globally about the systems at work in their lives—the idea that "systems are everywhere."

Time: 30 minutes

KEY DEFINITIONS

SYSTEMS THINKING

Identifying a system. Identifying a system and distinguishing it from other kinds of things that aren't systems. Specifically, a system is a collection of two or more components and processes that *interconnect* to *function* as a whole. Speed and comfort in a car for example are created by the interactions of the car's parts and thus are "greater than the sum" of all separate parts of the car. The way a system works is not the result of a single part but is produced by the *interaction* among the components and/or individual agents within it. A key way to differentiate things that are systems from things that aren't is to consider whether the overall way something works in the world will change if you remove one part of it.

Identify the way a system is functioning. The function of a system describes the overall behavior of the system—what it is doing or where it's going over time. A system's function might emerge naturally based on interconnections among components, or it might be the result of an intentional design (in which case, we might also refer to the function of a system as its goal). Regardless, the function of a system is the result of the dynamics that occur among components' interconnected behaviors.

Identifying components. Identifying the parts of a system that contribute to its functioning. *Components* have certain qualities and/or *behaviors* that determine how they *interconnect* with other components, as well as define their role in the system. Without being able to effectively identify the parts of a system, it's hard to understand how a system is actually *functioning* and how it might be changed.

Identifying behaviors. Identifying the specific actions, roles, or behaviors that a component of a system displays under various conditions. Being able to identify behaviors becomes important when we change systems, as often a component will look the same after the change, but its behavior will be different.

Identifying interconnections. Identifying the different ways that a system's parts, or *components*, interact with each other through their behaviors, and through those interactions, change the behaviors of other components.

Designing a system. Creating a system through engaging in an iterative design process, one that entails iterative cycles of feedback, troubleshooting, and testing. One of the most effective means of developing systems thinking is to regularly create and iterate on the design of systems, and doing so in a way that creates opportunities for students to think about generic systems models that apply across multiple domains and settings.

Distinguishing the goal of a system. The goal of the system is what a system that was intentionally designed is intended to do. Sometimes this might be the same as the functioning of the system … other times the goal and the *function* are not aligned. A given system might have multiple goals or purposes that are at play simultaneously, and come into conflict. Being able to understand system purpose or goal gives a sense of the ideal state of a system from a particular perspective.

Considering the role of system structure. Understanding that the ways that a system's *components* are set up in relation to one another gives insight into the *behavior* of those components and the overall *dynamics* and *functioning* of a system. When we try to understand and make changes in a system, it's more important to know about its structure than to just know the individual characteristics of the system's components. Often structures go unnoticed, but they have a big impact on what components in a system do.

STORYTELLING

Character. A real or imaginary person represented in a story.

Context. The circumstances in which an event occurs; a setting.

Narrative. An often-chronological sequence of real or fictitious events in a story, consisting of a context (or setting); a narrator, characters, or both; and an event sequence that has a beginning, middle, and end and includes a conflict and resolution.

Narrative conflict. Inherent incompatibility or tension between the goals of two or more characters or forces.

Narrator. A person who tells a story or gives an account of something.

Plot. The main events of a story, rendered by the writer as an interrelated sequence.

Resolution. A literary term; the goal of a narrative/story.

Storyboard. A panel of sketches that depict a sequence of action. Storyboards contain frames, and within each frame is a depiction of an important moment in the storyline. Storyboards often are used to plan the sequence and composition of a movie, video, or animated film.

COMMON CORE STATE STANDARDS	NEXT GENERATION SCIENCE STANDARDS
• RI.7.3	• 3-PS2–3
• RI.7.5	• 4-PS3–2
• W.8.6	• 3–5-ETS1–1
• RST.11–12.9	• 3–5-ETS1–2
• SL.6–12.4 (anchor standard)	• 3–5-ETS1–3
• SL.7.5	
• WHST.6–8.4	

MATERIALS OVERVIEW

- About 15 3" × 5" note cards
- About 75 3" × 5" sticky notes in at least four colors
- Paper and pencils
- Drawing pencils, colored pencils, and markers
- Adhesive tape
- Paper scissors or utility knives
- Digital projector

For each small group (two to three youths), you will need the following:

- A 22" × 28" piece of poster board for the recordable storyboard
- A 20-second recordable sound module with a 9V battery snap connector
- A 9V battery

HANDOUTS

- "Components and Resolutions"
- "Storyboard Template"
- "Diagram of a Recordable Sound Module"
- "Posting Your Speaking Stories"
- "Self-Reflection on 'Speaking Stories'"

OVERALL CHALLENGE PREPARATION

- Setting up a word wall can be helpful for integrating essential vocabulary into the activities in each challenge. Refer to the vocabulary often, and keep the word wall highly visible and clutter free. You can add new vocabulary in each unit to the terms already in use from previous Design Challenges.

- Fill out all the 3" × 5" sticky notes with "Component" texts (see the table in Part 1). Ideally, each of the four categories of component—character, object, event, and setting—is assigned its own color. Feel free to localize or customize the suggested text as desired.

- Fill out the 3" × 5" note cards with "Goal" text (see the table in Part 1). Localize or customize the text as desired.

- Create a demonstration storyboard with sound in advance (see Figure 6.1 for an example).

VOICES FROM THE FIELD

Students were able to recognize that a story is a system, and it has components that must be present in order for it to make a good story. They were able to relate to the incomplete stories and could recognize the components that were missing. Students completed their own stories and made storyboards representing the stories.

—LORI BELL, NATIONAL WRITING PROJECT

PART 1: WHAT'S THE STORY?

Youths are given a set of story components (two characters, a prop, a setting, and an event) and a goal/resolution and are asked to devise a coherent narrative structure from the relationships among the components. Retaining the same components, they then must create a new story that reaches a different outcome, which emphasizes the relationship between a story's structure and its goal. Ultimately, they transcribe one of their stories onto a nine-panel storyboard.

Time: 60 minutes

STUFF TO HAVE HANDY

- About 15 3" × 5" "Goal" note cards, which should be prepped already
- About 75 3" × 5" "Component" sticky notes in at least four colors, which should be prepped already
- Paper and pencils

HANDOUTS

- "Storyboard Template"
- "Components and Resolutions"

RESEARCH: STORIES—A STUDY IN RELATIONSHIPS—10 MINUTES

The goal of this activity is to show youths that systems thinking can be applied to systems outside of circuitry contexts and to elaborate on the storytelling activities introduced in Design Challenge 2. This activity will familiarize them with the components and vocabulary that are important to storytelling.

1. Before the activity begins, post the 75 "Component" sticky notes along a wall.

2. Begin with a group brainstorm about all the components of a story, writing youths' responses on the board. Answers might include:

   - Characters (e.g., protagonists, antagonists)
   - Settings or context
   - Important objects/props (e.g., King Arthur's sword, Jack's beanstalk, the materials that the three little pigs used to build their homes)

- Types of conflict or tensions (e.g., person versus person, person versus self, person versus environment, person versus technology)

- Basic sequencing (or plot) elements (e.g., beginning, middle, climax, end)

- Plot development techniques (e.g., foreshadowing and flashbacks)

3. Take a moment to read a familiar or simple story that youths might all know, such as a folk or fairy tale or a children's picture book. Some recommendations for picture books include:

- Crockett Johnson's *Harold and the Purple Crayon*

- Eric Carle's *The Very Busy Spider*

- Alice Schertle's *Little Blue Truck*

- Peggy Rathmann's *Good Night, Gorilla*

- Mo Willem's *Knuffle Bunny* or *Don't Let the Pigeon Stay Up Late*

4. Discuss how the narrative has a beginning, middle, and end. Highlight the conflict or tension in the story. How was this conflict or tension established? What is the conflict or tension? How does it get resolved?

VOICES FROM THE FIELD

I don't spend much time discussing conflict with my students. They think conflict means a fight between good guys and bad guys and that's it. But the notion of tension is one that they can really grab onto and actually use as they write. I explain it with rubber bands. As I hand them out, I tell my students to leave the rubber bands on their desks. "Don't touch them." Of course, they are jittery waiting to get their hands on the bands and "accidentally" shoot them off. As they wait, I take a large one and just dangle it on my finger. However, when I stretch it out and point it (not at a student), the rubber band suddenly becomes more interesting. It's the tension, the potential energy that rivets our attention. It's the same in their writing.

—SUZANNE LINEBARGER, NORTHERN CALIFORNIA WRITING PROJECT (PUBLISHED IN THE QUARTERLY, VOL. 23, NO. 3, 2001); NWP.ORG/CS/PUBLIC/PRINT/RESOURCE/QUARTERLY/2001NO3/LINEBARGER.HTML

5. Divide the youths into groups of two to three each. These groups will work together to create a story based on a fixed selection of components. Have a representative from each group select five "Component" sticky notes from the wall: 2 Characters, 1 Object, 1 Event, and 1 Context/Setting.

- Characters—the principal figures that the story is about. **Note:** One of these could be the e-puppet from Design Challenge 2.

- Objects—the important physical items that feature in the story.

- Events—something that happens/happened to the character(s) in the story.

- Context/Setting—Locations that the character(s) in the story will visit.

"Component" Sticky Notes (Customize as Desired)

	Character		Object	Event	Context/Setting
1	Brother/Sister	Child	Gift	Contest	Home
2	Frog	Horse	Key	Plan	Kitchen
3	Husband/Wife	Monster	Tree	Journey	Stairs
4	Orphan	Beggar	Spell	Dream	Road
5	King	Queen	Treasure	A Rescue	Cave
6	Prince	Princess	Axe	A Trap	River
7	Chef	Mother/Father	Door	A Pursuit	Mountain
8	Old Man	Old Woman	Boat	Something Is Revealed	Prison
9	Shepherdess	Bird	Sword	People Meet	Forest
10	Enemy	Stepparent	Book	A Fight	Palace
11	Giant	Thief	Window	An Argument	At Sea
12	Witch	Dragon	Crown	Time Passes	An Island
13	Musician	Knight	Ring	An Object Breaks	A Ruin
14	Merchant	Hunter	Fire	Someone Is Hurt	A Tower
15	Farmer	(The Character from Design Challenge 2)	Food	An Escape	Night

6. The components in a story exhibit explicit behaviors that have ramifications for the other components in the story. For example:

- Every significant event in a story has a cause and an influence on each character's present and future actions.

- Objects determine what a character is able to achieve.

- Settings can hold implications for plot, character, and theme in literary texts.

Reflect on the character profiles created in Design Challenge 2: His/her/its personality, likes, dislikes, history, and other elements all work together to define the behavior of a character, and what each character does, says, and thinks often has a direct impact on other characters in the story and the story's plot. Have groups think for a moment about how the behaviors connected to their "Component" sticky notes.

7. Tell youths that all stories have a resolution, the direction in which the narrative is heading (just as a circuitry system has a goal). Distribute one "Resolution" note card at random to each group. The words on each card are going to become the final sentence of each group's story, representing the components reaching a particular goal-state. Have groups take another moment to consider how the interconnections of their components need to change to produce this new goal.

3" x 5" Goal or Resolution Notecards (Localize/Customize as Desired)

	Story Goal/Resolution
1	... and he listened to his mother's advice from then on.
2	... they were never heard from again.
3	... so she revealed her true identity and they were married.
4	... so they changed places and everything was back to normal.
5	... and the flames rose higher and the evil place was destroyed.
6	... she never let it out of her sight again.
7	... he picked up his weapon and went on his way.
8	... and the kingdom rejoiced at the end of the tyrant's reign.
9	... and she was reunited with her family.
10	... but she still visited them from time to time.
11	... they thanked the hero who had saved them all.
12	... and for all I know, they may be dancing still.
13	... and they were blind for the rest of their days for their wickedness and falsehood.
14	... so they escaped their captors and fled home.
15	... but no matter how hard they searched, they were never able to find it again.

8. Youths may discover in this first brainstorm session that characteristics, objects, and events that they assigned to one character may need to be reassigned to another character to make the new narrative goal make sense. Perhaps the "Event" sticky note, originally used as the climax to the story, now is used to describe something that happened in one of the characters' past. These changes are considered modifications to a story's system structure—the particular way that all components in a system are set up. Structure plays a big role in determining the behaviors of the story's components, and the kind of interconnections that they have with one another.

> What is important in a story ... is not the plot, the things, or the people in the story, but the relationships between them.
>
> —FRITJOF CAPRA [1]

CREATE AND PLAY: INTERCONNECTIONS BETWEEN GOALS AND STRUCTURES—30 MINUTES

Youths will play with the story cards in a gamelike activity in small groups, iterating on the story structure in response to changing prompts. Ultimately, they will transcribe one of the stories from this activity into a nine-frame storyboard.

1. Pass out the "Components and Resolutions" handout, which is intended to guide youths' documentation of their stories, as well as to prompt them to think about how changing one element of a system (i.e., the resolution) affects the interconnections among the other components of the system.

2. Give youths five minutes to come up with a brief story in their small groups that contains their "Component" sticky notes and "Resolution" note card. They can create a story in any way they like, and they are not limited by the components on the table; they just need to ensure that their story includes all of those components and that it comes to a resolution. Inspire youths to experiment with various ways to arrange the components and see what structure brings the story to a sensible and satisfying conclusion. Be sure that at least one person in each group takes notes about the group's solution(s).

3. It may help to discuss briefly how plot elements in a story are often structured. A common sequence of plot elements are:

- **Beginning**: Where the author "sets the stage."

- **Rising Action**: Complications set up the conflict for the characters. Tension builds, and the story works its way up to the climax.

- **Middle/Climax**: The high point in the story, where the conflict or tension comes to a head.

- **Falling Action**: Events that happen after the climax, usually wrapping up the story and leading to the conclusion.

- **End/Resolution**: The point of closure, when the conflict is worked out.

4. When groups have completed (and documented) their stories, have them pass their "Resolution" cards to the group to their left. Retaining the same "Component" sticky notes, have groups come up with a second story in which the goal is the statement on their new card. What behaviors of the components need to change? In what way does the structure need to change to accommodate the new goal? Be sure that at least one person in each group writes down the group's solution(s).

5. Repeat the activity again, passing the "Resolution" card to the team on the left and writing a third story.

6. After groups complete their third story, distribute the "Storyboard Template" handout. Using this tool, groups will capture their favorite of their three stories in a nine-frame storyboard. Storyboarding provides youths with an avenue to combine linguistic and visual representations of their understanding of their story's structure.

Combine words and imagery to convey the structure of your story across nine panels.

Name of the Project   Music and Friends   Group Members   Anna, Marco, & Shawn

| 1 | Judd heard music across the valley. | 2 | It was his friend, Rowl, playing the saxophone. | 3 | Rowl was giving a concert for all of the animals in the valley. |

| 4 | Judd felt sad. He wanted to play along but didn't know how to play an instrument. | 5 | Leo the lion saw Judd standing there. "Wanna play, too?" he asked. | 6 | "You can try and play something on this recorder," Leo said. |

| 7 | Excited, Judd put the recorder to his lips and made up a tune. | 8 | Leo played the guitar with him. It sounded great! | 9 | Judd, Leo, and Rowl played the rest of the concert together. |

You can use this example as a model for your custom storyboard. In this story, a cow sees a penguin who plays a saxophone and has lots of friends. The cow is sad because he has no friends. Then he meets a lion who plays a guitar. The lion teaches him how to play the flute. They form a band with the penguin, and the cow is happy.

It can be a challenge to distill a story into nine frames for the first time, so you might want to help youths to think about where particular events should be located: Mapping some of the frames onto the basic plot elements described previously is a good place to start. You could do one of these as a whole group to model how a storyboard can work. Blank sticky notes can be used to draft a storyboard before drawing the nine panels.

SHARE: SOLICITING FEEDBACK AND CRITIQUE—20 MINUTES

Sharing your work in a group and listening to and incorporating feedback are important parts of the design process. Invite youths to share their work and listen to constructive feedback from their peers.

1. Invite groups to share their story templates.

2. Encourage peers to give both "warm" (constructive) and "cool" (positive) feedback to each other (See the Introduction to this book for more about feedback.) Have groups take note of the feedback that they received because they will have an opportunity to make changes to their storyboards based on this feedback in Part 2 of this Design Challenge.

3. Some suggestions for focused feedback at this moment include the following:

   • *Characterization:* Did you get a clear idea of the traits of each character? Were the relationships and motivations of the characters understandable? Why did the characters act the way they did?

   • *Conflict:* Was there a driving conflict or drama? Did the events in the story demonstrate convincing cause and effect?

   • *Outcome:* Did the ending make sense? Was there any transformation of the characters based on the events in the story? Was there a central message to the story?

   • *Structure:* Where can they tighten their story? Where can they use more detail?

VOICES FROM THE FIELD

Today the relationships and the community showed up in strong ways. Students encouraged each other to show their work when they were reticent. Lamaur said, "Come on, no one will laugh at you. We all can't draw that well."

—LAURA LEE STROUD, NATIONAL WRITING PROJECT

REFLECT: LET'S TALK—10 MINUTES

Begin a discussion about how youths' stories are like a system. Remind them of what was learned about systems in earlier Design Challenges.

The following questions can be used to facilitate the discussion:

- How is a story a system? (*Answer: Systems are made up of components with distinct behaviors that work together in a certain structure to achieve a goal.*)

- What are the components of the system? (*Answers will vary: the characters, actions, plot elements, settings, etc.*)

- How do components interconnect in a story? (*Answers will vary. Usually any "if … then …" statement will be accurate pertaining to the events or relationships between characters in a story.*)

- What would happen if you removed one component of the system? How would your story change? *(Answers will vary.)*

DESIGN CHALLENGE 3, PART 1

COMPONENTS AND RESOLUTIONS

STORY 1:

List the components and the resolution that your group is working with.

Use the space below to write the story that your group created that includes all the components and that resolution.

STORY 2:

What new resolution did you get?

Use the space below to write the story that your group created that includes all the components and that resolution.

How did you have to change your components for them to make sense with the new resolution?

STORY 3:

What new resolution did you get?

Use the space below to write the story that your group created that includes all the components and that resolution.

How did you have to change your components in order for them to make sense with the new resolution?

DESIGN CHALLENGE 3, PART 1

STORYBOARD TEMPLATE

STORYBOARD TEMPLATE

Combine words and imagery to convey the structure of your story across nine panels.

Name of the Project _____   Group Members _____

PART 2: MAKING CONNECTIONS

Youths use their prior circuitry knowledge to incorporate a recordable sound module into their storyboards. In this activity, they are challenged to make sense of a new electronic system based on the experience garnered from previous Design Challenges. Youths freely explore ways to enhance the communication of their story through the interconnections between visual and aural media. They also are given an opportunity to iterate on their storyboards based on feedback received in Part 1.

Time: 60 minutes

STUFF TO HAVE HANDY

- A 20-second recording module with a 9V battery snap connector (1 per group)

- A 9V battery (1 per group)

- A 22" x 28" piece of poster board for the recordable storyboard (1 per group)

- Drawing pencils, colored pencils, and markers

- Adhesive tape

- Paper scissors or utility knife

HANDOUTS

- "Diagram of a Recordable Sound Module"

RESEARCH AND PLAY: SOUND DESIGN CHALLENGE—15 MINUTES

Youths will use their prior circuitry experience to understand how an unfamiliar piece of electronic equipment works. Then they will play with many possibilities of enhancing their stories through sound—whether in the form of music, sound effects, or the spoken word.

1. Introduce the demonstration storyboard that you created in preparation for this activity and play the recordable sound module. The sound module is a fun way for youths to incorporate a level of interactivity to the storyboard; it also presents an opportunity to connect two systems (visual and sound) to enhance the communication of a story. Let youths know that they will be making a large storyboard like this, but that the current activity is just about how to work the recordable sound module.

2. Distribute the recordable sound modules (1 per group). Drawing upon what the youths know about circuits, ask them to attempt to explain all the components of the sound module—what are the names of the components? What are the components' behaviors, and how do they interconnect? Where does energy come from in the circuit, and where are any leverage points?

3. Distribute the "Diagram of a Recordable Sound Module" handout, explaining the various parts of the sound module and how it works.

	Recordable sound module	Records a limited amount of sound and can be played back when a button is pressed. We recommend a 20-second recording module with a 9V battery connector. Electronics123.com- #BR9

Components of the Recordable Sound Module:

	Circuit board	The central printed board that holds many of the crucial components of the system, providing connectors for other peripherals, such as LEDs, switches, and so on.
	9V battery	This battery is shaped like a rounded rectangular prism and has an output of 9 volts.

	9V battery clip	A component that allows a 9V battery to connect to the recordable sound module circuit. It contains a connection for both the positive and negative charges
	Push switch	This module requires two push switches; one (connected separately) for recording sound, and another (built into the circuit board) to trigger playback. When pushed, each switch reconnects (closes) its corresponding electrical circuit to play or record.
	Microphone	An instrument that converts sound waves into an electric current, usually fed into an amplifier, a recorder, or a broadcast transmitter.

	Speaker	An electroacoustic module that converts electrical signals into sounds loud enough to be heard at a distance.
	Recording LED indicator	A light-emitting diode (LED) that is connected to the push switch (Record) circuitry; this light is reconnected (and therefore lit) when the push switch (Record) button is pushed.

4. The recordable sound module comes fully assembled and tested; all youths need to do to turn it on is add a 9V battery.

5. To record, press and hold the "Record" switch (attached separately to the circuit board) and speak into the microphone. When the LED indicator turns on, you know it's ready to start recording. Release the switch to finish recording (the LED turns off to let you know that recording has stopped).

6. To hear what you've recorded, press the "Play" switch (mounted directly on the circuit board).

7. Have youths brainstorm within their groups some places in their story where sound could enhance the narrative impact. What would the presence of sound do for each of the nine frames in their storyboard?

8. Next, allow time for groups to work together and record the sound that they chose (using voices, instruments, or other sources). They should experiment with different sounds before they choose a final recording for their project.

VOICES FROM THE FIELD

Kennedy's story involves a woodpecker tap-tap-tapping on a tree through the wee hours of the night, preventing the protagonist from getting sleep. The protagonist learns from the experience to close her window at night. By contrast, Zach's story centered around an alien cat which had lost its ability to glow at the nose. In each frame of the story as the cat tries to reclaim its ability, other characters interact with the cat, to which it responds with a rather deep, masculine "meow."

—CHRISTINA CANTRILL, NATIONAL WRITING PROJECT

IMPORTANT TIPS FOR THIS ACTIVITY:

- The module can store only one audio file at a time, meaning that when youths press the "Record" switch, the previous recording gets erased.

- On the recordable sound module, the "Record" and "Play" buttons can be confused easily. If youths are having difficulty remembering which is which, consider marking one with a small sticker or a colored marker.

- To amplify the sound from the speaker, have youths create a conelike covering for the speaker out of paper. The sound will travel better if this simple device is taped onto the speaker.

- Throughout this volume, several different ways of converting energy have been discussed. For example, with LEDs, electrical energy is converted to create light (through a process called *electromagnetic radiation*). In this Design Challenge, electrical energy is converted to make sound through the vibration of the speaker membrane. Similarly, mechanical energy (like the vibration of the speaker) can be gathered to produce electrical energy.

- Did you also know that a standard type of speaker can be used as a microphone?

MOD THIS SESSION

Instead of incorporating a sound module into a paper product, a recordable module could be sewn into the e-puppet from Design Challenge 2 or a repurposed stuffed animal. In that way, the puppet or animal would appear to talk, sing, or play a musical instrument when the switch is pushed. Several of the youths' animals could be placed together to create a band or choir.

VOICES FROM THE FIELD

Through seeing his peers using their sound module as a repeating component of the story, Wilson began to iterate his story (about a football game) to include an audience cheering as characters in his story caught passes, scored touchdowns, and sacked quarterbacks.

—ERIC TUCK, NATIONAL WRITING PROJECT

ITERATE: FINALIZE STORIES—45 MINUTES

In this activity, youths create a final (and larger) version of their storyboards, enhanced by the addition of their sound module and incorporating any feedback from Part 1 of this Design Challenge.

1. Give each group a 22" x 28" piece of poster board, drawing pencils, colored pencils, and markers to make a poster-size version of its storyboard. Make adhesive tape and scissors (or a utility knife) available for groups to affix their sound modules to the backs of the boards, and cut a hole in the correct spot on the storyboard where the "Play" button will come through. *Safety note:* An adult should make the cuts if a utility knife is used in place of scissors.

2. When their large storyboard is complete, have groups incorporate their electronics in the appropriate frame. Youths can add the recordable sound module to the storyboard by pushing through and taping the "Play" button in the correct space. *Be careful to tape the "Play" button, not the "Record" button!*

VOICES FROM THE FIELD

During the share-out of their Speaking Stories, the student projects were a little short of the original goal of telling a complete story that incorporated sound as an integral part of the story. We discussed this as a group using one student's story. Through a guided exploration of possible iterations, one student easily discovered how to redesign her comic board to include the sound module as a valuable part of the story experience. Through her experience, peers quickly began to iterate and complete their designs, with several of the students meeting the original goal.

—ERIC TUCK, NATIONAL WRITING PROJECT

Sample projects:

Taping a sound module to the back of a small storyboard.

A student shares her small storyboard with the recordable sound module.

DESIGN CHALLENGE 3, PART 2

DIAGRAM OF A RECORDABLE SOUND MODULE

To record: Press and hold the "Record" switch and speak into the microphone. The LED indicator turns on when recording starts. Release the switch to finish recording, and the LED turns off.

To hear what you've recorded: Press the "Play" switch to play the complete message once.

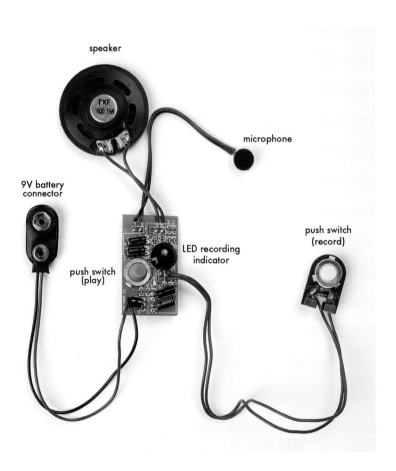

speaker

microphone

9V battery
connector

LED recording
indicator

push switch
(record)

push switch
(play)

PART 3: STORIES AS SYSTEMS

Youths present and reflect on their recorded sound modules and their storyboards. In the process, they draw parallels between story generation and the systems concepts explored in previous Design Challenges. Exploring the form that systems can take across domain contexts attunes youths to think more globally about the systems at work in their lives—the idea that "systems are everywhere."

Time: 30 minutes

STUFF TO HAVE HANDY

- The completed storyboards from Part 2, embedded with the recordable sound modules

HANDOUTS

- "Posting Your Speaking Stories"
- "Self-Reflection on Speaking Stories"

SHARE: PRESENTATION AND DISCUSSION—15 MINUTES

Give youths an opportunity to showcase their final projects.

1. Invite groups to present their completed work in the way that works best for your program. For instance, do the following:

- Groups can act out their stories, with one of the members playing the role of the narrator and the others as specific characters. Make sure that they demonstrate the sound module.

- Alternatively, create a gallery wall displaying the storyboards and have the youths independently visit the gallery, reading the stories and playing the sound modules.

- Have them share their storyboards on a pre-selected website (see suggestions at the Interconnections website, **digitalis.nwp.org/gnl**), using the "Posting Your Speaking Stories" worksheet to plan their posting.

2. In a large-group debriefing, invite youths to share what they did to iterate on their stories, based on either the feedback from Part 1 or new ideas that emerged from the incorporation of their sound modules in Part 2.

REFLECT: SELF-REFLECTION — 15 MINUTES

Have youths take a moment to think about the work that they've done for this activity and what they'd like to do in the future. Use the "Self-Reflection on Speaking Stories" worksheet to inform this reflection, or conduct a discussion with the following questions:

1. Describe one piece of feedback that you received from a peer or mentor during the design process that helped you improve your storyboard.

2. Describe one piece of feedback that you gave to a peer during the design process that you thought might help him or her to improve that story.

3. Why is sound an important component in the story that you created?

4. In what ways do you think that your story is a system?

5. Compare the sound recording module and the story in terms of the ways that they are systems:

   - How are the components between the systems the same or different?

   - How are the relationships between components in the systems the same or different?

   - How are the goals between the systems the same or different?

WHAT TO EXPECT

This worksheet is primarily designed to ensure that youths grasp the fundamentals of both creating a story and understanding it as a system. This is also an opportunity to get them thinking about how systems differ from other kinds of cause-and-effect relationships.

	Novice	Expert
Storytelling concepts	• Struggles to create a story or writes a story that fails to incorporate the designated components and goals • Does not demonstrate an understanding of the various parts of a story or how the pieces relate to each other • Never uses vocabulary that is important to how stories are put together • Struggles to communicate their story through writing, drawing, or oral presentation	• Is able to create a simple story from base components • Is able to make behaviors, components, and structure work logically toward a story's goal or resolution • Has a good grasp of the associated story vocabulary • Is able to communicate a message through written, verbal, and visual means
Circuitry concepts	• Sees no connection between the sound module's structure and components and those of previous circuits • Unable to envision how the recorded sound module might work based on prior experience	• Is able to apply and recognize components that previously were introduced, even though they look different (e.g., switches and buttons operate similarly) • Is able to make educated guesses about how components work based on prior observations of systems operation
Systems thinking concepts	• Unable to identify components, behaviors, interconnections, goals, and structure • Fails to see the systems thinking connections between stories, circuits, and other phenomena	• Is able to identify components, behaviors, interconnections, goals, and structure in multiple systems, including stories and circuits • Understands that systems thinking can be applied to a variety of phenomena, not just to their understanding of circuits

DESIGN CHALLENGE 3, PART 3

POSTING YOUR SPEAKING STORIES

Use this worksheet to help plan what you will say about your story on the chosen site.

GIVE YOUR PROJECT A NAME:

What will you call your story? Give it a unique and inspiring name!

WRITE A PROJECT DESCRIPTION:

1. What inspired you?

2. Tell about how adding sound improved your story.

3. Describe how your speaking story works and why.

PHOTO SHOOT PLANNING:

What should the photo(s) look like online? Below, sketch them out or write down a description of what they should look like. Should there be a video of the speaking story in action for the site? If so, what should show in the video?

DESIGN CHALLENGE 3, PART 3

SELF-REFLECTION ON SPEAKING STORIES

1. Describe one piece of feedback that you received from a peer or mentor during the design process that helped you improve your storyboard.

2. Describe one piece of feedback that you gave to a peer during the design process that you thought might help him or her to improve that story.

3. Why is sound an important component in the story that you created?

4. In what ways do you think that your story is a system?

5. Compare the sound recording module and the story in terms of the ways that they are systems:

- How are the components between the systems the same or different?

- How are the relationships between components in the systems the same or different?

- How are the goals between the systems the same or different?

DESIGN CHALLENGE 4 DIY FLASHLIGHTS AND SHADOW PUPPETS

Total Time: 265 minutes

OVERVIEW

The goal of this Design Challenge is for youths to learn about how a system's structure can determine specific component behaviors and larger system dynamics or interconnections. Youths experiment with different circuit structures and battery voltages to discover how circuits can be structured in series and parallel formations. They apply this understanding toward the design and development of flashlights made from inexpensive materials, and then they use their creations to put on a shadow puppet show.

PRODUCT

Youths will create a do-it-yourself (DIY) flashlight out of cardboard, light-emitting diodes (LEDs), a battery, and a slide switch. Then the flashlight will be used in the context of a storytelling/shadow-puppet activity.

TARGETED SYSTEMS THINKING CONCEPTS

A system's structure is determined by the particular way that its components are set up. The structure defines each component's specific behavior and its interconnections with other components. All components function together to accomplish the goal of lighting multiple LEDs in a single circuit.

PARTS

PART 1: EXPLORING SYSTEM STRUCTURES

The goal of this first activity is to introduce youths to the idea that a system's structure is determined by the particular way that components are set up. In this activity, youths will use identical components but will structure them in different ways to learn more about how the system's structure determines specific behaviors and interconnections in the system. They will learn specifically about how to build circuits in series and in parallel to meet the goals of the system (e.g., to light all of their LEDs). Youths will seek to balance the voltage of a battery with the number of LEDs in a circuit.

Time: 70 minutes

PART 2: DESIGN TIME—MAKING YOUR DIY FLASHLIGHT

In this activity, youths apply their new knowledge about systems structures to the creation of a useful tool—a flashlight—using simple materials. They will plan the design of their flashlights by creating a diagram, which also provides a convenient moment for assessment.

Time: 75 minutes

PART 3: TELLING STORIES WITH SHADOWS

In this activity, youths will use their DIY flashlights and incorporate the storytelling techniques they developed in previous Design Challenges to create a collaborative performance, this time employing shadow play and shadow puppetry techniques.

Time: 120 minutes

KEY DEFINITIONS

SYSTEMS THINKING

Identifying a system. Identifying a system and distinguishing it from other kinds of things that aren't systems. Specifically, a system is a collection of two or more *components* and processes that interconnect to *function* as a whole. Speed and comfort in a car for example are created by the interactions of the car's parts and thus are "greater than the sum" of all separate parts of the car. The way a system works is not the result of a single part but is produced by the *interaction* among the components and/or individual agents within it. A key way to differentiate things that are systems from things that aren't is to consider whether the overall way something works in the world will change if you remove one part of it.

Identify the way a system is functioning. The function of a system describes the overall behavior of the system—what it is doing or where it's going over time. A system's function might emerge naturally based on interconnoctions among components, or it might be the result of an intentional design (in which case, we might also refer to the function of a system as its goal). Regardless, the function of a system is the result of the dynamics that occur among components' interconnected behaviors.

Identifying components. Identifying the parts of a system that contribute to its functioning. *Components* have certain qualities and/or *behaviors* that determine how they *interconnect* with other components, as well as define their role in the system. Without being able to effectively identify the parts of a system, it's hard to understand how a system is actually *functioning* and how it might be changed.

Identifying behaviors. Identifying the specific actions, roles, or behaviors that a component of a system displays under various conditions. Being able to identify behaviors becomes important when we change systems, as often a component will look the same after the change, but its behavior will be different.

Identifying interconnections. Identifying the different ways that a system's parts, or *components*, interact with each other through their *behaviors*, and through those interactions, change the behaviors of other components.

Designing a system. Creating a system through engaging in an iterative design process, one that entails iterative cycles of feedback, troubleshooting, and testing. One of the most effective means of developing systems thinking is to regularly create and iterate on the design of systems, and doing so in a way that creates opportunities for youth to think about generic systems models that apply across multiple domains and settings.

Distinguishing the goal of a system. The goal of the system is what a system that was intentionally designed is intended to do. Sometimes this might be the same as the functioning of the system ... other times the goal and the *function* are not aligned. A given system might have multiple goals or purposes that are at play simultaneously, and come into conflict. Being able to understand system purpose or goal gives a sense of the ideal state of a system from a particular perspective.

Considering the role of system structure. Understanding that the ways that a system's *components* are set up in relation to one another gives insight into the *behavior* of those components and the overall *dynamics* and *functioning* of a system. When we try to understand and make changes in a system, it's more important to know about its structure than to just know the individual characteristics of the system's components. Often structures go unnoticed, but they have a big impact on what components in a system do.

Leverage points. Particular places within a system where a small shift in one thing can produce big changes in everything. Not every place in a system is a leverage point— sometimes changing one thing in a system will produce only small effects 'not felt throughout the system. Leverage points are important since they let us know where to focus our energies when we try to change systems.

CIRCUITRY

Series circuit. When components are wired in series within a circuit, electric current flows sequentially through those components in a continuous loop. This means that as the current travels from the battery through each LED, it loses some of its original "electrical charge," or energy (also known as *voltage*—see below), such that the amount of voltage available for each subsequent LED decreases with each one that it passes through.

Parallel circuit. When components are wired in parallel within a circuit, the electric current divides into two or more paths before recombining to complete the circuit. The current flows through three LEDs wired in parallel, and the electric current is split equally among the three of them. **Note:** The evenness of the split is contingent on the three LEDs being the same type and/or color.

Voltage. *Voltage* is the force that causes electric current to flow through a circuit. Increasing the voltage in a circuit without changing the resistance increases the current that flows through the circuit.

STORYTELLING

Script. A map or outline that a director or artist uses to create a movie, play, comic book, television show, or, in this case, a shadow puppet show.

Shadow play. A theatrical entertainment using the silhouettes of puppets or actors thrown onto a lighted screen.

Shadow puppet. A cut-out figure or object held between a source of light and a translucent screen.

COMMON CORE STATE STANDARDS	NEXT GENERATION SCIENCE STANDARDS
• RI.7.3	• 3-PS2–3
• RI.7.5	• MS-PS2–3
• RST.6–8.3	• 4-PS3–2
• SL.7.4	• 4-PS3–4
	• 3–5-ETS1–1
	• 3–5-ETS1–2
	• 3–5-ETS1–3
	• MS-ETS1–2
	• MS-ETS1–4

MATERIALS OVERVIEW

STUFF TO HAVE HANDY

You need to create a System Structure Kit for each youth that consists of a zip-closed baggie filled with the following system components:

- A 9V battery
- A 9V battery snap connector
- A 3V (coin cell) battery[1]
- A 3V battery holder[1]
- 6 two-pronged Super Bright LEDs (approximately 4V each)[2]
- Miniature slide switch
- A 500-ohm potentiometer

ADDITIONAL MATERIALS

- Digital projector
- Plenty of alligator clips (at least seven to eight per youth)
- Permanent markers
- Spools of insulated hook-up wire

- Diagonal wire cutters
- Wire strippers
- Needlenose pliers
- Electrical tape
- 8.5" x 11" sheets of cardstock (for the flashlight case)
- Arts and crafts materials like gift wrap, paint, and/or markers (to decorate the flashlight)
- Paper scissors
- Utility knife (to cut a hole for the switch in the flashlight case)
- Low-temperature glue guns and sticks
- Paper tape
- Pencils
- Storyboard from Design Challenge 3
- Cardstock and/or recycled manila folders for puppets
- Bamboo skewers with points removed (straws or other wooden sticks also can be used)
- Brads (paper fasteners with split legs)
- Hole punch or dowel for making holes
- Material for a shadow puppet stage; options can include:
  - Cardboard box (sized to be used as the stage) with wax paper for the screen, or
  - Thin cotton cloth pulled between a door frame and table
- *Optional:* Colored plastic for shadow highlights and lighting color changes

HANDOUTS

- "Switch Diagram" (from Design Challenge 2)
- "Multiple LEDs Diagram"
- "Series versus Parallel Circuits"
- "Diagram of Your LED Flashlight"
- "Diagram of a Circuit in an LED Flashlight"

- "Posting Your Shadow Play"
- "Self-Reflection and Review of LED Flashlight"
- "Shadow Puppet Template Inspirations"

OVERALL CHALLENGE PREPARATION

- Prepare Systems Structure Kits (1 per youth).

- Create a prototype of a sample circuit from Part 2 (see next) so that youths can see how the components interconnect, as well as the craft of applying electrical tape and affixing components together.

- Create a prototype of a DIY flashlight.

- Set up arts and crafts materials in a central location.

- Setting up a word wall can be helpful for integrating essential vocabulary into the activities in each Design Challenge. Refer to the vocabulary often, and keep the word wall highly visible and clutter free. You can add new vocabulary in each unit to the terms already in use from previous Design Challenges.

- On the 9V battery snap connector, it is important that the tips of the wires are exposed (uninsulated). If this is not the case, use wire strippers to expose the ends of the wires before the start of the activity.

PART 1: EXPLORING SYSTEM STRUCTURES

The goal of this first activity is to introduce youths to the idea that a system's structure is determined by the particular way that its components are set up. They will use identical components, but structure them in different ways to learn more about how a system's structure determines specific behaviors and interconnections in the system. They will learn specifically about how to build circuits both in series and in parallel to meet the goals of the system (e.g., to light all their LEDs). In addition, they will seek to balance the voltage of a battery with the number of LEDs in a circuit.

Time: 70 minutes

STUFF TO HAVE HANDY

- System Structure Kits (prepared in advance by the instructor; 1 per youth)
- Permanent markers
- Plenty of alligator clips (at least seven to eight per youth)

HANDOUTS

- "Switch Diagram" (from Design Challenge 2)
- "Multiple LEDs Diagram"
- "Series versus Parallel Circuits"

IMAGINE: DIAGRAMMING SYSTEM STRUCTURES—10 MINUTES

In this activity, youths learn how to build a circuit that can support multiple LEDs to help them connect the concepts of structure, components, interconnections, and behavior.

1. Begin by sharing the big idea for the day: namely, that a system's structure is determined by the particular way that its components set it up. That setup determines the specific behaviors and interconnections in the system. Remind youths that so far, they've built projects where multiple LEDs have been used, but now they will discover more about the relationship between the battery's voltage and the number of LEDs that it can support. It may help to reintroduce the "Switch Diagram" handout from Design Challenge 2.

2. Tell youths that they will build their own flashlights from scratch and then they will use their flashlights to create shadow puppets. They will need to incorporate more than one LED into their circuits so that their flashlights will produce enough light.

3. Ask the group what components they think that they'll need to make a flashlight. (It's okay if they don't know, but this is a nice opportunity to see if they can transfer their circuitry knowledge from previous Design Challenges.) They might guess batteries, LEDs, a switch, and connective wires. Let them know that a new component will be introduced into this challenge, a *potentiometer,* which regulates resistance in a circuit and thus can work to dim or brighten the light in flashlights.

4. Help youths to recognize that conceptually, they are dealing with a task that is very similar to Design Challenge 2 (the e-puppet)—building a circuit with a switch— with the addition of the new component, a potentiometer. However, even if there were no potentiometer, the interconnections still would have to change because they are adding more LEDs to the system, thus changing the system's structure.

5. Use the following questions to activate youths' prior knowledge. As you ask the questions, have them record their hypotheses on one of the handouts or on plain sheets of paper:

- How do you think the additional LEDs will be incorporated into the circuit? Do you think you could put them together any way you like?

- What kinds of interconnections do you expect to create when you add components to the circuit?

- Where do you think the switch should go?

Note: It probably will be helpful here to remind youths to label the positive and negative sides of the LEDs and battery, as well as point out where to incorporate a switch.

6. Invite youths to share their drawn circuits and ask them to explain their answers on the worksheet. [*Answers will vary. The goal is not for youths to necessarily get the "correct" answer here (they will be allowed to test their conjectures in the next section); the larger idea is about the system structures—the ways that a system's components are configured in relation to one another. The uniqueness of the structure will determine how those components behave, which will lead to specific ways that the overall system functions.*]

7. Explain that next, they are going to test their ideas to see what happens when systems are structured in different ways, with the aim of finding several different ways to illuminate multiple LEDs, as well as learn about some of the limitations of the components in the system.

VOICES FROM THE FIELD

Part of what I love about this activity is just watching how learners' ideas develop as they play and experiment with the materials. The kids had some experience already with circuits generally, but this is the first time they had to understand different circuit structures, and it's great that we didn't tell them up front about the difference between parallel and series circuits. I was able to see how they started with what they knew from the previous challenges, but then sort of had to stretch and expand their notions of how these materials operate when they're combined in new ways.

—RAFI SANTO, GRADUATE RESEARCH ASSISTANT AT INDIANA UNIVERSITY

PLAY: AN EXPERIMENT IN STRUCTURE—30 MINUTES

In this next part of the activity, youths will use the components in their System Structure Kits to experiment with the system's structure and try to discover working solutions to lighting more than one LED with a single power source.

1. Distribute the System Structure Kits to each youth. Explain the goal: Try to light as many of the LEDs as possible, using the materials in the kit. Encourage youths to collaborate and share ideas in the process of creation. Alternatively, they can work in groups of two or three if desired, or if materials are limited. Introduce components in the System Structure Kits as needed.

	Alligator clips	An electrical connector (named for its resemblance to the jaws of an alligator) attached to an electric cable for making a temporary connection to a battery or other component. Also called *alligator test leads*. SparkFun—PRT-11037
	9V battery	An energy source in which chemical energy is converted into electricity.

	9V battery snap connector	A snap connector is specifically designed to attach to a 9V battery. There are two wires (red is positive; black is negative) that can attach easily to the alligator clips or to other wires in your design. RS Electronics—HH-3449
	3V battery (also called "coin cell battery")	An energy source in which chemical energy is converted into electricity. We recommend using the common CR2032 type battery for e-textile projects (20 mm), which should power e-textile projects for weeks at a time. SparkFun—PRT-00338
	3V sewable battery holder	A holder for the common CR2032 type 3V battery. The holder has a neat pop-in, pop-out feature that makes changing the battery easy. The feet of the holder have two small holes that allow it to be sewn into e-textiles or other garments. SparkFun—DEV-08822
	White 5-mm Super Bright LED, clear white, 4V	An LED is a small device that lights up when an electric current passes through it. The positive end of the LED is the longer of the two legs. This LED is considered "super bright," brighter than the normal LED. NTE Electronics—NTE30045
	Miniature slide switch	This is a small slide switch that can be used as a simple on/off switch in the flashlight. GC Electronics—35–202

	Potentiometer, 500 ohm	This is an electrical component with a built-in knob or dial that can regulate changes in resistance. It can be used to increase or decrease the brightness of the light being emitted by LEDs. Parts Express—023–500

2. Hand out the "Multiple LEDs Diagram" worksheet. Instruct youths to discuss and sketch a couple of possible solutions to the problem. Warn them to leave extra room because after the experiment, they'll return to the worksheet and sketch what actually worked.

3. Instruct youths to put together the components to test their ideas, as well as experiment with new system structures (i.e., ways of putting the LEDs together). Have them record the outcomes of their systems when they are structured in different ways, noting the positive and negative sides of the battery and LEDs in their diagrams. Were they able to meet the goal of lighting multiple LEDs?

4. Point out that the 3V and 9V batteries don't just look different; they also have different *voltages*—the amount of force used to move an electric current through a conductor. Have youths look for at least one way to illuminate three LEDs using the 9V battery and at least one way to do so with the 3V battery. Things that they can experiment with might include:

   • The number of LEDs that they use

   • Which battery they use

   • Where the switch, potentiometer, and LEDs are placed in the circuit

   • How the LEDs are connected to one another and to the battery.

5. There are a couple of things that you can expect to see (see "possible solutions")

   • The 9V battery will be able to support up to three LEDs in series (with one LED connected to the next one in a line).

   • The 3V (coin cell) battery, however, will support only three LEDs if they are in parallel. Note that only one circuit in the diagram fails to light the LEDs.

POSSIBLE SOLUTIONS

9V

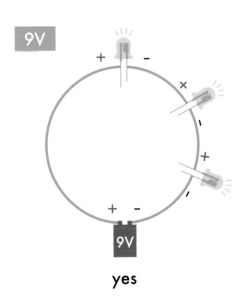

yes

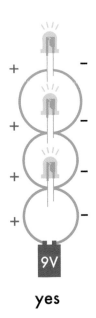

yes

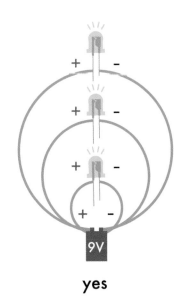

yes

3V

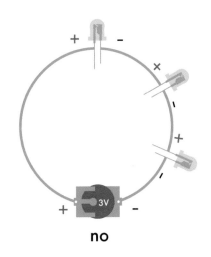

no

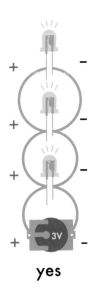

yes

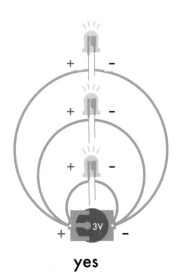

yes

6. Hopefully, some youths will "discover" both a series circuit structure and a parallel circuit structure in the process of experimenting. In case you do see any of the groups experimenting with changing the structure in these ways, note and name the kinds of structures for them as they emerge. Also, note the results of the various placement of the switch in the circuit.

7. As youths experiment, make sure that one person in each group is documenting successful solutions on their "Multiple LEDs Diagram" worksheet so that they can share it with the larger group.

IMPORTANT TIPS FOR THIS ACTIVITY:

- How can you identify positive and negative ends of the LEDs? If using the standard Super Bright LEDs, remind youths that the longer leg of the LED is the positive end. Because they will be bending the legs of the LEDs in this exercise and may have difficulty telling the positive and negative ends apart later, have them color the positive ends of the LED with a permanent marker to avoid confusion.

- When setting up a switch or a potentiometer, there are no inherently positive or negative ends. Just use two of the *adjacent loops*, attaching a wire or alligator clip to each. The center loop is always used; one of the other ones on either end will not be used. Youths likely will discover that the direction of the switch and potentiometer in relation to the battery will have no impact on the system's behavior (i.e., they should think about the switch as a gate that opens and closes in the circuit, and a potentiometer as regulating the amount of energy that goes through the circuit).

- Although you don't necessarily need to announce this to the group (as they should be able to discover it in their play), it is important to always orient the LEDs in the circuit with respect to the battery, *not* with the other LEDs, regardless of whether the circuit is in parallel or series. In other words, the positive side of the battery needs to be connected to the positive leg of the LED and the negative to the negative.

- In a series circuit, often the first LED will light up, but not the others if there isn't enough voltage in the battery.

- When multiple alligator clips are trying to connect to the same component, it's helpful to clip one alligator clip to the component and the other(s) to the jaws of the first clip.

Some alligator clips have an insulated plastic end, which can be slid back to expose the metal beneath if needed.

- Note that different colors of light require different voltage levels. Warmer colors (like reds, oranges, and yellows) are lower in frequency and require less voltage. Cooler colors (like purples, blues, and greens), by contrast, are higher in frequency and require more voltage.

- Likewise, youths may run into issues when combining multiple colors in one circuit (i.e., if red and blue LEDs were used in a single project, likely only the red LEDs would light).

SHARE AND RESEARCH: SERIES VERSUS PARALLEL—15 MINUTES

In this portion of the activity, youths will share their solutions and learn more about series and parallel circuits.

1. After the groups have had about 30 minutes to experiment and hopefully have at least two or three different successful structures diagrammed, conduct a discussion about the successful solutions, including diagrams and circuits.

2. Move among the groups, naming and sorting circuits that are in series, parallel, or hybrid arrangements.

3. What do youths notice? (*Answer: All functioning series solutions should include a 9V battery only. All the parallel formations may include either a 3V or a 9V.*) Why is that? (*Answer: This is because the battery needs to be in balance with the overall circuit design. You can use Ohm's Law. However, you can also more simply calculate the voltage needs in a circuit in series as 3V times the number of 3V LEDs used = the battery voltage needed to light the circuit. Therefore, if you would use three 3V LEDs in series, then you would need 9V to light them. However, in a parallel circuit, the current is divided equally across all of the LEDs and so you would only need 3V to light nearly any number of 3V LEDs placed in parallel. It's a more efficient circuit*).

4. This is a good time to introduce the "Series versus Parallel Circuits" handout and explain what is going on in both series and parallel circuit structures. See the box on the next page as you review the following:

- When components are wired in series within a circuit, electric current flows sequentially through those components in a continuous loop. This means that as the current travels from the battery through each LED, it loses some of its original electrical charge or energy (also known as *voltage*), with the result that the amount of voltage available decreases with each LED it passes through.

- When components are wired in parallel within a circuit, the electric current divides into two or more paths before recombining to complete the circuit. The current flows through three LEDs wired in parallel, and the electric current is split among the three of them equally. **Note:** the evenness of the split is contingent on the three LEDs being the same type.

- The key difference between series and parallel circuits relates to current flow. In a series circuit, there is only one pathway for energy to travel, and as energy passes from the battery to each LED, less and less of the battery's energy will be available to each subsequent LED in the circuit. On the other hand, in a parallel circuit, energy is able to travel directly to every LED without passing through others, allowing each to receive some amount of energy from the battery.

SERIES CIRCUIT STRUCTURE	PARALLEL CIRCUIT STRUCTURE
When components are wired in series within a circuit, electric current flows sequentially through those components in a continuous loop. This means that as the current travels from the battery through each LED, it loses some of its original electrical charge or energy (also known as *voltage*) such that the amount of voltage available for each subsequent LED decreases with each one it passes through. Note that this structure will not work with the 3V battery for this reason.	When components are wired in parallel within a circuit (as opposed to one right after another), the electric current divides into two or more paths before recombining to complete the circuit. This allows the same amount of energy or voltage to reach each LED.

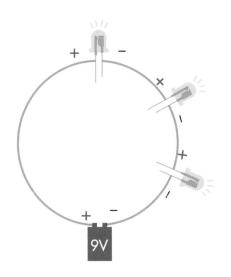 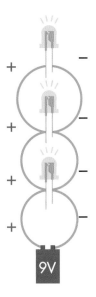

5. Ask youths to point out what they see as the major differences between the two circuit configurations (*Answers may vary, but they might be something like "A series has one big loop" and "A parallel circuit has a several smaller loops."*)

6. Inform youths that:

- In a *series* circuit, every component must function together to form a complete circuit.

- In a *parallel* circuit, each component makes its own complete circuit (trace the lines on the diagram to help point this out).

7. Ask the following questions:

- For each type of circuit, what would happen if one LED were to burn out? (*Answer: In the series circuit, it would break the circuit, while in a parallel circuit, any of the other two lights could be removed and the last one still would function.*)

- Why would lights continue to function in one and not the other? (*Answer: That's because the parallel circuit setup allows energy to flow to each LED separately.*)

Note: You may want to prebuild and demonstrate your own parallel circuit to model what would happen. It is very important that youths make the connection that the flow of energy is structured by the way that the system components are put together. This will allow them to understand later why the series circuit that they will build does not light all the LEDs in the circuit.

8. Allow youths more time to tinker with the materials with these ideas in mind. Make sure that each youth creates both a parallel and a series circuit, as they may not have had an experience with both types.

9. Reiterate the importance of system structures—that is, the way that a system's components are configured plays a role in determining the behaviors of the components and the dynamic interactions or interconnections that they have with each other.

Interconnections are often contextualized with "if/then" statements, such as: "If a circuit uses a parallel structure, then it requires less voltage to light up all LEDs than it would if it was structured in series."

—RAFI SANTO, GRADUATE RESEARCH ASSISTANT AT INDIANA UNIVERSITY

10. Prompt the group to try to think up other situations where a different configuration of identical components in a system could dramatically affect the ways that a system plays out.

- If they have trouble, have them consider the room that they're in, and ask what they could do to keep the same things in the room, but have them configured in such a way that the room would function in a totally different way. See if they can expand the idea to neighborhoods and the ways they're set up, or even cities.

REFLECT: LET'S TALK—15 MINUTES

Once everyone has created a functioning circuit in both parallel and series arrangements, conduct a large-group discussion. You can use the following questions to prompt the discussion (documenting their answers on the board):

- **What do we know about circuits as systems?**

  Answer: Circuits have components, like LEDs, batteries, switches, and alligator clips; circuits must be arranged in a closed loop to operate; if you incorporate multiple LEDs, you need to think about the system structure and the interconnections within the system between the battery and the LEDs; smaller batteries can't support multiple LEDs in a series, but larger batteries can; LEDs always have to be positioned with their positive and negative ends with respect to the battery.

- **Is the parallel LED circuit a system? Why or why not?**

  Answer: Yes, it is a system consisting of components with specific behaviors that interconnect to reach a goal (e.g., illuminating LEDs).

- **Is the series LED circuit a system? Why or why not?**

  Answer: Yes, it is also a system, consisting of components with specific behaviors that interconnect to reach a goal (e.g., illuminating LEDs).

- If the 9V series and 9V parallel circuits are *both* systems, are they the same system and structured differently, or are they actually different systems? How are their differences related to how the system works?

  Answer: While they are made of the same components, the fact that they are arranged in different ways means that as systems, they function differently, and so they could be thought of as different systems. The differences in the systems' structures produce different interconnections or interactions (i.e., whether the voltage is shared by the LEDs in series or distributed evenly across the LEDs in parallel).

- What are the goals of this system? How do components in this system interconnect to reach those goals?

  Answer: The goal of the system is to light up three LEDs; if the system is structured in series, then it needs a battery with enough voltage to power all components; if a system is structured in parallel, less voltage is required to power all LEDs.

WHAT TO EXPECT

The introduction of series and parallel circuits should help youths to understand that energy flows between components in a closed circuit and that energy in the system flows from the battery. *If that is not so, that is an indication that they are still working on their understanding of how a circuit functions.*

With respect to systems thinking concepts and vocabulary, the focus on system structure should hone youths' thinking on the interconnections among components. Specifically, asking them to think about *how* a new component is incorporated and how it changes the behavior of the system should help youths figure out how the behavior of one component affects the behavior of another component.

	Novice	Expert
Circuitry concepts	• Understands that in order for a circuit to be completed, it must be a closed loop, but is unable to create a system structure to support multiple LEDs • Finds difficulty grasping that energy in a closed circuit flows between components, and is not comfortable exploring electronic components • Is unable to diagram or prototype a working circuit • Doesn't appear to see interconnections between a battery's voltage and how many LEDs that it can support • Doesn't understand that a series circuit requires more power from the battery to illuminate multiple LEDs than a parallel circuit • Connects the battery to the LED(s) without taking into account the direction that energy flows in the circuit • Is unable to balance the system's interconnections to achieve the desired goal (using different numbers of LEDs, different voltages of batteries, and the system's structure as balancing mechanisms)	• Is comfortable playing with the electronic components in the process of exploring a wide number of solutions to create working circuits • Understands that there are at least two different structures that can be used in circuitry—series and parallel—and can diagram and/or prototype both • Understands that batteries have a particular voltage and that the amount of voltage determines how much power the battery has (and, in this case, how many LEDs that it can support) • Understands that each LED in a series circuit structure drains resources (voltage) available for other LEDs in the system • Understands that multiple LEDs can be supported in a single circuit easily by using a parallel circuit structure (and, therefore, is a more efficient way to operate a circuit than using a more powerful battery) • Has a good sense of the directionality of flow and the relationship of the battery to the LED(s) • Can use processes (e.g., tinkering or troubleshooting) to help move a system toward its goal—in this case, lighting multiple LEDs
Systems thinking concepts	• Is unable to identify and use basic systems thinking terminology to describe their circuit • Is unable to describe how a system's parts interact with each other through their behaviors • Fails to see connections between system structure and system dynamics and interconnections • Is uncomfortable troubleshooting a nonworking circuit	• Can easily identify and use basic systems thinking terminology (components, behaviors, and goals) to describe their circuit • Can identify different ways that the system's parts interact with each other through their behaviors, and begins to use terms like system dynamics and interconnections • Understands that the way that a system is structured affects the behaviors of the components and the kinds of interconnections or interactions that they have with one another; can contextualize this understanding in the discussions of their circuits, using phrases like "if a 3V battery is used, then the LEDs must be structured in parallel in order to light up"

ACTIVITY EXTENSION: MEASURING VOLTAGE DROP

One of the core ideas in circuitry that occurs naturally in the abovementioned activity is *drops in voltage.* Especially when wired in series with multiple LEDs, and when involving a potentiometer, the amount of voltage in the closed circuit changes depending on where you measure. In this extension, youths use a multimeter to measure voltage changes among different circuit configurations, including ones that include LEDs of different colors that use different amounts of voltage to light. Once you have measured a voltage drop across a single component, see what happens across the potentiometer. Measure the voltage drop on either side of the potentiometer and watch what happens to the voltage when the potentiometer's dial is turned. How can this be explained?

ACTIVITY EXTENSION: CREATING A SOFT POTENTIOMETER

Are you interested in creating your own potentiometer using soft materials like conductive thread or conductive fabric? Try this exercise; you can create a similar drop in voltage over these materials as they present a nontrivial amount of resistance. Cut a long piece of conductive thread or conductive piece of fabric. Measure the voltage from the farthest two points and then slide your measurements closer and closer together and note that the voltage drop will decrease incrementally as your measurements come together. How might you incorporate a soft potentiometer into your designs? What if you don't have these materials available? You can use a graphite pencil to create a shaded strip on a sheet of paper to produce a similar effect.

DESIGN CHALLENGE 4, PART 1

MULTIPLE LEDS DIAGRAM

Use this worksheet to diagram both your hypotheses and findings for your experiments to light multiple LEDs in a single circuit.

In the space below, share some of your ideas about how a system might be set up that will light at least 3 LEDs using (a) your 3V (coin cell) battery; (b) your 9V battery; or both.

After experimenting with the materials, diagram your successful solutions in this space. Do they look like the diagrams that you drew above? If not, how do they differ?

DESIGN CHALLENGE 4, PART 1

SERIES VERSUS PARALLEL CIRCUITS

When components are wired in series within a circuit, electric current flows sequentially through those components in a continuous loop. This means that as the current travels from the battery through each LED, it loses some of its original charge, or energy (also known as *voltage*), such that the amount of voltage available for each subsequent LED decreases with each one that it passes through.

When components are wired in parallel within a circuit, the electric current divides into two or more paths before recombining to complete the circuit. The current flows through three LEDs wired in parallel, and the electric current is split among the three of them equally. **Note:** The evenness of the split is contingent on the three LEDs being the same type. Otherwise, the current will flow more where it meets less resistance.

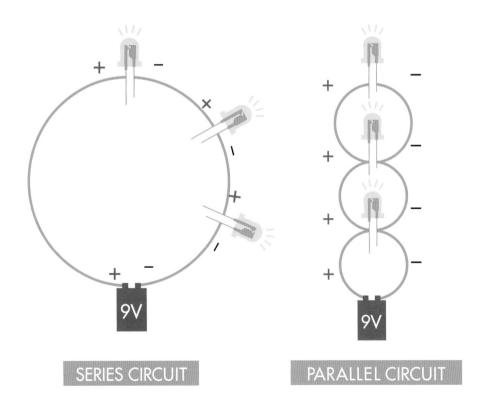

SERIES CIRCUIT   PARALLEL CIRCUIT

PART 2: DESIGN TIME—MAKING YOUR DIY FLASHLIGHT

In this activity, youths apply their new knowledge about systems structures to the creation of a useful tool—a flashlight—using simple materials. They will plan the design of their flashlights by creating a diagram, which also provides a convenient moment for assessment.

Time: 75 minutes

STUFF TO HAVE HANDY

- Prototype of a sample circuit with components affixed with electrical tape

- Prototype of a DIY flashlight prepared in advance

- System Structure Kits prepared in advance by the instructor; 1 per youth. **Note:** for this activity, remove the 9V battery and connector because the flashlight works best with a 3V battery so it won't overload the LEDs with voltage.

  - *OPTIONAL: If you plan to include the color mixing activity modification in this activity (see Mod This Session, later), replace the white Super Bright LEDs in the kits with one set each of red, green, or blue Super Bright LEDs. Restrict each kit to a single color, and prepare one third of the kits with red, one third with green, and one third with blue.*

- 3 alligator clips

- Permanent markers

- Spools of insulated hook-up wire

- Diagonal wire cutters

- Wire strippers

- Needlenose pliers

- Electrical tape

- 8.5" x 11" pieces of cardstock (for the flashlight case, one per youth)

- Arts and crafts materials like gift wrap, paint, and/or markers (to decorate the flashlight)

- Aluminum foil or other reflective material, such as empty metallic (silver-colored) potato chip bags, for the bulb area

- Paper scissors
- Utility knives (to cut holes for the switch and potentiometer in flashlight case cardstock)
- Low-temperature glue guns and sticks
- Paper tape (if cardstock is used for the flashlight case)
- Pencils

HANDOUTS

- "Diagram of a Circuit in an LED Flashlight"
- "Posting Your Flashlight"
- "Self-Reflection and Review of LED Flashlight"

IMAGINE AND CREATE: DESIGNING LED FLASHLIGHTS—45 MINUTES

In this activity, youths work individually to design and build a DIY flashlight. Applying their knowledge of circuitry toward the creation of a useful tool not only encourages youths to reassess the invisible systems that power the familiar artifacts in their environment, but also empowers them to think of themselves as "makers" who can take it upon themselves to build something from scratch, as opposed to relying on others to make it for them.

Youths will go through three phases in this activity:

1. **Diagramming** the configuration of the components of their flashlights
2. **Prototyping** the system in their flashlights using alligator clips
3. **Building** a final product based on the diagram and prototype

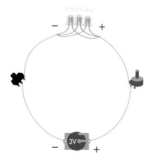

DIAGRAM

PROTOTYPE

BUILD

VOICES FROM THE FIELD

Going from the initial diagramming to the prototyping to the final flashlight design in this activity worked really well. I found that it was super important that our learners had a clear picture of how all of the core components of the flashlight fit together (the battery, LEDs, potentiometer, etc.) before they moved to actually having those components set up in a way that integrated the flashlight housing. Getting that prototype down and working, with a good understanding of what related to what, allowed learners to adapt once they hit the inevitable snags as they created the final product.

—RAFI SANTO, GRADUATE RESEARCH ASSISTANT AT INDIANA UNIVERSITY

1. Pose an initial question: What are the different components in a flashlight, and how might you make one using the materials that you just explored?

2. Using the "Diagram of a Circuit in an LED Flashlight" worksheet, have youths sketch a diagram of their proposed LED flashlight circuit. **Note:** This document also can be used as an assessment of youths' understanding at this point in the activity. Let them know that in order for the flashlight to generate enough light, they will need to use multiple LEDs.

3. Briefly share the diagrams as a whole group.

4. Show your prototype of a simple circuit with components affixed with either electrical tape or alligator clips to the group (which may differ from the circuit that the youths just created in their diagrams), in addition to your finished DIY flashlight. Show how the switch and potentiometer work in both the prototype and finished flashlight.

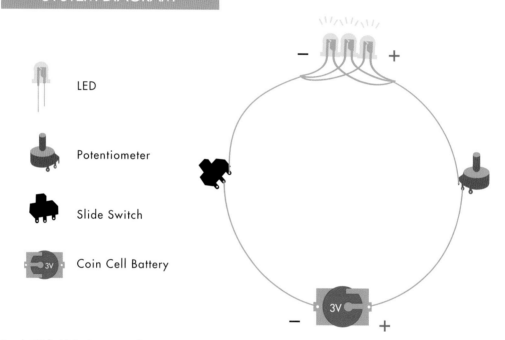

DIY FLASHLIGHT CIRCUIT SYSTEM DIAGRAM

LED

Potentiometer

Slide Switch

3V Coin Cell Battery

Sample DIY flashlight circuit system diagram.

5. Begin the prototyping phase with the group by returning to the modified System Structure Kits, if needed. First, have youths put together a circuit in any of the system structure configurations that they used before (parallel or series), using alligator clips to secure the connections. We suggest having them create a parallel circuit with the 3V battery in its holder, switch, potentiometer, and three LEDs (see Design Challenge 4, part 1) but they also may want to consult the notes they took on their "Multiple LEDs Diagram" worksheet in Part 1.

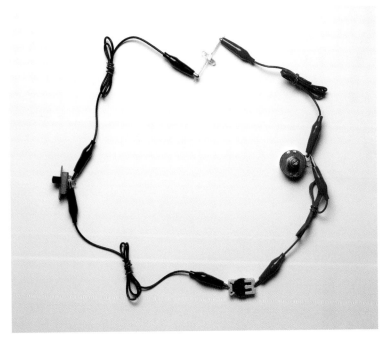

Sample flashlight circuit prototype.

> **TIP** Super Bright LEDs are more effective in a DIY flashlight than other LEDs because they produce more light. Super Bright white LEDs also work fine with 9V batteries, but Super Bright LEDs of other colors can burn out easily with a 9V battery if they are not paired with resistors, which is why we recommend a 3V battery for the DIY flashlight.

6. While youths are working, prepare the remaining materials for the next part of the activity and introduce them to the group as needed. We suggest having a glue gun station and wire cutting/twisting station somewhere in the room in an area with protected surfaces. We also suggest requiring youths to check in with you when they are ready to use the utility knife for the placement of their switch and potentiometer, to ensure adult supervision during this step.

	Wire stripper	A tool used to strip the plastic coating from insulated wires. Wire strippers typically have different gauge settings. We recommend the wire strippers from SparkFun, which feature six different gauge settings. SparkFun—TOL-08696
	Diagonal wire cutter	A tool specially designed to cut wire. SparkFun—TOL-08794
	Insulated hook-up wire	Insulated wire that can be cut into smaller pieces and incorporated into your projects. The protective coating is stripped away at the ends so the wire can be attached to components. SparkFun—PRT-08022
	Electrical tape	Provides an insulating barrier to any exposed wires in your projects, helping to prevent short circuits. SparkFun—PRT-10689

	Needlenose pliers	These pliers, named for their long, thin shape, are useful for craft and electrical projects to bend wire, completing fine detail work, or for bending the pins of two-pronged LEDs to make them sewable. SparkFun—TOL-08793
	Utility knife	An all-purpose blade useful for cutting holes in thick material. Local hardware store
	Low-temperature glue gun and sticks	A glue gun uses heat to melt a solid stick of glue that dries almost immediately after being applied to any surface. The glue can be used to affix loose items and/or act as an insulating barrier in projects. We recommend low-temperature glue for safety and to help prevent project components from being melted accidentally. Local arts and craft store

Once their circuits are completed and operational, have youths replace the alligator clips in their designs by following these steps:

7. Pass out one 8.5" x 11" sheet of cardstock to each youth. All youths will fold the cardstock cross-wise or cut it in half.

8. Using a sample switch and potentiometer as templates, help youths mark and cut with a utility knife two small holes—a square and a rectangle—in the side of one half-sheet of cardstock. See the example image for size and placement. Be careful not to make the holes too big, or the components might push through. Gradually increase the size of the hole as needed.

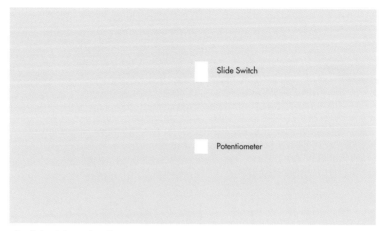

Slide Switch

Potentiometer

Holes cut into cardstock for slide switch and potentiometer.

9. Curl the cardstock into a short cylinder (about the size of a toilet tissue tube), and use tape to loosely hold it together. Youths should trace one end of their tube on the other piece of cardstock, creating a circle. Cut out the circle to create the LED-end of the flashlight and set the circle aside. *Optional: Youths can glue some reflective material to the circle (aluminum foil, the inside of a shiny chip bag, metallic wrapping paper, etc.) to help reflect the light from the LEDs.*

10. Remove the tape and uncurl the cardstock tube. Attach the switch and the potentiometer through the holes on the main cardstock rectangle, with the switch and the potentiometer's knob sticking through the front. Tape the switch on the front to hold it in place. Screw the potentiometer's washer onto the knob at the front of the cardstock to attach it. Set this piece aside.

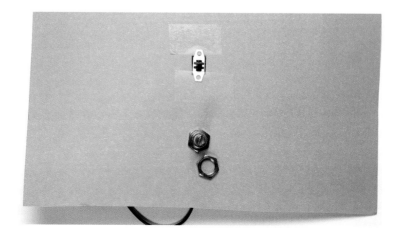

Note The following steps are specific to replacing the alligator clips in the prototype circuit with insulated wire, connecting the three LEDs, potentiometer, and switch. This example focuses on a parallel circuit, but the instructions can be generalized to other circuit configurations as well.

11. On each of the three LEDs, color the longer of the two legs (the positive end) with permanent marker to avoid later confusion.

12. Mark the cardboard circle with six spots to show where the positive and negative LED legs should poke through. (See the image for pinhole placement.)

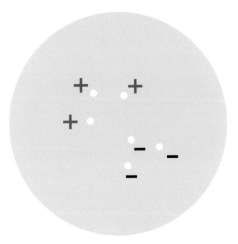

13. Push the legs of the LEDs one at a time through the cardstock circle, being careful to place them close enough so that the positive legs can be bundled and the negative legs also can be grouped together easily, while keeping the two sets of legs from touching. See the same diagram.

VOICES FROM THE FIELD

One of the trickiest parts of the flashlight activity is in placing the holes for the three LEDs in the cardstock circle correctly. The positive and negative legs have to be far enough apart so that they don't touch, but close enough to each other so that you can twist the three positive and three negative legs together in two bundles. The illustration is a great aid for that ... I recommend duplicating it as a template for youths to lay on their cardstock circles, poking holes right through both.

—JANIS WATSON, CURRICULUM SPECIALIST OF THE CREATIVITY LABS @ INDIANA UNIVERSITY

14. Twist together the positive (marked) legs of the three LEDs, and then twist the negative legs. Use the needlenose pliers to make sure that the bundles hold together.

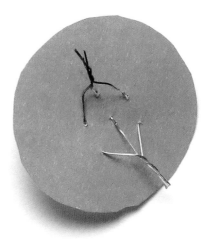

15. At this point, double-check the circuit by using two alligator clips to connect the positive and negative bundles to the battery in its holder. If the LEDs don't light, check the orientation (negative to negative; positive to positive) of the LEDs to the battery holder ends, as well as whether the legs are twisted together well enough to make a solid connection. When you have verified that the connection is good, remove the alligator clips and place the cardstock circle to the side.

16. Cut four 3-inch strips of hook-up wire. Use wire strippers to strip about a half inch of plastic insulation from each end of the wires.

17. Attach the positive (+) LED leg bundle to one wire using electrical tape, and the negative bundle to another.

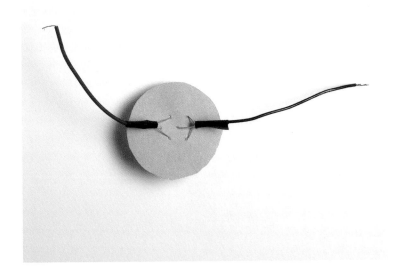

18. Connect the positive (+) wire from the LED cluster to one side of the switch.

19. Connect the negative (–) wire from the LEDs to one of the sides of the potentiometer. Twist the wires carefully to make a secure connection. Note that there are three connections on the potentiometer; one of the *outer* connections will not be wired into the circuit.

20. Connect the second wire from the potentiometer to the (–) lead on the 3V battery holder, and then connect the positive side of the battery holder to the center pin of the switch. Your circuit should resemble the image here:

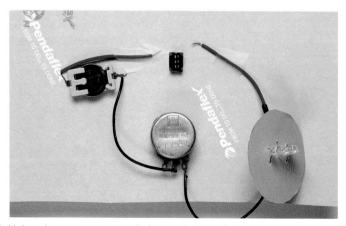

The inside of the flashlight, with most components attached. Notice that the red wires still need to be attached to the switch. Make sure the battery is taped down near the "top" edge of this rectangle, opposite the side where the lights will shine out.

21. With the 3V battery in its holder, double-check that the circuit still works, that the switch is operational, and that the potentiometer effectively changes the brightness of the LEDs. If not, try to debug the connections, looking for loose connections or issues with the orientation to the battery.

22. If the device is working, use small pieces of electrical tape to rewrap (insulate) the newly twisted joints of the circuit, making sure that no wire is left exposed. **Note:** Electrical tape around the joints will make the flashlight last longer. It also will help preserve the joints if the youths need to manipulate the circuit when attaching it to the cardboard housing.

23. Once youths have a working circuit, have them check the diagram against their final design in the "Diagram of a Circuit in an LED Flashlight" worksheet, using what they just built and noting any differences.

24. Position all the components in the tube and position the circle of cardstock so that the LEDs face out of the flashlight. Once the circuit components are reasonably positioned on both sides of the cardstock, affix the circle of cardstock well with tape or low-temperature hot glue, and roll the cardstock into a tube and tape it well to hold its shape.

Completed DIY flashlight, before final decoration.

25. Double-check that the flashlight still works and that none of the connections have become loose in the process.

26. And finally, allow time for youths to decorate their flashlight casings using the arts and crafts materials that you provided. The DIY flashlights are complete!

IMPORTANT TIP FOR THIS ACTIVITY:

In this activity, it's possible for youths to burn out an LED (e.g., if they were to wire just one LED to a 9V battery, there is a strong possibility that it will burn out). Typically, you will see a bright flash of light accompanied by a distinct smell (although it is not usually a hazard). If you're unsure, you can always try to light the LED using your 3V battery. If it doesn't work, it has burned out. However, be sure to celebrate these moments as opportunities for discovery! Electronics hobbyists burn out LEDs frequently, and it's useful to know how it happens in order to prevent it in the future.

MOD THIS SESSION

To add a collaborative aspect to this activity, introduce the science of color theory, and incorporate another opportunity to think about systems, try a modification where different flashlight kits include either red, green, or blue Super Bright LEDs, as opposed to white. In this modification, each youth will need to find two others with complementary colors after the single-color flashlights are completed, so that they can form a group with flashlights representing all three colors.

In this modification, youths have the opportunity to include color experimentation to the other learning activity. After the flashlights are operational, have them form into groups of three: one red, one green, and one blue flashlight. Each group should find a clear spot on a wall or tabletop to shine their lights, combining two and then all three colors and adjusting the color intensity with their potentiometers. With these three base colors and the ability to change brightness, each group should be able to create all the colors in the spectrum, as well as standard white light. This provides you with opportunities to introduce youths to the theory of light mixing color theory if you choose.

But beyond color mixing, be sure to watch the group interactions to see if youths notice the systemic nature of the activity. They should begin to see that each of the completed flashlights becomes a component in a new, larger system, and when they interconnect in the appropriate way (through calibrated light levels), those components work together toward the goal of creating different colors of light.

VOICES FROM THE FIELD

The flashlight activity calls for material like aluminum foil on the cardstock circle to aid in reflecting the LEDs' light ... but I found that if that isn't available, other reflective materials can be used, such as the reflective wrapping paper used in this robot flashlight.

—DIANE GLOSSON, GRADUATE RESEARCH ASSISTANT AT INDIANA UNIVERSITY

REFLECT AND SHARE: DOCUMENT YOUTHS' THINKING—30 MINUTES

You might want to consider having youths share their unique flashlight designs on an online community website! Distribute the "Posting Your Flashlight" worksheet. Ask them to complete the worksheet before they post their projects on a pre-selected website (see suggestions at the Interconnections website, digitalis.nwp.org/gnl). Remind them to refer to their notes about what makes a good post as they work on their own writing.

As a final activity, which can be used as an assessment, pass out the "Self-Reflection and Review of LED Flashlight" worksheet. Ask youths to fill these out individually. After the worksheets are completed, discuss youths' thoughts as a whole group. Ask volunteers to share something that they wrote in their self-reflection. Encourage the use of the following vocabulary terms introduced in Part 1:

- What was the *goal* of their circuit?

- What was the *voltage* of the batteries that youths employed?

- Where were the *leverage points* of the system?

- When youths made a change to the *system's structure*, how did the *system dynamics/interconnections* change in response?

WHAT TO EXPECT

In completing this activity, youths have had an opportunity to apply all the circuitry concepts covered thus far. This reflection will allow them an opportunity to express their conceptual understanding of a circuit as a system whose structure can vary.

The following table provides a description of the range of possible feedback from youths in response to the task on the "Diagram of a Circuit in an LED Flashlight" worksheet and the "What makes this flashlight a system?" question on the "Self-Reflection and Review of LED Flashlight" worksheet. These questions offer an excellent opportunity to evaluate youths' understanding of both circuitry and systems thinking concepts.

	Novice	Expert
Circuitry concepts	• Can identify the basic elements of an electronic circuit (i.e., LEDs, switch, potentiometer, battery, wire), but struggles to label important interconnections between components (such as the orientation of the LEDs and battery, the switch and the flow of the current in the circuit), or does so incorrectly • Cannot identify the structure of the circuit built (i.e., parallel or series) • Understands that in order for a circuit to be completed, it must be a closed loop; however, has difficulty incorporating more than one LED in a circuit in a system (in series or in parallel)	• Identifies all basic components of an electrical circuit, and can describe accurately the core interconnections between all components in the circuit (e.g., if a 3V battery is used, then you need to use a parallel structure to light more than one LED) • Readily identifies the structure of the circuit built (i.e., parallel or series) • Understands that in order for a circuit to be completed, it must be a closed loop, and can create a circuit and circuit diagram incorporating more than one LED in a circuit in a system (in series or in parallel)
Systems thinking concepts	• Describes the circuit simply as a collection of components with specific behaviors, with little attention given to how individual components interact to achieve the overall goal (e.g., lighting the LED) • Fails to see connections between system structure and system dynamics and interconnections • Is unable to identify potential leverage points, such as the voltage of the battery, the system's structure, or the switch	• Can explain a circuit in a way that conveys an understanding that a circuit is a system of multiple components, each with unique behaviors, and that it is the interconnections or interactions between these components (e.g., that the switch needs to be in the On position for the LEDs to turn on) that enables the system to achieve its goal (e.g., the LEDs to light up) • Understands that the way a system is structured affects the behaviors of the components and the kinds of interconnections or interactions they have with one another; can contextualize this understanding in the discussions of their circuits, using phrases like "if a 3V battery is used, then the LEDs must be structured in parallel in order to light up"

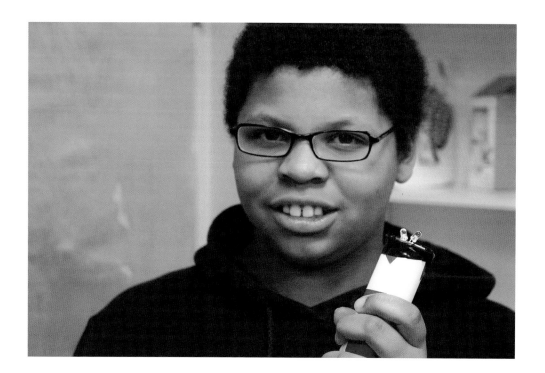

DESIGN CHALLENGE 4, PART 2

DIAGRAM OF A CIRCUIT IN AN LED FLASHLIGHT

Components and Behaviors of the System: Draw the diagram of your flashlight in the space below. Be sure to label your diagram with all the following components and note the behaviors of each component. Be sure to label the location and the interconnections among the components.

- Battery in holder

- Switch

- Potentiometer

- 3 LEDs

- Positive side (+) of components

- Negative side (-) of components

Name and explain some of the interconnections in this system.

DESIGN CHALLENGE 4, PART 2

POSTING YOUR FLASHLIGHT

Use this worksheet to help plan what you will say about your flashlight on the Interconnections site.

GIVE YOUR PROJECT A NAME:

What will you call your flashlight? Give it a unique and inspiring name!

WRITE A PROJECT DESCRIPTION:

1. What inspired you in designing your flashlight's case?

2. Tell us about the design decisions that you made. Did you start with a theme? Did you choose a particular color of LED for your flashlight?

PHOTO SHOOT PLANNING:

What should the photo(s) look like online? Sketch them out or write down a description of what they should look like, below. (Example: "Photo 1 should be the flashlight with the LEDs turned on in a dark room; Photo 2 should be the flashlight decorations showing in a lit room.") Should there be a video of the flashlight in action for the site? If so, what should show in the video?

DESIGN CHALLENGE 4, PART 2

SELF-REFLECTION AND REVIEW OF LED FLASHLIGHT

1. How did you decide on the design for your flashlight?

2. What was the hardest part of this activity for you? Why?

3. Describe and define what it means to wire LEDs "in series."

4. Describe and define what it means to wire LEDs "in parallel."

5. What makes this flashlight a system?

6. What makes this system different from the system(s) that you created in previous Design Challenges?

PART 3: TELLING STORIES WITH SHADOWS

In this activity, youths will use their DIY flashlights and incorporate the storytelling techniques that they developed in previous Design Challenges to create a collaborative performance, this time employing shadow play and shadow puppetry techniques.

Time: 120 minutes

STUFF TO HAVE HANDY

- Storyboards from Design Challenge 3
- Cardstock and/or recycled file folders for puppets
- Paper scissors
- Utility knives
- Bamboo skewers with points removed, drinking straws, or thin dowels of similar length
- Low-temperature glue gun and glue sticks
- Brads (sometimes called *paper fasteners* or *split pins*)
- Hole punch or tool for making holes in cardstock
- Material to create a shadow puppet stage, such as the following:
    - Cardboard box (large enough to serve as the stage for three or four shadow puppets) with waxed paper covering the front for the screen, or
    - Thin cotton cloth stretched across a door frame with a table
- *Optional:* Colored plastic for shadow highlights and lighting color changes

HANDOUTS

- "Shadow Puppet Template Inspirations"

RESEARCH: TELL A STORY WITH SHADOWS—10 MINUTES

Shadow puppetry presents an opportunity to enrich youths' understanding of how stories translate from a written format into a live performance. In the process, they gain new perspectives into how the components of a story look different when this translation takes place.

1. Begin by asking youths about their familiarity with shadow puppetry and other ways that they might have played with, or made, shadows. Discuss the different components that create a shadow (*Possible answers*: A shadow must have a light source, an object to block the light, and a surface on which the shadow forms). In shadow puppetry, the surface onto which shadows are cast is a screen. Puppets are manipulated between the screen and the light source, and the audience watches from the other side of the screen.

2. Discuss how stories can be shared in many ways and discuss the way that youths have created and shared stories thus far. **Note:** If you have completed Design Challenges 2 and 3, remind youths how they began with developing an e-puppet as a story character and then designed and storyboarded a story with audio enhancements. Encourage the group to think about shadows as another way to share a story. If possible, look for some sample shadow puppet videos on the web to familiarize them with this form of storytelling.

DESIGN AND ITERATE: DESIGN YOUR SHADOW STORY—60 MINUTES

Working in the same storyboarding groups formed in Design Challenge 3, youths should draw from their previous experiences with character development, stories, and storytelling—including their e-puppet and sound activities—to write a script for a shadow play. The storyboard created in Design Challenge 2 will be used as the narrative base of their shadow play. Mentor texts are another way to support thinking about how a script works versus other kinds of storytelling.

1. Ask each group to look at the storyboard that they created in Design Challenge 3 and imagine telling this story as a play. Does it require a narrator? Are there multiple settings? Should dialogue be added? What might be confusing to the audience if they couldn't look at the storyboard?

2. To help youths envision the translation of their storyboard into a script for performance, remind them that when someone writes a script, he or she is limited to writing what the audience can *see* (action and description) and *hear* (dialogue).[3]

SUGGESTIONS FOR SCRIPT WRITING AS A TEAM[4]

- All members of the team should review their storyboard silently.

- As a group, identify the main roles in the story (characters and objects) and divide them among the team.

- Outline the main events in the story, deciding which parts should be narrated (told by someone outside the story) and which should be dialogue (told by characters within the story).

- Decide what parts of the story can or must be cut (removed), depending on how many members of the team you have and what parts of the story have to be told.

- Try out the script by reading it out loud together. Go back and change it as needed.

VOICES FROM THE FIELD

Nudging some of the projects or their extensions towards explorations of identity or community/social issues might make the connections between digital and human systems more concrete (e.g. puppet shows about kids' dreams or concerns; fashion items that story-tell or symbolize identity or personal politics).

—CHAD SANSING, NATIONAL WRITING PROJECT

3. Once the script is ready, ask youths to write out a list of components that are important to telling their story—characters, props/objects, and important settings that might need to be shown in shadow. This list will be the beginning of their "make" list (i.e., what they need to make that will show up as a shadow). Encourage them to keep this list as simple as possible. **Note:** Scaffold the task as a large group by working together to create a sample list for a classic fairy tale or other well-known story.

4. Once groups have their "make" lists, they can begin to create their shadow puppets, starting with the main characters and any objects or props that are needed (see the suggestions in the "Making Simple Shadow Puppets" section, next).

5. After completing these elements of their story, youths can move on to making any scenery that will support the settings that are necessary for it.

MAKING SIMPLE SHADOW PUPPETS

Characters and objects can be simple or complex. Some simple characters are provided as a template in the "Shadow Puppet Template Inspirations" handout. Be thoughtful when planning the size of the puppets. Each has to fit behind the screen of your stage, and often more than one puppet or prop shadow will need to share the space.

1. Sketch a character/object on cardstock or recycled file folders. Referencing the "Shadow Puppet Template Inspirations" worksheet, note that characters or objects may include moving parts that are created separately.

    *   Sketch the main body and then any extra parts, making sure to mark where the parts will attach with circles and corresponding marks (such as the *x* and *o* used in some of the template examples).

    *   Be creative with what part moves; encourage youths to think about the ways that they think about character traits and actions that are an important part of telling the story and conveying how the character acts and feels.

Note: Suggest a limit of no more than two moving parts per character, as each requires manipulation during performance. With one moving part, two skewers (or straws or sticks) can be attached to the main body and the part. With two moving parts, the skewers should be attached to both parts to support the main body.

2. Cut out the body and parts with paper scissors.

3. Attach any parts to the body by creating a hole through both pieces using a hole punch or dowel for each part. Use a brad paper fastener to attach parts together.

4. Glue long narrow sticks, skewers, or drinking straws to the main body. Then glue a second stick to the moving part so that it can be manipulated separately. Encourage youths to practice moving the puppet with one or both hands and make any necessary adjustments (such as loosening the brads for easier movement).

IMPORTANT TIPS FOR THIS ACTIVITY:

*   *Enhance with Decorations:* Encourage youths to exaggerate any important features or descriptive elements that they think will make their character identifiable. For example, holes can highlight elements that allow light to pass through, such as eyes or clothing elements. Use decorative objects like feathers sparingly because they cast very abstract shadows. Translucent colored plastic can be used to project color highlights.

*   *Add Interest with Objects:* Items that a character would hold or use can help advance the narrative. Youths can also create cut-out words, sounds, or short phrases that a character would say or think. Symbols also can be be used here, such as a light bulb suddenly glowing to indicate that a character got an idea.

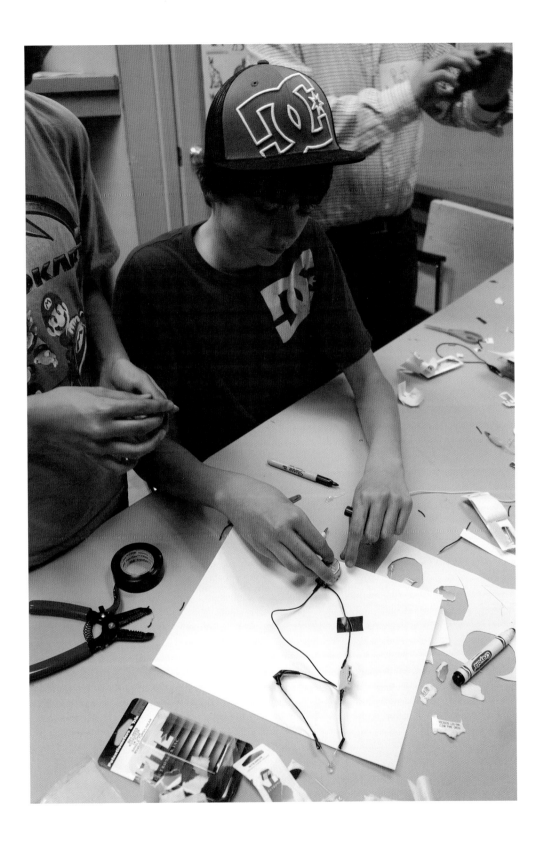

MOD THIS PROJECT

Youths can incorporate previously learned components, such as LEDs and audio switches, into their shadow puppets. This could bring an interesting modern element into a shadow puppet performance. In addition, youths might experiment with 3-D shadows, playing with toys or action figures to see what kinds of shadows they cast.

SET THE STAGE:

1. *Create a stage:* There are different options for making a shadow stage. These are a couple of ideas, but use what works best for your situation:

   • A taut piece of thin white cotton cloth stretched across a door, an old window frame, etc., usually will do.

- A smaller frame also can be created with a cardboard box and wax paper. To create a shadow box, find a box larger than the puppet interaction requires and do the following:

  - Cut out a window from the bottom of the box in the size you want.

  - Cover this window tightly with wax paper.

  - Place this box on its edge, with the wax paper facing the audience. Decorate if you want (although remember that shadow puppetry happens in the dark, so decorations will be seen only when the lights are on).

2. *Add the light source:* The DIY flashlight will give off light that will create the shadow. Set up your stage, puppets, and flashlight so that the shadow of the puppets shows up, but not the shadow of the puppeteer (unless that's what you want to show!). Let the youths experiment with their shadows and make adjustments as necessary.

3. *Creating scenery (optional):* It is usually best to wait until the puppets and props are completed and the screen is made before creating a scene (which is really a background frame for your story).

   - For some stories, such a background is not necessary, and simple objects can be used instead (e.g., a scene that takes place in a backyard might simply need a single tree object).

   - For more complete backgrounds, a simple but effective way is to make a shadow frame for your story. For instance, if the story takes place underwater, youths can create a frame around their screen that shows seashells along the bottom and a wave curve along the top. This will project the idea of an ocean while keeping the main area open for the characters to interact.

BRINGING IT ALL TOGETHER!

Encourage youths to practice their scene, working on the movement of their puppets and props to the best effect.

1. Ask them to experiment with the ways that shadows are created and the effects that can be achieved with light.

   - For example, sharp shadows that are the same size as the puppet can be achieved by keeping the puppet close to the screen.
   - Longer shadows and effects can be made by pulling the puppet away from the screen and blurring its shadow.

2. What impact does the positioning or moving of the flashlight have on the shadows?

SHARE: PERFORM YOUR SHADOW PLAYS—40 MINUTES

Now it's time to perform for others! Encourage youths to present their shadow puppet plays to the whole group. **Note:** You might consider recording the shadow plays for posting on the chosen website.

REFLECT: SHADOW STORIES AS SYSTEMS—10 MINUTES

As a final activity after they perform for each other, ask youths to reflect on their work together, using the following or similar prompts to guide reflection.

- What are the important components needed to tell a story with shadows?

- How could a change to any of the components make a change to the story? Give some examples.

- What systems did you notice within the shadow plays?

WHAT TO EXPECT

This activity is designed to ensure that youths grasp the fundamentals of both creating a story and understanding it as a system. This is also an opportunity to get them thinking about how systems differ from other kinds of cause-and-effect relationships and how different components and forms of storytelling (e.g., through shadows) introduce their own components and relationships into the mix.

	Novice	Expert
Storytelling concepts	• Struggles to create a story, or writes a story that fails to incorporate the designated components and goals • Does not demonstrate an understanding of the various parts of a story, or how the pieces relate to each other • Never uses vocabulary important to how stories are put together • Struggles to communicate their story through writing, drawing, or oral presentation	• Is able to create a simple story from base components • Is able to make behaviors, components, and structure work logically toward a story's goal or resolution • Has a good grasp of the associated story vocabulary • Is able to communicate a message through written, verbal, and visual means
Systems thinking concepts	• Is unable to identify components, behaviors, interconnections, goals, and structure • Fails to see the systems thinking connections between stories, circuits, and other phenomena	• Is able to identify components, behaviors, interconnections, goals, and structure in multiple systems, including stories and circuits • Understands that systems thinking can be applied to a variety of phenomena, including shadows and stories

DESIGN CHALLENGE 4, PART 3

SHADOW PUPPET TEMPLATE INSPIRATIONS

These templates offer ideas for how to design an effective shadow puppet. Note that the Xs indicate where the joints align for movement. When you design moveable parts in a shadow puppet, keep in mind that you have only two hands: one has to hold the puppet, leaving only one free to move any limbs or other parts.

DELVING DEEPER INTO SYSTEMS THINKING

The significant problems we face cannot be solved at the same level of thinking we were at when we created them.

—*Albert Einstein*

We are caught in an inescapable network of mutuality, tied in a single garment of destiny. Whatever affects one directly affects all indirectly.

—*Dr. Martin Luther King, Jr.*

So what is systems thinking, and why is it important? With so little time to cover what seems like so much, why should systems thinking get a seat at the educational table? We find the answer in part by looking at the vast problems in the world around us, which range from environmental degradation to global financial meltdowns, growing inequality to ballooning costs of health care, and so many more issues. At their core, these difficulties are about systems, and all can be linked fundamentally to perspective: people have a tendency to look at things in terms of isolated parts instead of interdependent wholes. In short, to solve these complex problems, we need to view the world as a set of complex systems.

We believe that teaching systems thinking holds promise for supporting the development of a generation of young people who look at things differently, through "new lenses" that will allow them to effectively meet the challenges of a world that is more connected than ever. These lenses involve looking before leaping, an orientation toward understanding the big picture, and the approach of *interpreting* things differently rather than *doing* them differently. After all, change in the ways we *do* things naturally follows from a change in the way we *see* things. Rather than focusing on a narrow analysis of phenomena that we too often assume are standing still, a systems thinking approach always assumes that the world is in constant motion, and that in that world, nothing exists in isolation. So the systems thinker learns to focus on the dynamics that surround, shape, and are shaped by whatever it is that we want to understand, whether it be in the realm of science, sociology, economics, or English literature. Systems thinkers seek to understand the impact of their actions on the often tightly interconnected system of which they are a part.

WHAT MAKES A SYSTEMS THINKER DIFFERENT? IT'S ALL ABOUT PERSPECTIVE!

As mentioned previously, much of systems thinking deals with changing our perspectives on situations and adopting the kinds of perspectives that people aren't often taught. Specifically, several practices are engaged in regularly by someone acting from a systems thinking perspective:

- Looking at the world in terms of integrated and interdependent wholes, as opposed to isolated parts

- Knowing that most complex problems involve dynamic systems that are in motion, rather than static parts that stand still

- Viewing situations from multiple levels of perspective, focusing on the connections between events and the underlying patterns, systemic structures, and assumptions from which those events emerge

- Considering how a particular stakeholder's position within a system will affect his or her ideas and assumptions about a system's function and how it should operate

- Adjusting the sense of time—by expanding the range of time considered when looking at a problem, you can gain insights into how certain actions in a system might have delayed effects

- Identifying the various dynamics, especially circular ones in the form of feedback loops, which lead a system to function in a particular way and move in a particular direction

- Focusing on finding leverage points that can be used to make lasting changes, as opposed to falling back on short-term fixes

- Considering the unintended consequences of intervening in a system

Think about the difference between a person who is able to do the things on that list and one who cannot. In an interconnected world, young people who are trained as systems thinkers have a powerful way of understanding, participating in, and changing the structures that affect their lives and those of people they care about.

WHAT MAKES A SYSTEM A SYSTEM?

A system isn't just a whole bunch of stuff that happens to be lumped together geographically or topically. It's not limited to what we usually call *systems* in our daily lives, such as when we refer to our education or healthcare systems, a computer system, or a heating system in a building (though these definitely *are* systems!). Systems have particular qualities, and knowing and being able to identify them is a key part of being able to look at things systemically.

Here's one definition of system that we like to use: A *system* is a collection of interacting *components* that interact to *function* as a whole, where the whole is always greater than the sum of its parts. If you changed one component, the whole would function differently. All these components are set up in a particular way, interacting in relation to one another, which is called a system's *structure.* The structure of a system determines the specific *behaviors* of different parts and the specific *system dynamics* that result from the interactions among the components. In a designed system, or one with intentional actors, these components work together to accomplish an intentional *purpose* or *goal* that someone brings to the system. But regardless of that intentional goal, a system always will function in a certain way that moves the system toward a certain state. (Note that these terms are defined in great detail in Appendix A.)

Linda Booth Sweeney, a leader in the field of systems thinking, likes to talk about the difference between systems and heaps (Sweeney 2001). Both, she says, contain lots of "stuff," or parts. But a heap won't be changed much if you take away some of its parts. Think of a pile of laundry. Add or take away a couple of shirts or a towel, and you still have a pile of laundry—not really a substantive change. Now think of a washing machine. Try taking off the door handle, adding a slot for detergent that doesn't connect to the rest of the machine, or changing the amount of electricity that feeds the machine. Good luck getting socks clean! That pile of laundry is a heap, where adding and taking away things won't really affect the pile very much (if at all) in terms of how it functions in the world. But a washing machine is a system—we can't just add, take away, or change components willy-nilly since these often are interconnected in specific ways, often feeding back on one another, and have specific roles or behaviors that allow the system to function in a particular way.

A SYSTEM'S GOAL, PURPOSE, AND FUNCTION: NOT ALL ARE CREATED EQUAL

One of the tricky things about systems is the fact that there's often a difference between the way that a system is *actually* working (its *function*) and how we *want* it to work (its *goal*). This is why so many of us try to intervene in existing systems—because they're not working well (or maybe they're working well for *some*, but not for all).

There are many cases where a system is functioning exactly as it was intended to do by someone designing or intervening in it. Let's take the example of a game. A game can be considered a system because how the game is played and how the game play unfolds are the results of multiple interactions among different components. The *function* of the system (the experience of playing the game) might be really difficult—and a designer might have meant it to be so (her *goal* might have been to create a difficult game). On the other hand, sometimes the overall function of a system is *at odds* with the intended goal that someone has for the system. For instance, from one perspective, the *goal* or purpose of a car is to take someone from point A to point B; but when the car's transmission gives out, the car will not *function* as a system to meet that goal.

It's important to be able to reflect not only on how a system might be functioning currently, but also on how a designer might have intended it to operate (or intended to change it). A given system might have multiple goals that are at play simultaneously, but come into conflict. The person who designed the washing machine has a pretty straightforward goal: get clothing clean (without destroying it in the process). Many systems are more complex than a washing machine, however, and have a less straightforward purpose. For example, the educational system has many components (e.g., teachers, youths, school buildings, assessments, and educational standards), all of which, presumably, are meant to work together in order to … do what? Well, that question is actually a matter of some dispute. Like many other systems, such as health care, social services, economies, businesses, and communities, the educational system has more than one person who acts as a "designer"—that is, there are multiple actors bringing varying goals and purposes to the design of a given system and contributing to the way that it is configured.

In the case of the educational system, some people believe that the purpose of being educated is to develop a population that is well prepared to engage in the project of democracy (this was Thomas Jefferson's view), while others see its purpose as preparing young people to compete in the global economy. These are only two possible goals, and while there might be some overlap of goals, we probably can agree that an educational system that aims at only one of the goals likely would look different from one that aims at the other. Knowing that any given system can have different stakeholders working toward different goals sometimes can help us understand why a system is not functioning as well as it could be. After all, not all goals are compatible.

Often, though, the way that systems actually operate is more organic than intentional. Many environmental issues involving the interaction of human behavior with natural ecosystems can be described as the result of systems whose functions are completely unintended. Global warming, for instance, results from the interaction of many components (human fossil fuel emissions, carbon dioxide's capacity to retain heat, the particular makeup of the Earth's atmosphere that captures certain gases, etc.), which all create a system that functions to increase global climate over time. Obviously, this was not anyone's intention, but it points to the fact that while many systems are designed and have intended goals or consequences (like that washing machine), others have their own logic and function that is driven by an emergent system structure (like economies and ecosystems).

SYSTEM STRUCTURE

The way that a system's components are set up in relation to one another, known as the *system structure,* is another important factor in understanding systems. On their own, components don't do very much. However, once they're connected to one another, they start to take on specific behaviors and roles within a system. These behaviors aren't a given, though; they depend on the way that the system is structured. For instance, if I take apart a car, lay out all the parts, and then put them back together in a different way, it's unlikely that the car will work the way that it did before or that the parts will exhibit their original behaviors. The relationships between the car parts are contingent on how they're structured.

Circuits offer a great example of this concept, and in Design Challenge 4 of this book, which addresses this idea of system structure, youths consider how a collection of the same components in a circuit, set up in different ways, result in very different systems. Specifically, they experiment with various circuitry components to see the differences between parallel circuits and series circuits.

In a *series circuit,* components (for example, light-emitting diodes/LEDs) are connected "in series," or one right after another, along a single path. When they are connected to a battery to form a closed circuit, the flow of electrons travels along one pathway in a continuous loop. Energy flowing from the battery travels sequentially through each of the LEDs along the circuit. As the current travels from the battery through each LED, more and more of the original electrical charge or energy (also known as *voltage*) is lost, and so the amount of energy available for each subsequent LED decreases. Depending on the voltage of the battery, the single current may not carry enough energy to light all the LEDs in the circuit.

On the other hand, in a *parallel circuit,* components are connected "in parallel," as opposed to one right after another. That is, rather than having one continuous loop, each LED is wired to the battery on a separate loop. This allows the same amount of energy or voltage to reach each LED.

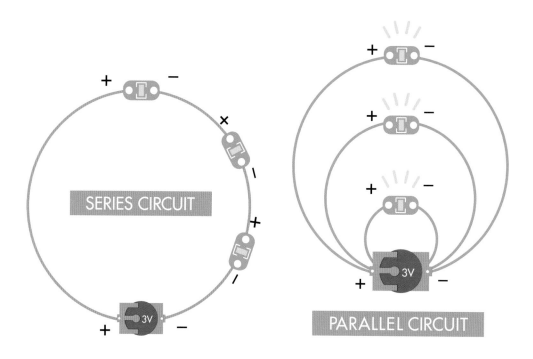

The key difference between the two types of circuits concerns *electron flow*. In a series circuit, there is only one pathway for energy to travel from the battery: As energy passes from the battery to the first LED, energy is used up, so less energy is available to the next LED in the circuit, and then the next gets even less, and so on. On the other hand, in a parallel circuit, energy is able to travel directly from the battery to each individual LED, allowing each to receive the same amount of energy.

This example of parallel versus series circuits can highlight for youths the important role that structure plays in the ways that systems function. A simple change in how a circuit is set up can mean the difference between lighting all the LEDs or only some.

STOCKS, FLOWS, AND LIMITED RESOURCES

Another set of ideas concerns the "stuff" of systems and how it moves across a system. The stuff of systems is called *stocks.* Stocks are an accumulated amount of something within a system (money in a bank account, fish in a pond, trees in a forest, jobs in an economy, and so on). A stock is always a *noun,* and it can accumulate or decrease. In circuitry, the amount of energy in a battery is a stock.

Flow is the rate at which a stock changes. Money comes in and out of a bank account due to wages paid, interest, and purchases. Fish come in and out of a pond due to birth rates, death rates, and fishing rates. A flow is always a *verb*, and it describes the rates of actions that influence stocks in a system. Flows describe "movement" within a system. In circuits, the rate at which a battery's energy is depleted when attached to an LED is a flow.

Understanding how the stocks and flows of a system operate is important due to a basic truth about systems: the concept of *limited resources.* In any system, the resources (stocks) are finite, meaning that at a certain point, they will run out. Many decisions about how to design and intervene in a system are based on trying to make the best use of that system's limited resources. Returning to the example of circuits, in an electronic circuit that involves a battery, the battery contains only a limited amount of energy, so when we design circuits (or any system, in fact), we must be aware of how the stock/flow dynamics work so that those limited resources aren't wasted.

LEVERAGE POINTS: INTERVENING AND CHANGING SYSTEMS

Understanding how systems work is all well and good, but if that insight isn't used to actually do something in the world, then it's just an academic exercise. Our vision of teaching systems thinking is rooted in the idea that young people eventually will become designers of new systems and redesigners of the systems that they inherit from us, and so some of the core ideas that we focus on are those related to how to change and intervene in systems.

When we think about changing systems, we think about *leverage points*. What makes a leverage point unique and powerful is that it's a place within a system where "a small change in one thing can produce big changes in everything," as activist and systems theorist Donella Meadows says. In a now-foundational book in the systems thinking world called *Leverage Points: Places to Intervene in a System* (1999), Meadows outlines different ways we can think about possible leverage points that range from less effective (e.g., changing the amount of "stuff" associated with certain parts of a system or changes to the structures that handle the movement of this "stuff") to more effective (e.g., changing the rules that govern a system, or better yet, the mindset that leads to things like rules, goals, and structure). While we won't go through all of the leverage points that Meadows outlined, we want to stress that focusing on leverage points isn't like generating any old solution to a problem; they are designed not only so you can remember the structures of a system, but also take advantage of these structures so that a little change can go a long way.

In a wonderful example of leverage points at work, Meadows shares the story of the Toxic Release Inventory, which required every factory that released air pollutants to document and report data on these pollutants publicly. When the inventory was instituted in 1986 by the US government, toxic emissions were reduced dramatically. The inventory didn't levy fines or make the process of releasing these chemicals into the air illegal—it simply made the information public. By 1990, toxic emissions in the United States dropped by 40 percent. Factory owners did not want to be known publicly as polluters, so they changed their practices. The availability of information to different stakeholders within a system (in this case, citizens) changed the way that this system operated. The Toxic Release Inventory targeted a leverage point: It didn't aim to remake the whole system to prevent pollution; rather, it just added one small part that wasn't there before. It was a minor change, but it had a big effect.

In the world of electronics and circuitry, we might think about a change to the structure of a system—as we mentioned earlier about parallel versus series circuits—as a leverage point. Nothing is being added or taken away from the system, but through a simple rewiring, the whole system functions differently and is more able to meet its goals.

One type of leverage point that comes up regularly when working with circuits is a *balancing feedback loop.* Balancing feedback loops are processes put in place to help move a system toward its goals or keep it at a desired state of equilibrium. Usually, balancing feedback loops stabilize systems by limiting or preventing certain processes from happening. Think about the way home heating systems work. A thermostat detects when the temperature drops below a preset level and reacts by turning on the heat. It continues to monitor the temperature, and once it reaches the preset level again, it turns off the heat. Eventually heat escapes (maybe because the temperature outside drops), and the process starts over. This is a good illustration of a balancing feedback loop, with the thermostat acting as the balancing mechanism.

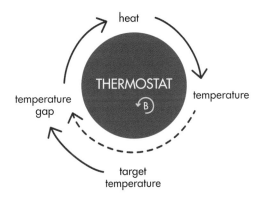

Balancing loops are sometimes harder to notice because, well, they're everywhere. Most systems contain many balancing feedback loops in order to continue functioning. Coolant in a car engine serves a "balancing" function by preventing the engine from overheating. Bathtubs have drains, which create balancing loops that prevent the tub from overflowing. Families who find themselves with a bunch of knickknacks hold yard sales (or these days, maybe they sell things on the Internet) to create more space. A human's or animal's body gets low on energy, so it sends hunger signals to the brain, which prompts eating to satisfy hunger (and keep nutrients and energy coming into the body) so that it can continue to function. In general, balancing feedback loops aim to keep or move a system toward some state of equilibrium that allows it to continue to meet its goals.

But people often try to create new balancing loops after things have gone very, very wrong. Think about bank runs—people fear that their money isn't safe in a bank, which causes them to remove the money they have. This weakens the bank because it has less capital to operate with and is less able to do things like make loans that keep it solvent. Other customers see this weakness, fear for their money, go and withdraw it, and start the whole cycle again until the bank collapses. This cycle is an example of a different type of dynamic: a *reinforcing feedback loop,* one that gets out of control and can derail a system from meeting its goal. We don't have bank runs in the United States these days because after the Great Depression (when they were common) the government created the Federal Deposit Insurance Corporation (FDIC), a balancing mechanism. If a bank is a member of the FDIC, all deposits are insured by the government for up to $250,000. This check on the system eliminates the possibility of bank runs because people don't need to fear that their money will be lost (so long as people have faith in the government's financial standing, anyway!). The presence of the FDIC created a balancing feedback loop, preventing the runaway situation of bank runs.

In the world of circuitry, balancing loops are also ubiquitous. The most common way that they're used as a leverage point in a system is through the inclusion of *switches*. Think about the way that a simple circuit (consisting of a battery, wires, and an LED) operates. If everything is connected, the light is always on, meaning that the very finite amount of energy in the battery will be depleted continuously—even when we don't need it. Enter the switch. The switch acts as a balancing mechanism to regulate when the light is on and when it's off. This allows the system to meet its goals in two ways: First, we can control when the light is on and when it's off (as with most lights, the goal is not to *always* have a light on). Second, the scarce energy resources in the system are conserved so that the system can better meet the goal of functioning and providing light when needed.

We find an even more powerful example of a balancing mechanism when we consider solar-powered cells (see Design Challenge 4 in our companion book, *Soft Circuits*). In contrast to a regular battery, which will eventually run out of energy and then fail to power an electrical system, a solar cell battery can be charged continuously by the Sun's energy. Using a solar cell creates a balancing loop that keeps an electrical system at its desired state: having power to function.

HANDLE WITH CARE: FIXES THAT FAIL AND UNINTENDED CONSEQUENCES

Part of the challenge of making a change in a system is that systems are complex, and we often don't know how they'll respond when we introduce new factors into them. Often, people try to go for simple solutions to problems not amenable to easy fixes and play into one of the common challenges associated with trying to change systems: inadvertently creating *fixes that fail*.

We're unfortunately all too familiar with these "solutions." Someone tries to pay off credit card interest by opening up a new credit card, only to find himself or herself with more interest to pay. A company tries to save money by cutting down on maintenance costs, but the machine malfunctions that result lead to more costs than they would have had in the first place. Traffic jams lead people to demand more roads, but when these new roads are built, they create more incentives to use cars instead of public transportation, and so congestion stays the same or even increases. Most of these involve a mode of thinking that's both short term (in terms of the time scale it envisions) and narrow (in terms of how it frames the problem).

Related to fixes that fail are *unintended consequences,* where one problem might be fixed, but it causes something else to happen in another part of a system that no one planned or even guessed would happen. For instance, in an effort to control cane field pests in Australia, cane toads were introduced, but not only did they fail to fix the pest problem, they became a serious problem in and of themselves. In another instance of unintended consequences Down Under, a law making bicycle helmets mandatory resulted in fewer young people cycling overall because they found it unfashionable, with counterproductive effects for the overall net health of that demographic. In international politics, counterterrorism analysts note the phenomenon of "blowback," where covert military operations meant to fight terrorism result in increased terrorist activity. One infamous instance of this, of course, was the covert US funding of the mujahideen forces that fought the Russian occupation of Afghanistan in the 1980s. The funding of the mujahideen eventually led to the rise of the Al Qaeda terrorist network, which was responsible for the September 11, 2001, attacks on the World Trade Center and the Pentagon, among other catastrophic attacks all over the world.

The ideas of leverage points and balancing loops can empower us to think about ways that we can make big changes, while the concepts of fixes that fail and unintended consequences point to how careful we need to be when we try to intervene in systems. Ideally, a systems thinker keeps both sides of this coin in mind, understanding how important it is to be deliberate and conscientious when interacting with systems, but not shying away from acting within them when intervention is needed.

Appendix A

GLOSSARY OF KEY TERMS

SYSTEMS THINKING

Identifying a system.   Identifying a system and distinguishing it from other kinds of things that aren't systems. Specifically, a system is a collection of two or more *components* and processes that *interconnect* to *function* as a whole. Speed and comfort in a car for example are created by the interactions of the car's parts and thus are "greater than the sum" of all separate parts of the car. The way a system works is not the result of a single part but is produced by the *interaction* among the components and/or individual agents within it. A key way to differentiate things that are systems from things that aren't is to consider whether the overall way something works in the world will change if you remove one part of it.

Identify the way a system is functioning.   The function of a system describes the overall behavior of the system—what it is doing or where it's going over time. A system's function might emerge naturally based on interconnections among components, or it might be the result of an intentional design (in which case, we might also call refer to the function of a system as its goal). Regardless, the function of a system is the result of the dynamics that occur among components' interconnected behaviors.

Distinguishing the goal of a system.   The goal of the system is what a system that was intentionally designed is intended to do. Sometimes this might be the same as the *functioning* of the system ... other times the goal and the *function* are not aligned.

A given system might have multiple goals or purposes that are at play simultaneously, and come into conflict. Being able to understand a system's purpose or goal gives a sense of the ideal state of a system from a particular perspective.

Identifying components.   Components are the parts of a system that contribute to its functioning. *Components* have certain qualities and/or *behaviors* that determine how they *interconnect* with other components, as well as define their role in the system. Without being able to effectively identify the parts of a system, it's hard to understand how a system is actually *functioning* and how it might be changed.

Identifying behaviors.   Behaviors are the specific actions or roles that a component of a system displays under various conditions. Being able to identify behaviors becomes important when we change systems, as often a component will look the same after the change, but its behavior will be different.

Identifying interconnections.   Interconnections are the different ways that a system's parts, or *components,* interact with each other through their *behaviors,* and through those interactions, change the behaviors of other components.

Considering the role of system structure.   Understanding how a system's *components* are set up in relation to one another gives insight into the *behavior* of a component. A system's structure affects the behaviors of its components and the overall *dynamics* and *functioning* of a system. For instance, how a city's highway system is structured affects overall traffic patterns and car movement within it. Being able to see a system's structure gives insights into the mechanisms and relationships that are at the core of a system, which can be leveraged to create systemic changes.

Make systems visible.   When we learn to "make the system visible"—whether modeling a system on the back of a napkin, through a computer simulation, a game, a picture, a diagram, a set of mathematical computations, or a story—we can use these representations to communicate about how things work. At their best, good pictures of systems help both the creator and the "reader" or "audience" to understand not only the parts of the system (the components), but also, how those components work together to produce a whole.

Balancing feedback loops.   Feedback loops are circular, cause-and-effect processes that create stability by counteracting or dampening change. These processes keep a system at the desired state of equilibrium, the system goal. Usually, balancing feedback processes stabilize systems by limiting or preventing certain processes from happening.

Having a sense of how balancing feedback loops operate can give a person a sense of what will make a system stable.

Stocks & flows.   Stocks are an accumulated amount of something within a system (like money in a bank account, fish in a pond, trees in a forest, or jobs in an economy), and flows are the rate at which stocks in a system change either through increasing or decreasing (money comes in and out of a bank account due to wages paid, interest, and purchases. Fish come in and out of a pond due to birth rates, death rates, and fishing rates, etc.). Stocks are always nouns; they're the "stuff" of systems, while flows are always verbs; they're the "movement" of systems. Understanding stocks and flows gives someone an angle into how different parts of the system change over time.

Limited resources.   In any system, it is important to understand which resources are finite, ones that run out at a certain point. Keeping in mind which resources are limited helps people make decisions about how best to maximize resources.

Nested systems.   Systems that are a smaller part of other systems. Almost all systems are nested within larger systems. With nested systems, a larger system will affect the way that a subsystem behaves, and the subsystem will affect the way that the larger system behaves. Having a sense of nested systems helps people keep an eye on how systems interconnect and are always part of bigger pictures.

Dynamic equilibrium.   A state in which stocks and flows are balanced so the system is not varying widely, but still has internal dynamic processes that are continually in flux even though the system is stable overall. For example: in economics dynamic equilibrium might be used to talk about the constant flux of money movement in otherwise stable markets; in ecology, a population of organisms stabilizes when birth rate and death rate are in balance.

Designing a system.   Creating a system through engaging in an iterative design process, one that entails cycles of feedback, troubleshooting, and testing. One of the most effective means of developing systems thinking is to regularly create and iterate on the design of systems.

Leverage points.   Particular places within a system where a small shift in one thing can produce big changes in everything. Leverage points are difficult to find because they often lie far away from either the problem or its obvious solution. It is because of the multitude of cause-and-effect relationships, feedback loops, and system structures that a seemingly small change can be amplified, often in unexpected ways. Not every place in a system is a leverage point—sometimes changing one thing in a system creates only small effects that aren't felt throughout the system.

CIRCUITRY

Amp. A unit of measure of the number of electrons flowing through a wire (thread) per unit of time.

Battery. An energy source that converts chemical energy into electrical energy.

Conductivity. The degree to which a material transmits electricity. Conductivity is inversely related to resistance.

Conductor. A material through which electric current flows easily.

Current. A flow of electric charge through a medium; e.g., wire, conductive fabric, or a light-emitting diode (LED).

Current flow/flow. The rate at which an electric charge passes through a point in the circuit.

Debug. The iterative process of identifying and removing errors from hardware or software designs.

e-Textiles. Everyday textiles and clothes that have electric components embedded in them; also known as *electric textiles* or *smart textiles.*

Electronic circuit/circuit. An unbroken path capable of carrying an electric current (i.e., a *loop*). Typically, an electric circuit contains a source of power (e.g., a battery).

Lead. A wire that conveys electric current from a source to a component in the system, or that connects two points of a circuit.

Load. A device (like a lightbulb or motor) that requires electric current passing through it to give it power.

Multimeter. A handheld device with a negative and a positive probe, which is designed to measure electric current, voltage, and resistance to help determine whether a material or artifact is conductive or not.

Parallel circuit. When components are wired in parallel within a circuit, the electric current divides into two or more paths before recombining to complete the circuit. The current flows through three LEDs wired in parallel, and the electric current is split equally among the three of them. **Note:** The evenness of the split is contingent on the three LEDs being the same type and/or color.

Resistance. A measure of how difficult it is to "push" current through a circuit. A *resistor* is a component in a circuit that limits, but doesn't stop, the flow of electric current.

Series circuit. When components are wired in series within a circuit, electric current flows sequentially through those components in a continuous loop. This means that as the current travels from the battery through each LED, it loses some of its original electrical charge or energy (also known as *voltage*) such that the amount of voltage available for each subsequent LED decreases with each one it passes through.

Short circuit (or "short"). A low-resistance connection between the two sides of the battery that causes the energy of a battery to drain or terminate completely.

Solar panel. A thin, semiconductor wafer specially treated to form an electric field when struck by light (with a positive charge on one side and a negative one on the other). When activated, electrons are knocked loose from the atoms in the material. If conductors are attached to the positive and negative sides, forming a closed circuit, the electrons can be captured in the form of electric current.

Switch. A component that controls the flow of current by opening and closing a circuit.

Volt. A unit of measure of the amount of voltage in a circuit.

Voltage. *Voltage* is the force that causes electric current to flow through a circuit. Increasing the voltage in a circuit without changing the resistance increases the current that flows through the circuit.

MODKIT AND LILYPAD

Block. A puzzle-piece shape that is used to create code and programs in Modkit. Blocks connect to each other like a jigsaw puzzle, preventing common syntax errors.

In Modkit, there are six categories of blocks: Setup, Output, Input, Operators, Control, and Variables.

Code. Language that describes the instructions or program used in software; in the examples in this book, code is created in Modkit to tell the LilyPad Simple how to behave.

Microcontroller. A small computer on a circuit board, containing a processor core and memory, which can be programmed for various types of hardware like LEDs, speakers, and other devices like temperature and light sensors. One example of a microcontroller is the LilyPad Simple.

Petal. A silver shape that lines the outside of the LilyPad Arduino and other LilyPad components. Each petal can be programmed independently within Modkit to send signals to a particular input or output device, like an LED. (Also called *pins* in Modkit.)

Programming. The act or process of writing sequences of instructions that are designed to be executed by a computer.

Script. An automated series of instructions carried out in a specific order, created in Modkit Micro and carried out by the LilyPad Simple.

STORYTELLING

Character. A real or imaginary person represented in a story.

Character trait. A distinguishing feature or specific quality of a character that influences a character's actions.

Context. The circumstances in which an event occurs; a setting.

Narrative. An often-chronological sequence of real or fictitious events in a story, consisting of a context (or setting), a narrator, characters, or both; and an event sequence that has a beginning, middle, and end and includes a conflict and resolution.

Narrative conflict. Inherent incompatibility or tension between the goals of two or more characters or forces.

Narrator. A person who tells a story or gives an account of something.

Plot. The main events of a story, rendered by the writer as an interrelated sequence.

Resolution. A literary term; the goal of a narrative/story.

Script. A map or outline that a director or artist uses to create a movie, play, comic book, television show (or in the examples in this book, a shadow puppet show).

Shadow play. A theatrical entertainment using silhouettes thrown by puppets or actors onto a lighted screen.

Shadow puppet. A cut-out figure or object held between a source of light and a translucent screen.

Storyboard. A panel of sketches that depict a sequence of action. Storyboards contain frames, and within each frame is a depiction of an important moment in the storyline. Storyboards often are used to plan out the sequence and composition of a movie, video, or animated film.

Appendix B

ADDITIONAL RESOURCES

Here is a selection of videos, links to other resources, and inspirations that you might use in your classroom to help students better understand electric circuits. You also can search online for other similar resources using key terms such as "electric circuits," "electricity," "power source," "switch," "conductivity," "load," "batteries," and "current."

DESIGN CHALLENGE 1

ADDITIONAL INSPIRATION

BRAINPOP: ELECTRIC CIRCUITS AS AN INTRODUCTION

Electrical circuits are mighty important—but how do they work? Includes components of a circuit.

   www.brainpop.com/science/energy/electriccircuits

Video: 3 minutes, 45 seconds
Requires subscription, or sign up for a five-day free trial

BRAINPOP: BATTERIES

They power everything from flashlights to submarines, but how do batteries work?

www.brainpop.com/science/energy/batteries

Video: 2 minutes, 24 seconds
Requires subscription, or sign up for a five-day free trial

BRAINPOP: ELECTRICITY

Light up my life! General information about electricity.

www.brainpop.com/science/energy/electricity

Video: 2 minutes, 24 seconds
Requires subscription, or sign up for a five-day free trial

BILL NYE THE SCIENCE GUY: ELECTRIC CIRCUITS

Electricity might seem mysterious, but once you understand the science, the light goes on (so to speak).

www.youtube.com/watch?v=rg-XFXdtZnQ

Video: 23 minutes

EXPLORING CONDUCTIVITY: KID CIRCUITS

Video from PBS Kids *ZOOM*. Youths become conductors for a broken circuit by holding hands and using a lemon battery.

www.teachersdomain.org/resource/phy03.sci.phys.mfe.zcircuit

Video: 3 minutes, 23 seconds

DESIGNING ELECTRIC CIRCUITS: DOOR ALARM

Video from PBS Kids *ZOOM*. Youths use electrical circuits to create door alarms out of a variety of materials.

www.teachersdomain.org/resource/phy03.sci.phys.mfw.zalarm

Video: 3 minutes, 47 seconds

ENERGY QUEST: CHAPTER ON CIRCUITS

Energy Quest is the energy education website of the California Energy Commission. It is very thorough and informative.

www.energyquest.ca.gov/story/chapter04.html

Energy Story website, Chapter 4

HOW STUFF WORKS: HOW BATTERIES WORK

A text-based resource with information on how a battery works to create an electro-chemical charge.

www.howstuffworks.com/battery.htm

Website essay

DESIGN CHALLENGE 2

REFERENCES

WARM/COOL FEEDBACK

nsrfharmony.org

The information on this topic found in Design Challenge 2 was derived from the essay "Tuning Protocol," by Joseph McDonald and David Allen, found at the National School Reform Faculty website (see link above).

ADDITIONAL INSPIRATION

THUMB FU!

Thumb wrestling with puppets wired for sound and lights!
Video: 1 minute, 26 seconds

vimeo.com/12271372

MY FIRST LOOPIN

An educational textile electronics toy developed by ZippyKit. It Includes everything you need to build your own "Loopin."
Video: 8 minutes, 32 seconds

www.youtube.com/watch?v=dwBjzdBimW0

FASHIONINGTECH: SOFT CIRCUIT KIT

Salt 'n' Peanut are a mother and baby elephant duo that love to be in constant contact. When the trunk of Salt (the mother elephant) and the trunk of Peanut (the baby elephant) connect, the LED in Peanut's chest illuminates, signifying love and joy. (Available at Maker Faires)

soft-circuit.com/tutorials/peanut

DESIGN CHALLENGE 3

INSTRUCTIONAL RESOURCES

LEDS FOR BEGINNERS

This instructable website shows in a basic and clear way how to wire up one or more LEDs.
(Note that these resources feature resistors, which are not needed for the project presented in this challenge.)

- Step 7: Wiring up multiple LEDs in series.

    instructables.com/id/LEDs-for-Beginners/step7/Wiring-up-multiple
    -LEDs-in-series/

- Step 8: Wiring up multiple LEDs in parallel.

    instructables.com/id/LEDs-for-Beginners/step8/Wiring-up-multiple
    -LEDs-in-parallel/

ADDITIONAL INSPIRATION

COLOR ADDITION: THE PHYSICS CLASSROOM

www.physicsclassroom.com/class/light/u12l2d.cfm

Learn about how colors can be added to create new colors, in Lesson 2 of the "Light Waves and Color" Chapter of The Physics Classroom.

DESIGN CHALLENGE 4

REFERENCES

We recommend reviewing *Script Frenzy* workbooks and lesson plans for ideas. (The site is no longer supported, but the books are still available.)

- Workbooks: **ywp.scriptfrenzy.org/workbooks**
- Lesson plans: **ywp.scriptfrenzy.org/lesson-plans**

Adapted from *Readers Theater: Stories on Stage* ("Appendix: From Story to Script"), by Aaron Shepard

- Found at: **aaronshep.com/rt/books/StoriesOS_old.html**

GENERAL DIY ELECTRONICS RESOURCES

ANIOMAGIC.COM

Aniomagic kits and pieces. Aniomagic is a commercial company that sells e-textile kits that are unique in themselves but are somewhat similar to the LilyPad Arduino materials. Kits and parts are available through the Aniomagic website as well as SparkFun.com.

MAKERSHED.COM

Kits and books. MakerShed is the commercial arm for MakerMedia and offers an array of kits and books that they have self-published in the areas of robotics, crafts, and related areas.

CRAFTZINE.COM

Daily source of craft projects and inspiration

SHORT CIRCUITS FORMAL ASSESSMENT

Name: _____   Date: _____

You will need to reference the following components to answer some of these questions.

3V battery in holder   Switch   LED   9V battery in holder

1. Use one 3V battery in a battery holder, one switch, and one LED to draw a *working circuit*. **Note:** Draw the components that you see above, or write their names in a box within your circuits—whatever method is easiest for you. Don't forget to draw the connections between the components and mark the positive and negative ends!

2. Use one 9V battery in a battery holder, one switch, and three LEDs to draw a *series circuit*. **Note:** Draw the components you see above, or write their names in a box within your circuits—whatever method is easiest for you. Don't forget to draw the connections between the components and mark the positive and negative ends!

3. Use one 3V battery in a battery holder, one switch, and three LEDs to draw a *parallel circuit*. **Note:** Draw the components you see above, or write their names in a box within your circuits—whatever method is easiest for you. Don't forget to draw the connections between the components and mark the positive and negative ends!

4. Use one 9V battery in a battery holder, one switch, and two LEDs to make a *broken circuit* (i.e., one that will not work.) **Note:** Draw the components you see above, or write their names in a box within your circuits—whatever method is easiest for you. Don't forget to draw the connections between the components and mark the positive and negative ends!

5. What is the relationship between the following three things? You can explain your answer in words or pictures.

    (a) studying, (b) grades, and (c) interest in the subject matter

Based on your answer, what do you think would happen to your studying effort and grades if your interest in the subject matter went *down*?

6. *David has not been doing well in school this year, and many of the students in David's class make fun of him. This makes David act out, often getting into fights. As a result, he has gotten suspended several times. Being suspended keeps him out of class and causes his grades to drop even further.*

What is the best way for David to improve his grades? (Circle one choice.)

(a) Get David a tutor.

(b) Tell the other students to stop teasing David.

(c) Continue to punish David.

(d) Do nothing. The situation will eventually clear up on its own.

Why do you think your answer will work?

7. What is the relationship between the amount of grass that is growing in a field, the number of rabbits that live in the area (rabbits eat grass), and the number of wolves in the area (wolves eat rabbits)? Explain your answer in either words or pictures.

If someone decided to kill all the wolves, what would happen to the rabbits and the grass?

8. *There's a rumor spreading around school that Jamie has a crush on Frankie. Jamie is very upset about this. Jamie's friend told her not to worry because by tomorrow, everyone will be talking about something else. She explained that rumors spread quickly because they're interesting and because it's fun to tell "secrets." However, once everyone knows, rumors just aren't interesting anymore because they're no longer secret.*

How does this explain why Jamie shouldn't worry?

SYSTEMS THINKING CONCEPT CARDS: SHORT CIRCUITS

The following cards have been included for you to use any way that works well in your setting, such as printing a set for each youth, creating a classroom deck to store in a resource center, or even using them as game cards for a whole-group games or activities (like *Jeopardy!*, *Flyswatter*, *Baseball*, *and so on*).

SYSTEMS THINKING CONCEPT CARDS: SHORT CIRCUITS

01.

IDENTIFYING A SYSTEM

Identifying a system and distinguishing it from other kinds of things that aren't systems. Specifically, a system is a collection of two or more components and processes that interconnect to function as a whole. Speed and comfort in a car for example are created by the interactions of the car's parts and thus are "greater than the sum" of all separate parts of the car. The way a system works is not the result of a single part but is produced by the interaction among the components and/or individual agents within it. A key way to differentiate things that are systems from things that aren't is to consider whether the overall way something works in the world will change if you remove one part of it.

SYSTEMS THINKING CONCEPT CARDS: SHORT CIRCUITS

02.

IDENTIFY THE WAY A
SYSTEM IS FUNCTIONING

The function of a system describes the overall behavior of the system—what it is doing or where it's going over time. A system's function might emerge naturally based on interconnections among components, or it might be the result of an intentional design (in which case, we might also refer to the function of a system as its goal). Regardless, the function of a system is the result of the dynamics that occur among components' interconnected behaviors.

SYSTEMS THINKING CONCEPT CARDS: SHORT CIRCUITS

03.

DISTINGUISHING THE GOAL
OF A SYSTEM

The goal of the system is what a system that was intentionally designed is intended to do. Sometimes this might be the same as the functioning of the system... other times the goal and the function are not aligned. A given system might have multiple goals or purposes that are at play simultaneously, and come into conflict. Being able to understand system purpose or goal gives a sense of the ideal state of a system from a particular perspective.

SYSTEMS THINKING CONCEPT CARDS: SHORT CIRCUITS

04.

IDENTIFYING COMPONENTS

Identifying the parts of a system that contribute to its functioning. Components have certain qualities and/or behaviors that determine how they interconnect with other components, as well as define their role in the system. Without being able to effectively identify the parts of a system, it's hard to understand how a system is actually functioning and how it might be changed.

SYSTEMS THINKING CONCEPT CARDS: SHORT CIRCUITS

05.

IDENTIFYING BEHAVIORS

Identifying the specific actions, roles, or behaviors that a component of a system displays under various conditions. Being able to identify behaviors becomes important when we change systems, as often a component will look the same after the change, but its behavior will be different.

SYSTEMS THINKING CONCEPT CARDS:
SHORT CIRCUITS

06.
IDENTIFYING INTERCONNECTIONS

Identifying the different ways that a system's parts, or components, interact with each other through their behaviors, and through those interactions, change the behaviors of other components.

SYSTEMS THINKING CONCEPT CARDS:
SHORT CIRCUITS

07.
PERCEIVING DYNAMICS

Perceiving a system's dynamics involves looking at a higher level at how the system works. Dynamics in a system are often characterized by circles – patterns that feed back on another. These are called feedback loops. Understanding dynamics gives insights into the mechanisms and relationships that are at the core of a system and can be leveraged to create systemic changes.

SYSTEMS THINKING CONCEPT CARDS:
SHORT CIRCUITS

08.
CONSIDERING THE ROLE OF
SYSTEM STRUCTURE

Understanding how a system's components are set up in relation to one another gives insight into the behavior of a component. A system's structure affects the behaviors of its components and the overall dynamics and functioning of a system. For instance, how a city's highway system is structured affects overall traffic patterns and car movement within it. Being able to see a system's structure gives insights into the mechanisms and relationships that are at the core of a system, which can be leveraged to create systemic changes.

SYSTEMS THINKING CONCEPT CARDS:
SHORT CIRCUITS

09.
MAKE SYSTEMS VISIBLE

When we learn to "make the system visible" – whether modeling a system on the back of a napkin, through a computer simulation, a game, a picture, a diagram, a set of mathematical computations, or a story–we can use these representations to communicate about how things work. At their best, good pictures of systems help both the creator and the "reader" or "audience" to understand not only the parts of the system (the components), but also, how those components work together to produce a whole.

SYSTEMS THINKING CONCEPT CARDS:
SHORT CIRCUITS

10.
SYSTEMS DIAGRAM

Is a diagram used to visualize the dynamics that occur between components in a system, intended to capture how the variables interrelate. One way of diagramming a feedback loop uses an "R" with a clockwise arrow around it to indicate a reinforcing feedback loop. A "B" with a counterclockwise arrow around it would indicate a balancing feedback loop, which "counters" something in a system. The plus sign indicates an increase in that amount of a component in a system, and a minus sign indicates a decrease in the amount of a component in a system. There are other ways to create systems diagrams, but the most important thing about a good systems diagram is that it not only shows the components in a system, but is able to show the relationships between the components through the arrows, symbols, and text.

SYSTEMS THINKING CONCEPT CARDS:
SHORT CIRCUITS

11.
FEEDBACK LOOPS

Are relationships between two or more components of a system, where actions by these components interact in a circular fashion – something that component A does effects component B, which then circles back and effects component A. There are two types of feedback loops, Balancing and Reinforcing.

SYSTEMS THINKING CONCEPT CARDS: SHORT CIRCUITS

12.

REINFORCING FEEDBACK LOOPS

Relationships where two or more components of a system cause each other to increase, such as in escalation cycles, or decrease, such in resource drain cycles, in a way that's "out of control" or creates a "snowball effect". Reinforcing loops encourage a system to reproduce certain behaviors, though these behaviors always "exhaust" themselves after the resources fueling the growth or diminishment run out. This is also called "limits to growth". There are two types of reinforcing feedback loops: "vicious" cycles and "virtuous" cycles.

SYSTEMS THINKING CONCEPT CARDS: SHORT CIRCUITS

13.

VICIOUS CYCLES

Reinforcing feedback loops that cause a negative outcome in terms of the perceived goal of the system. One thing to keep in mind is that the same thing might be a vicious cycle to one person, but a virtuous cycle for another person who has different goals.

SYSTEMS THINKING CONCEPT CARDS: SHORT CIRCUITS

14.

VIRTUOUS CYCLES

Reinforcing feedback loops that cause a positive outcome in terms the perceived goal of the system. One thing to keep in mind is that the same thing might be a virtuous cycle to one person, but a vicious cycle for another person who has different goals.

SYSTEMS THINKING CONCEPT CARDS: SHORT CIRCUITS

15.

BALANCING FEEDBACK LOOPS

Relationships where two or more elements of a system keep each other in balance, with one (or more) elements leading to increase, and one (or more) elements leading to decrease. These processes keep a system at the desired state of equilibrium, the system goal. Usually, balancing feedback processes stabilize systems by limiting or preventing certain processes from happening. Having a sense of how balancing feedback loops operate can give a person a sense of what will make a system stable.

SYSTEMS THINKING CONCEPT CARDS: SHORT CIRCUITS

16.

STOCKS & FLOWS

Stocks are an accumulated amount of something within a system (like money in a bank account, fish in a pond, trees in a forest, or jobs in an economy), and flows are the rate at which stocks in a system change either through increasing or decreasing (money comes in and out of a bank account due to wages paid, interest, and purchases. Fish come in and out of a pond due to birth rates, death rates, and fishing rates, etc.). Stocks are always nouns; they're the "stuff" of systems, while flows are always verbs; they're the "movement" of systems. Understanding Stocks and Flows gives someone an insight into how different parts of the system change over time.

SYSTEMS THINKING CONCEPT CARDS: SHORT CIRCUITS

17.

LIMITED RESOURCES

In any system, it is important to understand which resources are finite, ones that will run out at a certain point. Keeping in mind which resources are limited helps people make decisions about how best to maximize resources.

SYSTEMS THINKING CONCEPT CARDS:
SHORT CIRCUITS

18.
NESTED SYSTEMS

Systems that are a smaller part of other systems. Almost all systems are nested within larger systems. With nested systems, a larger system will affect the way that a subsystem behaves, and the subsystem will affect the way that the larger system behaves. Having a sense of nested systems helps people keep an eye on how systems interconnect and are always part of bigger pictures.

SYSTEMS THINKING CONCEPT CARDS:
SHORT CIRCUITS

19.
DYNAMIC EQUILIBRIUM

A state in which stocks and flows are balanced so the system is not varying widely, but still has internal dynamic processes that are continually in flux even though the system is stable overall. For example: in economics dynamic equilibrium might be used to talk about the constant flux of money movement in otherwise stable markets; in ecology, a population of organisms stabilizes when birth rate and death rate are in balance.

SYSTEMS THINKING CONCEPT CARDS:
SHORT CIRCUITS

20.
DESIGNING A SYSTEM

Creating a system through engaging in an iterative design process, one that entails iterative cycles of feedback, troubleshooting and testing. One of the most effective means of developing systems thinking is to regularly create and iterate on the design of systems, and doing so in a way that creates opportunities for students to think about generic systems models that apply across multiple domains and settings.

SYSTEMS THINKING CONCEPT CARDS:
SHORT CIRCUITS

21.
FIXES THAT FAIL

Any kind of solution to a problem that fixes the problem temporarily but fails fix it in the long term, and might even make it worse over time. Fixes that Fail are often put in place quickly, usually without much reflection on what consequences they'll have for the system. They're important to see since they're often the ways that people respond to problems in a system.

SYSTEMS THINKING CONCEPT CARDS:
SHORT CIRCUITS

22.
LEVERAGE POINTS

Particular places within a system where a small shift in one thing can produce big changes in everything. Leverage points are difficult to find because they often lie far away from either the problem or the obvious solution. It is because of the multitude of cause and effect relationships, feedback loops and system structures that a seemingly small change can be amplified, often in unexpected ways. Not every place in a system is a leverage point – sometimes changing one thing in a system will just have small effects that aren't felt throughout the system. Leverage points are important since they let us know where to focus our energies when we try to change systems.

SYSTEMS THINKING CONCEPT CARDS:
SHORT CIRCUITS

23.
UNINTENDED CONSEQUENCES

The unexpected result of an action taken in a system that the actor taking that original action did not want to happen. Unintended Consequences are often the result of fixes that fail or someone aiming to find a leverage point in a system but not considering long-term implications to those actions — someone failed to keep in mind time horizons. Having a good sense of potential unintended consequences means that someone will carefully consider before too hastily intervening in a system.

SYSTEMS THINKING CONCEPT CARDS:
SHORT CIRCUITS

24.

CONSIDERING HOW MENTAL MODELS SHAPE ACTION IN A SYSTEM

The ability to consider the assumptions, ideas, and intentions that a given actor might have in relation to a system, and how these affect that actor's behavior within the system. Mental models are often correct about what components are included in a system, but frequently draw wrong conclusions about a system's overall behavior.

SYSTEMS THINKING CONCEPT CARDS:
SHORT CIRCUITS

25.

LOOKING AT A SYSTEM FROM MULTIPLE PERSPECTIVES

The ability to understand that different actors in a system will have different mental models of the system and consider each of these perspectives when engaging in action within a system. This is also called "thinking across the table."

SYSTEMS THINKING CONCEPT CARDS:
SHORT CIRCUITS

26.

CONSIDERING MULTIPLE LEVELS OF PERSPECTIVE

The ability to move fluidly between different levels of perspective within a system, from events, to patterns to system structures, to mental models. The most visible level of systems are events, visible instances of elements interacting in a system. Using the metaphor of a system as an iceberg, events are "above the waterline" – they're easy to see. When we start to think "below the waterline," we start to see three other levels of perspective: patterns (recurring sets of events), structures (ways the elements are set up in a system which give rise to regular patterns), and mental models (which shape systems structures). Switching between different levels of perspective when looking at a system deepens understanding of how a system operates.

SYSTEMS THINKING CONCEPT CARDS:
SHORT CIRCUITS

27.

TIME DELAYS

Are the time lag between an action in a system and the evidence of its effects. For example, there's a long delay between the point when you plant a seed in the ground and the appearance of a fruit-bearing tree.

SYSTEMS THINKING CONCEPT CARDS:
SHORT CIRCUITS

28.

TIME HORIZONS

Are the overall period of time that you look at something in order to understand it. For example, if we only look a complex system like an economy for a short period of time, we might misunderstand how it's behaving and miss the effects of actions taken far into the past.

SYSTEMS THINKING CONCEPT CARDS: SHORT CIRCUITS

UNDERSTANDING SYSTEMS:
DIGITAL DESIGN FOR A COMPLEX WORLD

SHORT CIRCUITS CHALLENGE CARDS

Short Circuits challenge cards offer a series of jumping–off points for the creation of projects using micro-electronics and found materials. The cards in this deck allow budding designers of all levels to combine circuitry and physical materials to create many different kinds of open-ended projects. Challenges are rated from easy to hardcore and come with some hints to help get things started. All can be modified to include alternative materials so let your imagination run wild!

LEVELS

- ● EASY
- ✦ MEDIUM
- ✿ HARD
- ❋ HARDCORE

WHERE TO GO FOR MATERIALS

Radio Shack
radioshack.com

SparkFun
sparkfun.com

Jameco
jameco.com

Adafruit LED tutorial:
http://tinyurl.com/7ssqzgv

Lessons in Electric Circuits:
http://tinyurl.com/3bvvjs

SHORT CIRCUITS CHALLENGE CARDS

OVERVIEW

This deck contains 5 different categories of challenges from which to pick:

CATEGORIES

MINI-CHALLENGES
If you're just warming up, or need a bit of a challenge, these activities will get your brain working and test your knowledge of circuits and components.

HACK IT!
Give your old electronics new life by hacking them apart and using the components inside for your own projects!

EXPLORE COMPONENTS
Components are the building blocks of circuits. If you don't understand them, you won't get far! These challenges look more closely at the components you've used in Short Circuits.

SCIENCE (FICTIONAL) DEVICES
Time to use your imagination! The future is here—and you're the engineer. Design the world of tomorrow today!

MICROCONTROLLER CHALLENGES
These activities will use a micro-controller that will allow you to use sensors and switches to create complex circuits with ease! You'll also need a computer to do some programming.

TIPS

SAFETY TIPS

Put your safety goggles on. Cutting metal and plastic can result in small flying bits of material. Soldering irons "spit" sometimes as well.

Never use a sharp tool without someone else around.

Never use a tool you haven't used before, or which you are uncomfortable using. Ask someone for help.

Never use a damaged tool. If a tool is damaged, stop using it and tell an adult. If no adult is present, then mark the tool so you or someone else won't use it later.

Make sure that the path around you is clear when using sharp tools or soldering irons. It is important that people do not bump into you. It's easy to be injured or injure some-one else who isn't paying attention.

SOLDERING TIPS

Never touch the end of the soldering iron. It is about 600 degrees and will burn you!

Hold wires to be heated with tweezers or clamps, not your hands. Wires get hot, too.

Always return the soldering iron to its stand when not in use. Never put it down on your workbench.

Work in a well-ventilated area. Avoid breathing any smoke or fumes by keeping your head to the side of, not above, your work.

Make sure to throw out any solder, wires, or bits of metal in the trashcan. Don't leave it sitting around.

Be sure to wash your hands after solder-ing. Don't even think about putting them near your mouth until you do!

01 PAPERCRAFT/ MINECRAFT

LEVEL

EASY

CATEGORY

MINI-CHALLENGES

Bedazzle a paper-foldable with lights!

EXPLANATION

These 3-D foldable toys are fun to make but are often missing the magic of light. Imagine a way to add lights and incorporate a paper switch that makes your papercraft even hotter!

HINTS

Make sure your paper creature can hold your components without breaking. Connect conductive fabric to either side of the paper battery holder; then drop the 3V coin cell inside!

COMPONENTS

LEDS, 3V coin cell battery, white construc-tion paper that can be used in your print-er, tape, Internet, scissors, color or black and white printer, conductive fabric.

SYSTEMS THINKING SPOTLIGHT

component relationships, designing a system

02 POTATO BATTERY

LEVEL

EASY

CATEGORY

MINI-CHALLENGES

Create a working battery out of a potato and a few components.

EXPLANATION

Potato juice contains many water-soluble chemicals that may cause a chemical reaction with one or both of our electrodes.

HINTS

Make sure to use a fresh potato—it needs to be juicy to work well!

COMPONENTS

potato, copper nails, zinc nails, multimeter, alligator clips

SYSTEMS THINKING SPOTLIGHT

component relationships, designing a system, identifying behaviors

03
LEMON BATTERY

LEVEL

EASY

CATEGORY

MINI-CHALLENGES

Create a battery with a real lemon and some everyday components you can find around the house.

EXPLANATION

The two nails work as electrodes connecting the non-metallic parts of the lemon, causing an electro-chemical reaction, which generates a small potential difference or charge.

HINTS

Make sure to use a fresh lemon: it needs to be juicy to work well!

COMPONENTS

lemon, copper nails, zinc nails, plastic coated wire

SYSTEMS THINKING SPOTLIGHT

component relationships, designing a system, identifying behaviors

---

04
LIE DETECTOR

LEVEL

HARDCORE

CATEGORY

MINI-CHALLENGES

Create a working lie detector with a few cheap components!

EXPLANATION

This works by testing your galvanic skin response for sweat or moisture.

HINTS

Be sure to securely attach the contact wires to the foil using hot glue.

COMPONENTS

4.7K resistor, 82K resistor, 0.01uF capacitor, 2N3904 and 2N3906 transistors, 2-AA battery holder, small breadboard, 8 ohm speaker, aluminum foil

SYSTEMS THINKING SPOTLIGHT

component relationships, designing a system, considering a system's purpose or goal

---

05
CONTINUITY TESTER

LEVEL

MEDIUM

CATEGORY

MINI-CHALLENGES

Create a simple continuity tester with a few cheap components and a battery.

EXPLANATION

e-Crafters need a good continuity tester. In this challenge, the circuit tries to pass a small current through the item being tested and the LED will light brightly, dimly, or not at all according to the resistance of the item.

HINTS

Be sure to unclip the battery or attach the leads to cardboard to stop them from touching when not in use — or you'll drain your battery if they accidentally touch!

COMPONENTS

390 ohm resistor, LED, 9V and battery clip, alligator clips, breadboard

SYSTEMS THINKING SPOTLIGHT

component relationships, role of system structure, system dynamics/interconnections

06
CONTACT MIC

LEVEL

MEDIUM

CATEGORY

MINI-CHALLENGES

Create a contact microphone to listen to everyday objects and hear the unexpected!

EXPLANATION

A contact microphone senses audio vibrations through solid objects. It listens to everything you attach it to!

HINTS

Be sure to check connections with a multimeter before taping, hot gluing, or otherwise sealing away your wires.

COMPONENTS

piezo transducer (RadioShack 273-073A), 1/4" audio cable (e.g. RadioShack 42-2381A), tape, solder, soldering iron, hot glue, heat shrink tubing, etc.

SYSTEMS THINKING SPOTLIGHT

component relationships, role of system structure, designing a system

---

07
PENCIL RESISTORS

LEVEL

EASY

CATEGORY

MINI-CHALLENGES

In this experiment you will test if the physical length of a pencil resistor affects the output of a circuit.

EXPLANATION

The graphite properties of a pencil are similar to a resistor. You can vary the length of the pencil and vary the resistance.

HINTS

Be sure to use an electric sharpener on both ends of the pencil. You'll want a nice exposed piece of graphite to connect to the alligator clips.

COMPONENTS

#2 pencils (without erasers or with the eraser ends removed), insulated alligator clip set, 9V battery and clips, small 9V light bulb and holder, ruler, pencil sharpener, Popsicle stick

SYSTEMS THINKING SPOTLIGHT

component relationships, role of system structure, designing a system

---

08
FLASH 555

LEVEL

HARD

CATEGORY

MINI-CHALLENGES

Create a flashing light with an LED, a 555 timer, and a few cheap components.

EXPLANATION

Use the timer to help control the on and off flashing of an LED light.

HINTS

Make sure the 555 chip is facing the right direction. Look at the little notch at one end. That is the top of the chip. Directly to the left of that notch is pin number 1.

COMPONENTS

NE555 Bipolar Timer, LED, 470K resistor, 1K resistor, 1uF capacitor, 9V battery

SYSTEMS THINKING SPOTLIGHT

balancing feedback loop; system dynamics/interconnections, designing a system

09
RE-ANIMATOR 1

LEVEL

EASY

CATEGORY

HACK IT!

Take apart an old game controller in search of its vibration motor.

EXPLANATION

Even if a controller is broken there are plenty of useful parts inside. So open it up and look around.

HINTS

Carefully snip or desolder the wires connected to the circuit board. Be sure not to damage the motor. Use desoldering braid and the iron to help remove soldered joints on the controller. Use one of these controllers: PS1, 2, or 3; Xbox 360; or Wii remote.

COMPONENTS

Controllers, snips, soldering iron, braid

SYSTEMS THINKING SPOTLIGHT

identifying components, identifying behaviors, identifying a system, role of system structure

---

10

RE-ANIMATOR 2

LEVEL

EASY

CATEGORY

HACK IT!

Now that it is free, bring the vibration motor back to life using your imagination, a 3V coin cell battery—and even a switch.

EXPLANATION

These motors don't require a lot of power (they're low voltage). Use anywhere from 3-5 volts to re-animate.

HINTS

Be sure you have the positive and negative leads or wires matched up correctly. The wires are usually red (positive) and black (negative/ground).

COMPONENTS

motor, 3V coin cell battery, momentary switch

SYSTEMS THINKING SPOTLIGHT

designing a system, system dynamics/interconnections, considering a system's purpose or goal

---

11

STEP-BY-STEP 1

LEVEL

MEDIUM

CATEGORY

HACK IT!

Take apart any modern printer and you'll see buttons, LEDs, gears, and stepper motors.

EXPLANATION

Old printers are often discarded, but they have plenty of useful parts left, especially the stepper motors.

HINTS

Every printer is different. Be careful when taking out the motors and gears—you don't want to damage them!

COMPONENTS

Screwdriver, snips, printer

SYSTEMS THINKING SPOTLIGHT

identifying components, identifying behaviors, identifying a system, role of system structure

12
STEP-BY-STEP 2

LEVEL
HARDCORE

CATEGORY
HACK IT!

Make something with a stepper motor

EXPLANATION
The amazing thing about stepper motors is that they can be operated precisely. But you'll need a micro-controller and a few components on a breadboard.

HINTS
This is a complicated electronics project. Experience with Arduino UNO is needed.

COMPONENTS
stepper motor, Arduino, wires, h-bridge, breadboard

SYSTEMS THINKING SPOTLIGHT
designing a system, system dynamics/interconnections, role of system structure

---

13
REMOTER PROMOTER 1

LEVEL
EASY

CATEGORY
HACK IT!

Take apart an old TV remote. Desolder or snip the infrared (IR) LEDs at the top of the remote.

EXPLANATION
TV remotes use infrared light (IR) that we cannot see. Although it's invisible to the eye the light can control the television's volume, channels, etc.

HINTS
Be careful not to damage the LED when removing it. Also, are the positive and negative leads (or wires) labeled on the board? If so, take note!

COMPONENTS
TV remote, snips, screwdriver

SYSTEMS THINKING SPOTLIGHT
identifying components, identifying behaviors, identifying a system, role of system structure

---

14
REMOTER PROMOTER 2

LEVEL
EASY

CATEGORY
HACK IT!

Point your IR LED into your laptop's webcam, draw a picture in the air and watch it come to life!

EXPLANATION
Webcams pick up different frequencies of light than your eyes. So turn on your webcam and bask in the invisible yet visible infrared light.

HINTS
Make sure you have the positive and negative leads on the correct sides of the coin cell battery.

COMPONENTS
IR LED, 3V coin cell battery, webcam

SYSTEMS THINKING SPOTLIGHT
system dynamics/interconnections, role of system structure, considering a system's purpose or goal

15 RAINBOW WIRES

LEVEL

EASY

CATEGORY

HACK IT!

Open up an old computer and cut off the headers of the ribbon wires for free bundled wire.

EXPLANATION

Old computers are full of useful parts. Open one up and see what you can find. There are usually a few strips of bundled ribbon wires. These can be useful for many electronics projects. You can strip off wires a few at a time, if needed.

HINTS

Be careful when opening the computer. There are many sharp edges inside. Make sure the computer is unplugged when you open the case!

COMPONENTS

snips, various screwdrivers, old computer, wire stripper

SYSTEMS THINKING SPOTLIGHT

identifying components

---

16 RECYCLED ART

LEVEL

MEDIUM

CATEGORY

HACK IT!

Take apart any old electronic object and make a new sculpture, piece of jewelry, or a collage from its components.

EXPLANATION

Even if you can't fix a piece of broken electronics, you can appreciate the beauty of some of the components. Take something apart, investigate how it fits together, and then use a few choice old parts to create a new work of art! Use hot glue guns to put your pieces back together into something new.

HINTS

Don't use parts like batteries, which may leak, or glass parts, that may break.

COMPONENTS

Any piece of electronic equipment, but make sure it's something you don't need! Hot glue gun, hot glue, snips, screwdrivers.

SYSTEMS THINKING SPOTLIGHT

modeling a system

---

17 CONDUCTIVITY CHALLENGE

LEVEL

EASY

CATEGORY

EXPLORE COMPONENTS

Using a multimeter and your favorite room, find five conductive surfaces.

EXPLANATION

Multimeters have two leads, and can be placed on a surface to see if it is conductive or a component that will transmit electricity.

HINTS

You will need to put the multimeter in Continuity Mode, and it should beep or light up when you touch both leads to a conductive material.

COMPONENTS

Multimeter, various surfaces and materials

SYSTEMS THINKING SPOTLIGHT

component relationships; system dynamics/interconnections

18
DR. RESEARCH

LEVEL

MEDIUM

CATEGORY

EXPLORE COMPONENTS

Using a variety of coin cell batteries and resistors, light up a multi-colored selection of LEDs.

EXPLANATION

Using an LED, a battery, and a resistor figure out which voltage works best with which LED colors. What about resistors? Can you figure out the resistor names based on the brightness of the LED?

HINTS

Be careful not to use batteries of a high voltage, like 9V, or you may burn out your LED.

COMPONENTS

resistors, LEDs, coin cell batteries (3-5 volts)

SYSTEMS THINKING SPOTLIGHT

component relationships; system dynamics/interconnections, role of system structure

---

19
SCULPTURE WIZARD

LEVEL

HARD

CATEGORY

EXPLORE COMPONENTS

Make an LED sculpture using parallel circuits and an LED calculator, called the "Planning Wizard."

EXPLANATION

Use the Planning Wizard LED calculator to create a sculpture with common electronic components.

HINTS

Parallel circuits use one wire to connect a number of LEDs using positive leads.

COMPONENTS

LEDs, batteries (various voltages), assorted resistors, Planning Wizard

SYSTEMS THINKING SPOTLIGHT

component relationships, designing a system, role of system structure

---

20
SCULPTURE WIZARD 2

LEVEL

HARD

CATEGORY

EXPLORE COMPONENTS

Make a serial LED sculpture using the Planning Wizard.

EXPLANATION

Use the Planning Wizard LED calculator to create a sculpture with your leftover components.

HINTS

Make sure to follow the diagrams carefully before you solder everything together!

COMPONENTS

LEDs, batteries (various voltages), assorted resistors

SYSTEMS THINKING SPOTLIGHT

component relationships, designing a system, role of system structure

21 SWITCH IT UP

LEVEL

EASY

● ● ✦ ☀

CATEGORY

EXPLORE COMPONENTS

Use a multimeter to test out different switches and buttons to see how they work.

EXPLANATION

You can use a multimeter to test out the way electricity flows through a button or switch.

HINTS

You will need to put the multimeter in Continuity Mode, and it should beep or light up when there is a connection between both leads.

COMPONENTS

various switches (momentary push-button switches, SPST and SPDT switches), multimeter

SYSTEMS THINKING SPOTLIGHT

identifying components, identifying behaviors, system dynamics/ interconnections

---

22 WATER

LEVEL

EASY

● ● ✦ ☀

CATEGORY

EXPLORE COMPONENTS

Make a circuit diagram with plastic tubes and water that demonstrates a circuit with a switch.

EXPLANATION

Make a circuit diagram with water moving in one direction. Create switches by blocking and unblocking the water's path. Let the water represent the flow of electricity. The tubes represent the conductor, like wires. Blocking and unblocking the water's path is similar to how a switch works.

HINTS

Try creating a resistor, or something that slows the flow of water in your "circuit," like a smaller tube or a sponge.

COMPONENTS

plastic tubes, water, scissors, hot glue guns

SYSTEMS THINKING SPOTLIGHT

modeling a system, considering a system's purpose or goal, role of system structure

---

23 SOLAR ONE

LEVEL

MEDIUM

● ● ✦ ☀

CATEGORY

EXPLORE COMPONENTS

Draw two pictures that detail how a solar-powered calculator works.

EXPLANATION

Sensors are everywhere, hidden behind everything just waiting to be used! Describe your thinking and then draw a schematic to illustrate your explanation.

HINTS

These sensors are called solar cells.

COMPONENTS

paper, pencil

SYSTEMS THINKING SPOTLIGHT

modeling a system, considering a system's purpose or goal, role of system structure

SHORT CIRCUITS CHALLENGE CARDS

24 SWIPE

LEVEL
MEDIUM

CATEGORY
EXPLORE COMPONENTS

Ever wondered how a swipe or credit card worked? How about RFID tags in library books? We've wondered about that stuff, too! Can you figure out how they work?

EXPLANATION
There are electronics and sensors being used all around us. Use what you know so far about sensors and short circuits to come up with your own solution.

HINTS
Describe your thinking and then draw a schematic to illustrate your explanation.

COMPONENTS
paper, pencil

SYSTEMS THINKING SPOTLIGHT
modeling a system, identifying components, identifying behaviors, role of system structure

---

SHORT CIRCUITS CHALLENGE CARDS

25 CONDUCTIVITY EXPERIMENT

LEVEL
EASY

CATEGORY
EXPLORE COMPONENTS

Use batteries to light up a flashlight bulb, using aluminum foil

EXPLANATION
The aluminum foil strip is conductive and makes a path for the energy in the battery to follow. The energy follows the path and lights up the bulb.

HINTS
Start by folding the aluminum foil to make a long strip and figure out how to light up the battery. Now that you've made it light up, can you create a switch?

COMPONENTS
batteries, aluminum foil about 4" x 12", flashlight bulbs

SYSTEMS THINKING SPOTLIGHT
role of system structure, system dynamics/interconnections

SHORT CIRCUITS CHALLENGE CARDS

26 CAPACITOR CYLINDER

LEVEL
EASY

CATEGORY
EXPLORE COMPONENTS

Create a paper capacitor out of nested paper cylinders

EXPLANATION
Capacitors store energy with layers of conductive and nonconductive materials.

HINTS
Be sure to label each part so it is clear how each part of the component works.

COMPONENTS
paper, pencils, markers or colored pencils, tape

SYSTEMS THINKING SPOTLIGHT
designing a system, component relationships, role of system structure, nested systems

27
MODEL RESISTOR

LEVEL

MEDIUM

CATEGORY

EXPLORE COMPONENTS

Create a paper resistor model with layers that show how a resistor functions.

EXPLANATION

Resistors are devices that make use of poor conductors to limit the flow of electricity through a circuit.

HINTS

Be sure to label each part so it is clear how each part of the component works.

COMPONENTS

paper, pencils, markers or colored pencils, tape

SYSTEMS THINKING SPOTLIGHT

modeling a system, component relationships, role of system structure

---

28
MODEL BATTERY

LEVEL

EASY

CATEGORY

EXPLORE COMPONENTS

Create a paper battery model with layers to show how a battery functions on the inside.

EXPLANATION

Batteries turn stored chemical energy into electrical energy.

HINTS

Be sure to label each part so it is clear how each part of the component works.

COMPONENTS

paper, pencils, markers or colored pencils, tape

SYSTEMS THINKING SPOTLIGHT

modeling a system, component relationships, role of system structure

---

29
SWITCH MODEL

LEVEL

MEDIUM

CATEGORY

EXPLORE COMPONENTS

Create a paper model of a switch that will show how the inside of an actual switch works.

EXPLANATION

Switches work by connecting or disconnecting parts of a circuit.

HINTS

Be sure to label each part so it is clear how each part of the component works.

COMPONENTS

paper, pencils, markers or colored pencils, tape

SYSTEMS THINKING SPOTLIGHT

modeling a system, component relationships, role of system structure

30
LEGO® CIRCUITS

LEVEL

HARD

CATEGORY

EXPLORE COMPONENTS

Find a simple circuit diagram and create a Lego® diagram that mimics it.

EXPLANATION

Circuit diagrams are very specific. Find the right Legos® to represent each component.

HINTS

Can you make a working switch? How about multi-Lego battery with layers?

COMPONENTS

Legos®, circuit diagrams

SYSTEMS THINKING SPOTLIGHT

modeling a system, component relationships, role of system structure

---

31
MISSING PARTS

LEVEL

EASY

CATEGORY

EXPLORE COMPONENTS

Fill in the blanks on a circuit diagram, drawing in the proper components to complete it.

EXPLANATION

Every circuit must have the right balance of components to function properly.

HINTS

Choose from the bank of listed components to complete the circuit.

COMPONENTS

circuit diagrams, pen or pencil

SYSTEMS THINKING SPOTLIGHT

modeling a system, component relationships, role of system structure

---

32
ELECTRONIC SYMBOLS MINI-GAME

LEVEL

EASY

CATEGORY

EXPLORE COMPONENTS

Create flash cards for basic electrical components.

EXPLANATION

Draw the diagram on one side and label the component on the other.

HINTS

If you have space, write a small definition for the component on the back as well.

COMPONENTS

paper, pencils, markers or colored pencils

SYSTEMS THINKING SPOTLIGHT

identifying components, identifying behaviors, identifying a system

33
INVISIBLE FORCES

LEVEL

EASY

CATEGORY

EXPLORE COMPONENTS

See an invisible magnetic charge by sprinkling steel bits onto a piece of paper with a magnet underneath.

EXPLANATION

The filings will take the shape of a "figure eight," which is the lines of force of the magnetic field.

HINTS

Be careful when ripping apart the steel wool. Wear protective gloves and goggles and don't get any in your eyes!

COMPONENTS

protective gloves, protective eyewear, paper, magnet, steel wool (ripped apart until you have small pieces)

SYSTEMS THINKING SPOTLIGHT

modeling a system, identifying behaviors, system dynamics/interconnections

---

34
PAPER POTS

LEVEL

MEDIUM

CATEGORY

EXPLORE COMPONENTS

Create a paper potentiometer with paper and a brass fastener for the paper "wiper."

EXPLANATION

Potentiometers have variable resistance based on the wiper position, so focus on that mechanism.

HINTS

Be sure to label each part so it is clear how each part of the component works.

COMPONENTS

brass fasteners, paper, pencils, markers or colored pencils

SYSTEMS THINKING SPOTLIGHT

component relationships, designing a system, role of system structure

---

35
TO FLY

LEVEL

EASY TO MEDIUM

CATEGORY

SCIENCE (FICTIONAL) DEVICES

Design a flying skateboard or vehicle and show us how it works inside!

EXPLANATION

Will you use fans? Magnets? Jets? Design the device on paper and explain how it works.

HINTS

Try to include components you already use—and give details about new ones you dream up!

COMPONENTS

paper, pencils, markers or colored pencils

SYSTEMS THINKING SPOTLIGHT

designing a system, modeling a system

36 LIGHTSABER

LEVEL

MEDIUM

CATEGORY

SCIENCE (FICTIONAL) DEVICES

How does a lightsaber work? Create a technical diagram to show us the details.

EXPLANATION

You've seen them in *Star Wars*. Now, design the device on paper and explain how it works.

HINTS

Try to include components you already use—and give details about new ones you dream up!

COMPONENTS

paper, pencils, markers or colored pencils

SYSTEMS THINKING SPOTLIGHT

modeling a system, identifying components, identifying behaviors, role of system structure

---

37 "LIGHTENING" BOLT

LEVEL

MEDIUM

CATEGORY

SCIENCE (FICTIONAL) DEVICES

Design a shoe where the LEDs light up only when you run.

EXPLANATION

Design the device on paper. Then draw a schematic or detailed example so we can see how everything works inside!

HINTS

Try to include components you already use—and give details about new ones you dream up!

COMPONENTS

paper, pencils, markers or colored pencils

SYSTEMS THINKING SPOTLIGHT

designing a system, system dynamics/interconnections

---

38 FUTURE NOW

LEVEL

HARD

CATEGORY

SCIENCE (FICTIONAL) DEVICES

What type of futuristic technological device do you wish existed? Draw it and create a diagram of its inner workings.

EXPLANATION

Design the device on paper and explain how it works.

HINTS

Try to include components you already use—and give details about new ones you dream up!

COMPONENTS

paper, pencils, markers or colored pencils

SYSTEMS THINKING SPOTLIGHT

designing a system, considering a system's purpose or goal, role of system structure

39
DRYER GUTS

LEVEL

HARDCORE

CATEGORY

SCIENCE (FICTIONAL) DEVICES

Draw a schematic to show how automatic faucets and hand dryers work.

EXPLANATION

Draw a design for these devices on paper and explain how they work.

HINTS

Remember, these devices exist today: what type of sensors do you think they use?

COMPONENTS

paper, pencils, markers or colored pencils

SYSTEMS THINKING SPOTLIGHT

modeling a system, identifying components, identifying behaviors, role of system structure

---

40
SENSING
LIGHTS

LEVEL

HARD

CATEGORY

SCIENCE (FICTIONAL) DEVICES

Draw a schematic to show how automatic lights / light dimmers work.

EXPLANATION

Draw a design for these devices on paper and explain how they work.

HINTS

Remember, these devices exist today: what type of sensors or components do you think they use?

COMPONENTS

paper, pencils, markers or colored pencils

SYSTEMS THINKING SPOTLIGHT

modeling a system, identifying components, identifying behaviors, feedback loops

---

HOW DOES
IT WORK?

LEVEL

HARD

CATEGORY

SCIENCE (FICTIONAL) DEVICES

How do car / fridge / microwave door lights work? Draw a diagram to show us!

EXPLANATION

Draw a design for these devices on paper and explain how they work.

HINTS

Remember, these devices exist today— what type of switches or components do you think they use?

COMPONENTS

paper, pencils, markers or colored pencils

SYSTEMS THINKING SPOTLIGHT

modeling a system, identifying components, identifying behaviors, feedback loops

42
TELEPORTATION DEVICES

LEVEL

MEDIUM

CATEGORY

SCIENCE (FICTIONAL) DEVICES

Create your own teleportation device and make a diagram to explain how it works, in detail.

EXPLANATION

Imagine a machine that warps you from one place to another. Design the device on paper and explain how it works.

HINTS

Try to include components you already use—and give details about new ones you dream up!

COMPONENTS

paper, pencils, markers or colored pencils

SYSTEMS THINKING SPOTLIGHT

designing a system, modeling a system, component relationships, considering a system's purpose or goal

---

43
SHRINKINATOR— GROWINATOR

LEVEL

HARD

CATEGORY

SCIENCE (FICTIONAL) DEVICES

Create a device that will grow or shrink people and things. Create a technical drawing to explain how it works.

EXPLANATION

Imagine a device that can make you as small as an ant or as large as a house. Design the device on paper and explain how it works.

HINTS

Try to include components you already use—and give details about new ones you dream up!

COMPONENTS

paper, pencils, markers or colored pencils

SYSTEMS THINKING SPOTLIGHT

designing a system, modeling a system, component relationships, reinforcing feedback loops, system dynamics/interconnections

---

44
DETECTION DEVICE

LEVEL

HARD

CATEGORY

SCIENCE (FICTIONAL) DEVICES

Design a device to help you find lost keys, socks, or other objects.

EXPLANATION

Think of a device to help you find lost objects. Design the device on paper and explain how it works.

HINTS

Try to include components you already use—and give details about new ones you dream up!

COMPONENTS

paper, pencils, markers or colored pencils

SYSTEMS THINKING SPOTLIGHT

designing a system, component relationships, considering a system's purpose or goal

45
SWITCH IT UP

LEVEL

MEDIUM

CATEGORY

MICROCONTROLLER CHALLENGES

Use a momentary pushbutton switch to turn on/off an LED.

EXPLANATION

A switch can help you turn on or off an LED, depending on its position. Build the circuit from "Lights On" and then insert your switch on the power or ground side!

HINTS

Make sure the switch is aligned correctly. Feel free to experiment with different pins on the switch until you get it right!

COMPONENTS

Arduino, breadboard, 220 ohm resistor, LED, switch, wire

SYSTEMS THINKING SPOTLIGHT

designing a system, component relationships, role of system structure

---

46
SMOOTH IT OUT

LEVEL

HARD

CATEGORY

MICROCONTROLLER CHALLENGES

Use a potentiometer to fade an LED.

EXPLANATION

Hook up an LED on pin 9. Next, hook up a potentiometer to one of the analog inputs. This will be used to control the brightness of the LED.

HINTS

Look at the AnalogIn example that comes with Arduino for some help and example code.

COMPONENTS

Arduino, breadboard, 220 ohm resistor, LED, 10k potentiometer, wire

SYSTEMS THINKING SPOTLIGHT

designing a system, component relationships, reinforcing feedback loops

---

47
STEP IT UP

LEVEL

MEDIUM

CATEGORY

MICROCONTROLLER CHALLENGES

Make a foot controlled switch out of simple parts

EXPLANATION

Put a small strip of foil around your shoe and connect it to one side of your "Switch It Up" circuit. Make a pad of foil and connect it to the other side. Congratulations, you've created a foot-controlled switch. What else can you use it for?

HINTS

Remember, to create a switch you must allow current to flow through conductive materials. Make sure once the aluminum foil pieces are touching that one is connected to the power side of the LED, the other to ground.

COMPONENTS

Arduino, breadboard, 220 ohm resistor, LED, wire, aluminum foil

SYSTEMS THINKING SPOTLIGHT

designing a system, component relationships, role of system structure

NOTES

DESIGN CHALLENGE 1

1. The LilyPad Arduino is a microcontroller board designed for wearables and e-textiles. It can be sewn to fabric and similarly mounted power supplies, sensors and actuators with conductive thread. LilyPad Arduino components can be ordered through SparkFun Electronics.

DESIGN CHALLENGE 2

1. To help avoid shorts, you may want to insert the battery in the battery holder before beginning the activity.

2. If more than one LED is used in the puppet, it will be important for youths to understand how to place the LEDs in a parallel circuit to the battery in order for them to light. See Design Challenges 4 and 5 of this book for more information.

3. National Council for Teachers of English (NCTE), found at: http://www .readwritethink.org/files/resources/lesson_images/lesson175/RWT186-1.pdf

DESIGN CHALLENGE 3

1. *Uncommon Wisdom: Conversations with Remarkable People* as quoted in Linda Booth Sweeney, *When a Butterfly Sneezes: A Guide for Helping Kids Explore Interconnections in Our world through favorite stories.* (2001). Waltham, MA: Pegasus Communications.

DESIGN CHALLENGE 4

1. Because 3V batteries can short easily, we recommend inserting the 3V battery into the holder before placing it in the zip-closed bag.

2. The LED Series/Parallel Array Wizard tool (http://led.linear1.org/led.wiz) is useful for calculating the number of LEDs and resistors needed for varying amounts of voltage when arranging LEDs in series.

3. We recommend reviewing Script Frenzy workbooks and lesson plans for ideas, found at http://2012.ywp.scriptfrenzy.org/views/curricula_el.

4. Adapted from *Readers Theater: From Story to Script*, by Aaron Shepard, http://www.aaronshep.com/rt/sheets.html.

REFERENCES AND PHOTO CREDITS

REFERENCES

Baafi, E., and A. Millner. 2011. Modkit: A toolkit for tinkering with tangibles and connecting communities. *Proceedings of Tangible, Embedded, and Embodied Interaction* (TEI). doi 10.1145/1935701.1935783

Brown, A. L. 1992. Design experiments: Theoretical and methodological challenges in creating complex interventions in classroom settings. *Journal of the Learning Sciences* 2 (2): 141–178.

Brown, Gordon S. 1990. The genesis of the system thinking program at the Orange Grove Middle School, Tucson, Arizona. Personal report. 6301 N. Calle de Adelita, Tucson, AZ 85718: March 1.

Buechley, L. 2006. A construction kit for electronic textiles. In *2006 10th IEEE International Symposium on Wearable Computers*, 83-90.

Colella, V. 2000. Participatory simulations: Building collaborative understanding through immersive dynamic modeling. *Journal of the Learning Sciences* 9 (4): 471–500.

Colella, V. S., E. Klopfer, and M. Resnick. 2001. Adventures in modeling: Exploring complex, dynamic systems with StarLogo. Williston, VT: Teachers College Press.

Danish, J. A., K. Peppler, D. Phelps, and D. Washington. 2011. Life in the hive: Supporting inquiry into complexity within the zone of proximal development. *Journal of Science Education and Technology* 20 (5): 454–467.

Draper, F. 1989. Letter to Jay Forrester. Personal communication, Orange Grove Junior High School, 1911 E. Orange Grove Rd., Tucson, AZ 85718. May 2, 1989.

Goldstone, R. L., and U. Wilensky. 2008. Promoting transfer by grounding complex systems principles. *Journal of the Learning Sciences* 17 (4): 465–516.

Hmelo-Silver, C. E., and M. G. Pfeffer. 2004. Comparing expert and novice understanding of a complex system from the perspective of structures, behaviors, and functions. *Cognitive Science* 28 (1): 127–138.

Hmelo-Silver, C., R. Jordan, L. Liu, and E. Chernobilsky. 2011. Representational tools for understanding complex computer-supported collaborative learning environments. *Computer-Supported Collaborative Learning Series* 12 (Part 1): 83–106. doi:10.1007/978-1-4419-7710-6_4

Kafai, Y. B. 2006. Constructionism. In K. Sawyer (Ed.), Cambridge Handbook of the Learning Sciences, 35–46. New York: Cambridge University Press.

Lenhart, A., and M. Madden. 2007. Social networking websites and teens: An overview. Washington, DC: Pew Internet and American Life Project.

Lyneis, D. (2000). Bringing system dynamics to a school near you: Suggestions for introducing and sustaining system dynamics in K-12 education. International System Dynamics Society Conference. Bergen, Norway.

Maloney, J. H., K. Peppler, Y. Kafai, M. Resnick, and N. Rusk. 2008. Programming by choice: Urban youth learning programming with Scratch. *ACM SIGCSE Bulletin* 40(1): 367–371.

Meadows, D. 1999. Leverage points: Places to intervene in a system. Hartland, VT: Sustainability Institute.

Papert, S. 1980. Mindstorms: Children, computers, and powerful ideas. New York: Basic Books, Inc.

Papert, S., and I. Harel. (1991). *Constructionism.* New York: Ablex Publishing Corporation. http://www.papert.org/articles/SituatingConstructionism.html

Peppler, K. A., and Y. B. Kafai. (2007). From SuperGoo to Scratch: Exploring creative digital media production in informal learning. *Learning, Media and Technology* 32(2): 149–166.

Resnick, M., et al. 2009. Scratch: Programming for all. *Communications of the ACM* 52 (11): 60–67.

Rusk, N., M. Resnick, and S. Cooke. 2009. Origins and guiding principles of the Computer Clubhouse. In Y. Kafai, K. Peppler, and R. Chapman (Eds.), The Computer Clubhouse: Constructionism and creativity in youth communities. New York: Teachers College Press.

Salen, K. 2008. Toward an ecology of gaming. In K. Salen (Ed.), The ecology of games: Connecting youth, games, and learning. Cambridge, MA: The MIT Press.

Salen, K., R. Torres, R. Rufo-Tepper, A. Shapiro, and L. Wolozin. 2010. Quest to learn: Growing a school for digital kids. Cambridge, MA: MIT Press.

Sweeney, L. 2001. When a butterfly sneezes: A guide for helping kids explore interconnections in our world through favorite stories. Waltham, MA: Pegasus Communications.

Wilensky, U. 1999. NetLogo [Computer Program]: Center for Connected Learning and Computer-Based Modeling. Northwestern University, Evanston, IL.

Wilensky, U., and M. Resnick. 1999. Thinking in levels: A dynamic systems perspective to making sense of the world. *Journal of Science Education and Technology* 8 (1): 3–19.

SPARKFUN PHOTO CREDITS

The following photographs of electronic components found in this volume are the creative copyright of Sparkfun Electronics (https://sparkfun.com):

9V Battery: SparkFun Electronics, Juan Pena, Product SKU-10218

9V Snap Connector: SparkFun Electronics, Juan Pena, Product SKU-00091

Alligator Test Leads: SparkFun Electronics, Juan Pena, Product SKU-11037

Coin Cell Battery: Two views: SparkFun Electronics, Juan Pena, Product SKU-00337

Conductive Fabric: SparkFun Electronics, Juan Pena, Product SKU-10056

Conductive Thread: SparkFun Electronics, Juan Pena, Product SKU-11791

Diagonal Cutters: SparkFun Electronics, Juan Pena, Product SKU-08794

Digital Multimeter: Two views: SparkFun Electronics, Juan Pena, Product SKU-09141

Electrical Tape: SparkFun Electronics, Juan Pena, Product SKU-10689

Hook-up Wire: SparkFun Electronics, Juan Pena, Product SKU-00023

LED–Basic Blue: SparkFun Electronics, Juan Pena, Product SKU-11372

LED–Basic Red: SparkFun Electronics, Juan Pena, Product SKU-09590

LilyPad Arduino Simple Board: SparkFun Electronics, Juan Pena, Product SKU-10274

LilyPad Button Board: SparkFun Electronics, Juan Pena, Product SKU-08776

LilyPad Buzzer: SparkFun Electronics, Juan Pena, Product SKU-08463

LilyPad Coin Cell Battery Holder: SparkFun Electronics, Juan Pena, Product SKU-10730

LilyPad FTDI Basic Breakout board: SparkFun Electronics, Juan Pena, Product SKU-10275

LilyPad LED White: SparkFun Electronics, Juan Pena, Product SKU-10081

LilyPad LiPower: SparkFun Electronics, Juan Pena, Product SKU-11260

LilyPad Slide Switch: SparkFun Electronics, Juan Pena, Product SKU-09350

Mini Power Switch: SparkFun Electronics, Juan Pena, Product SKU-00102

Needlenose Pliers: SparkFun Electronics, Juan Pena, Product SKU-08793

Polymer Lithium Ion Battery: Two views: SparkFun Electronics, Juan Pena, Product SKU-00341

Rotary Potentiometer: SparkFun Electronics, Juan Pena, Product SKU-09939

Sewing Snaps: SparkFun Electronics, Juan Pena, Product SKU-11347

Super Bright LED: SparkFun Electronics, Juan Pena, Product SKU-00531

USB Mini-B Cable: SparkFun Electronics, Juan Pena, Product SKU-00598

Wire Strippers: SparkFun Electronics, Juan Pena, Product SKU-08696

INDEX

INTERCONNECTIONS CURRICULA SUMMARY SHEET:
SHORT CIRCUITS

WHAT IS THE INTERCONNECTIONS CURRICULA?

Interconnections: Understanding Systems through Digital Design is a collection of curricula that support students to develop critical 21st century skills—systems thinking and digital design—by engaging in rich project-based learning using the latest technologies.

WHAT'S SYSTEMS THINKING, AND WHY IS IT IMPORTANT FOR MY STUDENTS?

As the world gets more complex and interconnected, we need to help our kids to understand and positively impact the dizzying number of systems around them. Systems thinking is a set of ideas and practices that allow kids to see through the "lens" of systems: how to take a "big picture" view of complex social structures and technologies, how to see the patterns and dynamics that drive systems, how to understand that the whole is usually greater than the sum of its parts.

HOW IS DIGITAL DESIGN DIFFERENT FROM OTHER USES OF EDUCATIONAL TECHNOLOGY?

Digital design is all about getting students the skills they need in order to be innovative, creative, and entrepreneurial thinkers. Rather than educational technologies that replicate a consumer mentality around learning—dumping information into students' brains—digital design activities put them in the driver's seat, having them come up with the ways technology can look in the world and preparing them for a world that increasingly expects them to engage in creative processes.

CIRCUITRY, REALLY?

There are lots of great reasons we've found in our work to use physical computing and circuitry as the foundation for a classroom curriculum. Technologies like these are incredibly engaging, are an integral part of youth culture, and can be leveraged to get students excited about entering into some pretty important academic practices: giving and getting feedback, revising drafts, making arguments, problem solving, and more.

DOES THIS ALIGN TO STANDARDS?

Yes! All the Interconnections curricula have been aligned to the Common Core State Standards in areas including language arts, history and science, as well as the Next Generation Science Standards.

HOW MUCH TIME DOES THIS TAKE?

The *Short Circuits* curriculum is designed to take about 20–30 hours overall, but of course can and will be adapted to fit your students' needs and abilities as well as your school culture. This means that we fully expect that you might take certain parts and extend them, cut other parts, or repurpose them to fit existing units of study.